PILLS, PETTICOATS, AND PLOWS

pills, petticoats, & plows

THE SOUTHERN COUNTRY STORE

Thomas D. Clark

FOREWORD BY JOHN D. W. GUICE

UNIVERSITY OF OKLAHOMA PRESS
NORMAN AND LONDON

This book is affectionately

dedicated to my wife

ELIZABETH TURNER CLARK

Library of Congress Catalog Card Number: 64–11333

ISBN: 0–8061–1093–7

 First printing by the University of Oklahoma Press, 1964; second printing, 1974; third printing, 1989.

CONTENTS

Foreword, by John D. W. Guice vi
Preface x
1. The Country Store 3
2. Behind Battered Faces 17
3. Stove or Shady Porch 35
4. The Walls Grow Long Paper Tails 55
5. Social Correspondents 67
6. Ten Gross June Bugs, Assorted 84
7. A Little Bit of Santa Claus 98
8. Under the Sign of the Stud Horse 114
9. Big Hogs Grew in Iowa 126
10. Mr. McGuffey at the Crossroads 143
11. Admiral Dewey Corsets and Bonton Petticoats 159
12. Gentle Jackson in a Devil of a Fix 172
13. The Halt, the Lame, and the Bilious 189
14. The Farmer and His Almanac 212
15. Death Always Came at Night 224
16. Heavy Goods in the Corner 238
17. Money Catchers 257
18. An Ought's an Ought 271
Bibliography 292

FOREWORD

"'S WONDERFUL! 'S Marvelous! . . ." These superlatives of pleasure from George Gershwin's charming and frequently revived 1927 musical *Funny Face* accurately describe Thomas D. Clark's *Pills, Petticoats, and Plows: The Southern Country Store.* Of Clark's twenty-four single-authored books that were published 1933–84, *Pills, Petticoats, and Plows* is the most wonderful and marvelous of them all. For in it he deals with a subject that was a part of his life and the lives of his pioneer ancestors who cultivated in Mississippi plots of the virgin soil that the Choctaw ceded in the 1830 Treaty of Dancing Rabbit Creek.

Clark lived on a cotton farm until he entered high school as a boarding student. So he had firsthand knowledge of the postbellum southern country store. In addition, Clark had access to a wide variety of records from over seventy stores, and he leisurely visited several dozens of them over the course of a year while on a leave of absence. Never an armchair historian, Clark was a pioneer practitioner of "oral history," as well as an avid manuscript collector. As such, he acquired dozens of collections from country stores for the archives of the University of Kentucky, where he taught for thirty-seven years and where he served as department head for over two decades. It is amazing that Clark's treatment of a subject to which he was so close is as objective and critical as it is entertaining and empathetic.

The topic, prose, and analysis all contribute to the fascination of this study, the sixth book that Clark wrote within a dozen years of receiving the doctorate from Duke University. Anyone fortunate enough to have lingered a while in an authentic crossroads store realizes what a conglomeration of items the merchants jammed onto the shelves, stacked in the aisles, hung from the rafters, or stored in adjoining sheds. In cleverly designed chapters with equally fetching titles, Clark describes this bewildering array of merchandise—from stove bolts to spectacles, from condoms to coffins. And he leaves no doubt that the country store was the most important social and economic institution in the South between Appomattox and World War I.

Simply stated, it is fun to read *Pills, Petticoats, and Plows.* No academician is more entertaining than Tom Clark at the podium, and he writes in the same colorful, descriptive, down-home manner. There is hardly a "plain vanilla" or "B-flat" sentence in the entire book. No matter what the topic, he appeals to the senses as well as the sensitivities. Yet for a scholarly study written nearly a half century ago, PP&P is a bit risqué. The introductory sentence in chapter 5, "Social Correspondents," reads, "Love in the cotton fields of the South was a throbbing thing which required vigorous expression." Chapter 6 on the role of the drummer begins with a "traveling salesman and farmer's daughter" story. Though Clark takes every opportunity to inject tasteful humor into his prose, he writes with considerable poignancy as he deals with topics such as Christmas, drug addiction, education, and death in the southern countryside.

Because of the folksy style of the author and his decision not to include citations to his complex manuscript sources, some errant readers fail to recognize the depth and breadth of Clark's scholarship. PP&P is not only one of the best social histories of the late-nineteenth-century South, but it is an excellent interpretation of economic and political conditions as well. The stocks of these crossroads emporia offer silent testimony to literally every aspect of the lives of their patrons. Could they talk, the porches of the square-fronted buildings and the warm spaces around the potbellied stoves inside would reveal all of the social and political secrets of the trading area.

In an insightful chapter entitled "An Ought's an Ought," Clark offers a penetrating commentary on the oft-maligned "lien" system that, in a sense, enslaved so many Southerners, white and black. Biological as well as economic survival in the post-war South, however, depended on the extension of credit by local merchants who were part of a national financial network. The opening of a petty sharecropper account anywhere in the deep South created a tiny ripple that was felt ultimately all the way to the nation's financial center in Manhattan. Without a doubt, it was a flawed economic system, one in which the store owners appeared to be the villains. In reality, as Clark explains, merchants were just one link in a financial chain that stretched northward through manufacturers and distributors all the way to the nation's most powerful financial institutions.

Though many authors demonstrate a mastery of their subjects, few can match Tom Clark's descriptive powers. In part, one can attribute this to the depth of his empathy. Instead of reading history, time and time again the reader of PP&P has the sensation of watching a play or a "video," to be more contemporary. Whether the situation is lighthearted, serious, or sad, Clark leaves the reader with the impression that he is shining a light into the very souls of his subjects. Another explanation of his verbal power is his handiness with the vernacular of the period and place. For instance, he seems as much at home with the nomenclature of the hardware and machinery as one of the store clerks or farmers. And, of course, there is the hereditary factor; garrulousness seems to be part of Clark's genetic structure. Though his words flow as if their source is endless, he chooses them carefully—as an artist does pigments—so that they create in the reader sensations of smell, sound, and sight. And at the right time his verbiage recreates within us the appropriate emotion.

Not only does Tom Clark salt, pepper, and spice his prose in this book as naturally as good cooks do their favorite dishes, but he repeatedly composes enticing topic sentences and ferrets out quotes that are as entertaining as they are enlightening. From among the many thousands of extant orders scribbled by the generally illiterate customers, Clark selects the most illustrative and, according to the situation, the most humorous or pathetic. He includes a generous selection of pertinent quotes from storekeepers to vividly drive home his points. Liberally sprinkled throughout the book are imaginative similes such as: "Along one side feed or shed rooms leaned against the main building like architectural quotation marks."

Though Clark addresses problems that are peculiar to the post-Civil War South, he treats an institution that in many ways was a national one. While the lien system did not prevail in other regions, all country stores during the second half of the nineteenth century bore marked similarities. Everywhere, merchants of that era extended credit, and their stores served as social and political centers. Farming implements used in Alabama differed from those in Kansas or Vermont, but most Americans bought similar home remedies, notions, housewares, and countless other items. Despite regional variations in tastes and customs and the impact of climatic differences, country stores across the land shared a number of universal characteristics. A 1944 reviewer in the *Boston Globe* made this point. "Any damyankee who ever knew a New England general store," he wrote, "will find this book to be the genuine article, right out of the cracker-barrel."

While the post-Civil War South was largely populated by recently freed slaves and Confederate veterans, it was a frontier nevertheless. Indeed, it had been a frontier since 1607, and many parts of the South would remain a frontier until as late as World War II. The census officials may have declared that a frontier line no longer existed in the United States after 1890, but there were numerous counties in the South where lifestyles and attitudes had changed hardly at all in the century preceding World War I. While not a Turnerian, Clark is a scholar of the West as well as of the South; in 1959 he authored *Frontier America*—one of the first texts used in courses on the American West. Students of the Westward Movement, as well as those of the South, will enjoy *Pills, Petticoats, and Plows.* As the *Boston Globe* writer recognized, "There is a lot of fun to be had from the hundreds of customers' orders Prof. Clark has collected."

University of Southern Mississippi JOHN D. W. GUICE
April 14, 1989

PREFACE

OCCASIONALLY in isolated areas of the modern South ancient country stores hold on in spite of chain-store competition. Some of them were founded in the 1870's and 1880's, and there may still be a few which antedate the Civil War. The modern American in search of local color regards these anachronisms in present-day chain-store glitter and commercial rivalry as sources of antique merchandise, antiquated human relics, and rural wit and wisdom. Newspaper feature writers stalk these veterans for stories for nostalgic readers of Sunday supplements. The square box front, narrow front porch, rusting signs, and pungent smells all represent what most people believe was a better day.

Fewer visitors now have the background knowledge and experience to get a view of the past from littered counters, shelves of disarranged merchandise, and cluttered walls. The country store in a way was far more symbolic of the southern way of rural life than were other institutions. Even the church and school were often administered as much from the store as from their own buildings. The storekeeper was all things to his community. He served as school trustee, deacon or steward, railway agent, fertilizer salesman, social adviser, character reference, politician, lodge master, and general community "obliger." His store was the hub of the local universe. It was market place, banking and credit source, recreational center, public forum, and news exchange. There were few aspects of farm life in the South after 1870 which were uninfluenced by the country store.

In a light and romantic vein the southern country store was a place where the countryman made contacts with industrial and commercial America. It was his refuge in time of trouble, the source of his pleasures, a place to hear a favorite candidate speak, and a point of departure for all his travels. Here it was that he bought his first "long" pants, drank his first liquor, compared notes on his romance with a local belle, bought a postage stamp, a coffin, a wagon, a necktie, a can of sardines, or a pistol. He secured credit to make a tobacco or cotton crop, to buy a few "little extras" for the children at Christmas time, and bought almost everything else that he used.

An older generation of southerners still recalls the heady smells of apples, cheese, tobacco, oranges, salt mackerel, axle grease, soap, and kerosene. This was an incongruous mixture, but the blended smells gave the southern country store a pungent aroma which lingered on in memory as a warm spot in community life, but its romance was one of a frugal sort of rural plenty.

The heyday of the southern country store was also the age of triumph of that jovial but fraudulent American who promised a curative remedy for all human diseases, including those of psychological origins. Barn and store walls, fences, trees, and even natural landmarks were plastered with advertisements which promised sound health fresh from the cauldrons of mountebank and quack. Every other sharper in the country looked upon the country store as a means of direct touch to the rural hayseed. Account books were filled with the stories of rural Americans seeking restoration of health, escape from the withering bloom of womanhood, the loss of manhood, and the horrors and insidiousness of incurable diseases.

Behind the box façade of the country store was also enacted much of the vital drama of the agricultural South. Where the store was the connecting link between the rascals of the medicine and easy-money trades and their victims, it was also a direct tie with eastern bankers, manufacturers, and distributors of all sorts of goods. The opening of a petty sharecropper account in Gee's Bend in Alabama was ultimately noted in a banking house in New York. Banks accepted the discounted notes of merchants and distributors to secure their debts. The whole southern agricultural credit system hinged on the extension of credit by local merchants. Local bankers were far less important in the economic affairs of their communities than were the furnishing merchants. Much has been written in fact, and in fiction, about the usury of storekeepers. No doubt a large number of the accusations were true. Merchants made high profits from price mark-ups, exhorbitant interest rates, and time differentials in credit terms. Many of them dealt sharply with their customers, making profits from every credit and market transaction. Yet storekeeping in the post–Civil War South was for many a precarious business. It took sharp management over the years to earn a profit in many stores. Often merchants found themselves in the same economic straits as their customers.

It was also true that many storekeepers became the local "rich men." In many cases they lived in the best houses. They and their families lived well. They were generous contributors to local churches, and because of their "wealth" they often ran local political and social affairs. This was to become an accepted pattern of social status and organization throughout the South. Whether it was in village, town, or crossroads there was the merchant "kingpin" who lived in the big house and who was influential in all matters in his community. Many southern families who now enjoy high social status began their rise to respectability behind counters in country stores. Many large mercantile organizations and industries had their beginnings at the same place. Among these were the Cannon Mills, Cone Mills, the International Shoe Company, and the Fels-Naptha Company.

The southern store was a focal center of rural social intercourse. It was both a pleasant gathering place and a place where downtrodden farmers learned the brutal facts of regional staple-crop failure. Largely because of this there grew up about the stores an appreciable amount of folklore. Some originated with the sharp trading practices of merchants, and some sprang from the fertile wits of sentimental and jocular customers.

Historians of the New South have tended to pass over the enormous volume of firsthand materials available in the stores themselves in writing their essays and books. They have tended to generalize about the economy of the agrarian South between 1870 and 1930 without seeing the record. Much of what they have said is wrong, and some factual materials are superficially interpreted without benefit of adequate understanding. The period 1870–1920 was one in which southerners struggled to create a regional economy that would sustain them without completely destroying the South's resources. This they almost failed to accomplish. The land was gutted in an attempt to keep the little farmer solvent while he was enslaved to a system of farm credits designed to make him a peon.

The appearance of the boll weevil in the lower Mississippi Valley South, the arrival of sawmills which slashed away the great stands of pine and cypress, the inflation accompanying World War I, the coming of chain stores with cheaper cash prices, and a changing credit structure in the nation marked the approaching end of the cross-roads furnishing merchant. With him went most of his customers, his stocks of goods, and his ruinous credit system.

The migration away from the South, which began in 1910, gained momentum during the war and throughout the 1920's. Not all the migration which ultimately hurt the old-line storekeepers, however, was away from the region—an even larger portion of it was away from the farm itself into towns and cities. Improved roads, the rise of industry, changing forms of agriculture, and the failure of farm tenancy in the great depression, sealed the fate of the country stores. The economic change which began in 1910 was also a social revolt, as was subsequently to be reflected in the steps toward the epic Supreme Court decision of *Brown* versus *the Topeka School Board* in 1954 and in the continuing judicial shattering of the "traditional southern way of life."

This is a study drawn from the original records of the stores. In many cases I was fortunate to be able to interview old storekeepers, and to rummage through the remains of their stock of merchandise which were offered customers of another day. An attempt is made here to balance the romance and color of the southern country store with the grim realities of its confiscatory credit system. It would be easy to condemn this mode of merchandising for its many weaknesses and failures, but to do so would require a much firmer answer to the question of where rural people, in a financially straitened South, could have found more generous creditors who would have advanced credit on shaky liens or promissory notes secured by unplanted crops of cotton and tobacco.

There were enough color and excitement about the southern country store to make it a central institution in the memories of older southerners. The smells of oranges, kerosene, new leather, glaze on cloth, ripe cheddar cheese, and salt mackerel still touch off a flood of reminiscences about "the good old days when folks didn't have much, but they enjoyed what they had." The stores supplied the things country people needed. But in the South the country store was a more intimate and functional part of the social and economic lives of customers than were country stores in any other section of the country. This work undertakes to reveal the economic importance of the store to Southern economy, while preserving something of the human flavor of both store and customer.

THOMAS D. CLARK

Lexington, Kentucky

PILLS, PETTICOATS, AND PLOWS

1

THE COUNTRY STORE

ROBERT SOMERS, an English traveler in the United States in 1870, stumbled along the muddy streets of Atlanta. Five years before, the town had been prostrate from Sherman's raid, but now this traveler could detect little of its story of destruction. As he walked down the bustling, partially completed streets, Somers philosophized that "one receives at every step a lively impression of the great power residing somewhere in the United States of filling the most distant and unpromising places with wares and traffiickers of all kinds." Opening onto the sidewalks, the store doors overflowed with goods from everywhere. Piled high upon the rough walks were "northern notions" from New York, Baltimore, Cincinnati, Chicago and Boston. New York oyster saloons were crowded with hurrying people, and their doorjambs were piled high with empty oyster shells shipped in from Savannah and Charleston. Drummers swarmed over the town displaying the very latest in patented devices, and at nights they were crowded into stuffy hotel rooms where they carried on their poker playing and eternal yarn spinning.

In one wholesale house the Englishman halted to inspect the wares of an imaginative agent of a Yankee manufacturer. Before he could begin his inspection of the goods, he was regaled with a long dissertation on the new safety kerosene lamp. It was the most perfect device to come from the lampmaker's shop. Safety, in fact, was its cardinal virtue. Already drummers had sold much of the rural South on the idea of using patent lamps, but there had appeared a serious drawback. Everywhere it was said that the new lamps were dangerous. Leaning back against hundreds of kitchen walls in homemade hickory chairs, dramatic bumpkins repeated to their neighbors hair-raising stories of exploding lamps. Flimsy pine-plank houses burned to the ground in a twinkling of an eye, all due to the use of kerosene.

Families were horror-stricken when flame followed a wick downward into the bowl of their lamps. Old folk accounts are filled with the heroism of brave persons who rushed up just in time to grab a flaming missile with a pair of fire tongs and throw it high into the air to explode like Confederate cannon fire, and then shed its fiery drops of oil over the ground like pieces of brimstone on the day of final wrath. This could not be true of the lamps which Robert Somers inspected. To prove it, the glib salesman lighted three or four of them and nonchalantly tossed them around the store to burn at will.

While the lamps safely burned away in their respective corners, the enterprising representative turned his attention to other wonders. There was a patented washing machine which was to be as much a factor of emancipation for southern womanhood as the Emancipation Proclamation had been for the Negro slave. It was a marvelous machine which "promised to make its way against all competition." Then there was a patented pothook which was to keep women enchained to the old-fashioned kitchen fireplace, but as a gesture to progress it had an ingenious cradle attachment for weighing the baby.

That morning the querulous English traveler saw the true symbols of the New South: Atlanta, a newly patented safe kerosene lamp, and piles of goods in wholesale houses for the southern country stores. It was not so much a matter of mystery that quantities of goods were found on the Atlanta market as was the fact that these goods were effectively put into channels where they were sold directly to small customers. Actually the English visitor had picked the mercantile story up in the middle. He understood neither its beginning nor its end.

Already the shadow of reconstruction was showing its outline. The old system of southern economy was in an advanced stage of deterioration. Large plantations were being broken into smaller units, and communities predominantly yeoman became more important factors in southern civilization.

Immediately after the war numerous villages and towns came into existence almost overnight. Crossroads stores popped up like mushrooms. Small purchasers were far removed from the source of goods. No longer were there plantation owners and factors who moved in supplies in large quantities. The whole picture of trade was changed.

As large landholdings were broken up into moderate farms, there was an increasing demand for merchandise in smaller individual quantities. Southern people found themselves isolated; they had to have stores near by, and "near by" to the postwar southerner meant the maximum distance which could be traveled in a brief space of time by a Negro boy on a mule.

Merchants who formerly supplied the southern trade through middlemen or factors were now concerned about the convenience of the stores to their customers. Drummers in two-horse buggies struggled over the miry roads of the South searching for crossroads where progressive customers could begin storekeeping. Their unexpressed motto was "A store within reach of every cabin in the South." They were agents of a new industrial age. For them, reconstruction was not alone a matter of political and social change.

Manufacturing companies and wholesale houses constantly sought new outlets for their goods. They were anxious to supply both stock and capital if bright young men would open stores in their communities and get the local business. In every section railroads were being built, and as their lines were extended, they needed both freight and freight agents. Selecting strategic points along their newly built lines, company representatives encouraged the building of warehouses, stores and railway stations. At Dewey Rose, Georgia, railroad officials encouraged young T. J. Hewell to open a store, and when he demurred that he might go broke, he was asked if he had money. When he said, "No," the promotion agent asked, "How in hell can you go broke when you ain't got nothing?" This young Hewell had never pondered. At any rate such a philosophy evidently put the proposition in a new light, for soon a long-barreled house was serving a thriving trade as both freight station and store.

Elsewhere in the South stores were springing up in almost every location where there were enough people to buy a profitable quantity of goods. These crossroads emporiums of cheap merchandise rapidly became symbolic of the creation of a new southern economic system from the wreckage of the old. Perhaps no other southern institution more nearly embodied so much of the intimate story of the New South.

Plantation owners, army sutlers, adventurous former soldiers, Alsatian Jews and enterprising native yeoman sons opened stores. Sidney Andrews, a northern newspaper reporter, saw northern men coming south with their stocks of goods and capital to begin new businesses.

The Union Army took men across the South, and many of the soldiers saw in it a land of opportunity. When the war was ended, they came back to cast their lot with the region which they had helped to overrun. Already, in many instances, they had established pleasant relations with the people in the community, and upon their return they were able to make a quick start. At Glymp's store in South Carolina a New Jersey Jew spotted an opportunity to make a fortune, and hardly had the surrender occurred before he was back. He bought the old stand which had been started in 1845 and expanded it into a big general merchandise store.

At Shuqulak, Mississippi, young E. F. Nunn came home from the Confederate Army to reorganize a business which he had left in the hands of his mother. Fortunately, he had used good business judgment when he sold his slaves and bought cotton with the money. With the capital from the sale of cotton he bought more cotton, chickens, eggs, hides, and everything else that could possibly be sold to produce merchants in Mobile. His accounts showed that he was in constant communication with his former Alabama neighbors, A. P. Bush and Company, who, until the end of the war, were country merchants themselves at Pinckneyville on the east side of the Tombigbee River. All around young Nunn in Mississippi, country stores were coming into existence. Confederate veterans everywhere turned to storekeeping as a side line to operating disorganized plantations. Jewish newcomers in search of opportunity picked out likely places and imported stocks of merchandise from relatives and friends in New Orleans, Mobile and Charleston.

Many of the southern stores had their beginnings in humble peddler's packs. Alsatian Jewish peddlers bumped over impossible roads in one-horse wagons loaded with lines of cheap goods, or in winter floundered in bottomless mudholes to reach their customers. Sometimes they came on foot with packs strapped securely to their weary backs. These peddlers were postwar counterparts of the shrewd Yankees who had once swarmed over the land with their numerous gadgets, tin pans, buckets, clocks, and shoes. The Jews were of a similar humorous turn of mind. Also like the Yankee they had their eyes fastened on the main chance, but unlike him they were unable to whistle through their teeth in the face of adversity.

Southern country folk found these peddlers interesting. They laughed at their strange European accents and the bargain-driving shrugs of their shoulders. They made them the butts of crude practical jokes, but always their visits were welcomed and exciting. Nothing brought a rural family quite the same thrill as having a peddler open his pack before the fireplace. Beds were pushed back, chairs squared around, and the peddler was given a place of honor in the middle of the floor. With a flourish he undid his stout leather fastenings and then rolled back the awning-striped cover of his pack to expose his wares. With subtlety he placed his bright-colored cloth in the first bag to be opened and in one deft movement revealed its colorful bolts of goods. When his canvas roll was opened, there came a rush of smells. Odors of sachets, cheap perfumes, soaps, leather goods, and spices filled the room. It was like bringing a store right up to the most isolated country hearth.

Jostling around the countryside, these peddlers dreamed of the day when at last they could back their wagons under the shed and turn their horses out to graze. They searched for just the right spots to open stands, and when they finally located them, emptied their packs onto store shelves and went into business in a permanent location.

Already the peddlers knew their trade. They had learned whom to trust and whom to watch. Old friends who had traded generously with them in their horse-and-wagon days, were given slight advantages of lower prices and, frequently, little presents or lagniappes for old time's sake.

There was, however, an original sin back of the beginning of many of the country stores. It was one of thievery and debauchery of a most rancorous sort. Some of the crossroads castles started out ingloriously as deadfalls of the senseless period of reconstruction. Since cash was scarce in the South, and especially in the rural districts, customers offered produce for exchange in lieu of money. This was both a convenient and tempting practice for the newly freed slaves. Also, it was a lucrative field for economic exploitation for the "fly-by-night" carpetbag merchant. Thus it became a simple matter for a Negro or a scalawag white man to steal a few hundred pounds of cotton at night during picking time and carry it off to an illicit "night" store or deadfall for sale. Cotton in open fields was great temptation when an unscrupulous merchant was near by. In a North Carolina community in 1868, Leon Stevenson saw several Negro women waddling across his field in a most peculiar manner. When he searched their clothing he found that their petticoats were stuffed with his cotton.

The whole produce business was early tied up with the nefarious deadfall practice. Many a southern farmer gave up trying to have poultry and eggs for the reason that they were stolen and taken off to the stores for sale. Deadfalls operated in out-of-the-way places and often under cover of darkness. Some of them were portable or traveling stores fitted into wagons and canal boats. In the Louisiana sugar belt, barge store-boats eased along the back ways of sugar plantations receiving stolen goods for which the merchants exchanged wares from their shelves with great profit to themselves.

Sitting around the stores, cotton farmers watched Negroes and suspicious white people come and go. A guilty-looking freedman stumbled in with a bag across his shoulder and shuffled off into the side room of the store. The farmer gave "a poke at the ribs of the merchant half in fun, half in earnest," wrote one witness, "and would like to know whose cotton or corn. The merchant with downcast eyes and the slightest possible purple mounting on his face, makes a semi-poke and says, that 'there are large crops.' " Stores themselves were victims of the deadfall customers, and their windows were universally barred with strong diagonal iron straps which at least kept thieves from easy access to the buildings.

For many years the southern people had been forced to do without consumer's goods. During four years of war when stocks were exhausted and could not be replaced, most of them were unable to buy even the most commonplace and necessary goods. When the war ended, these customers were again ready buyers. Most southerners were without money, but as a result of the lien laws recently passed by the state legislatures, they were able to purchase astounding amounts of merchandise. Everywhere there was an anxiety to buy new goods, even if buying meant going hopelessly into debt; large piles of goods stacked on the Atlanta, Mobile, New Orleans, and Charleston shelves and sidewalks, melted overnight. Where there had been one store before the war, there were now ten. A flush postwar market had created thousands of outlets.

Of course the Negro, hampered by both war and slavery, had felt the pinch even more than the white man. Now the freedom of going into a country store and looking over its crowded shelves was for him nothing short of a trip to heaven. Long shelves of bright-colored goods and piles of fat meat; the smell of lard, the rich, heavy overtone of tempting salt herring and mackerel spiced with the celestial odor of sardines and cheese; the mouth-watering sight of big boxes of crackers and tantalizing glass jars of long sticks of striped candy were entirely too much temptation for the impractical man of either race. Political rights and freedom meant nothing in the face of this maddening intoxication. Quickly Negroes became the stores' best customers, buying what they wanted rather than what they needed. It was a joyous, heady experience! Here was freedom of the most tangible sort, and the store was the one place in the new order where the Negro knew he would suffer least from racial discrimination. His money was as good as that of the white man, and in some few instances he had more of it for the moment. But like his hang-over from cheap water-spiked whisky, his cash was soon gone and his spending habits threw him upon the unrelenting mercy of the lien laws. Soon he was back in slavery, not to a plantation master, but to a conscienceless counterbook.

Young men of the ante bellum South looked forward to professions of law, medicine and the ministry, or to running a plantation; their sons now found clerking a gentlemen's trade. Scarcely had the news of Lee's surrender cleared the wires before the editor of the Milledgeville *Federal Union* was saying that nine out of every ten young men in the southern towns were going into the business of clerking.

Frantically editorial prophets of the New South looked about for opportunities which would ease the economic strain of their bankrupt people. While exploiters were grabbing at political and social advantages, these editors mapped their courses of future economic pursuits. In Louisville, Cincinnati, Charleston, Baltimore, New York, and Chicago, money making became their theme and they often adopted the more conciliatory doctrine of new business opportunities. The editor of the Baltimore *Gazette* surveyed the southern field and decided, "What with carpet bag officials, scalawag judges, and Negro representatives, there is but one liberty left South Carolina. That is the liberty of making money. . . ."

Louisville wholesale distributors, for instance, were quick to realize that the southern trade was a rich plum. If only they could hold the "Cincinnati Yankees" off until they thrust their powerful Louisville and Nashville railroad southward, prosperity would be assured them. During the war the city had been under the control of the Union Army, but now it was the best Rebel city outside of Richmond. George Prentice's *Journal* spread the cheering news that Kentucky had plenty and to spare. The editor of the Barnwell (South Carolina) *Sentinel* published the fact that "Kentucky had an enormous surplus of corn and meat this season, and she intends to give liberally of them to her suffering brethren in the South. For this purpose societies are being organized throughout the state, and before the close of the year we hope to hear of one in every county."

Louisville was a big-hearted city. Immediately after the close of the war Atlanta was in ruins and her poor people were walking the streets in dejection and hunger. Louisville businessmen sent $2,500 to help out until conditions could be improved. When prominent Confederate soldiers died, store doors in the Falls City were closed out of respect. Drummers for Kentucky houses were selected first because they were good Confederates and second because they were salesmen.

Poor roads and a lack of railways encouraged new stores. Back of this, however, was the demand for an agency which could exchange small quantities of goods for equally small amounts of diverse rural produce. At the same time cotton selling and buying was now removed from the larger towns and cities to crossroad villages. Reconstruction credit legislation forced upon the country merchant the necessity of buying produce of every sort. Thus it was that the stores became not alone sources of supply for merchandise, but likewise community markets for almost everything that could be sold for a profit.

There were country stores in the ante bellum South, but as a part of the whole economic picture they were of relatively minor significance. Goods were distributed by cotton factors and merchants in the towns, and because of their larger volume of trade they were powerful competitors of the rural storekeepers. The early southern country stores, except for those which were well located, were frontier trading posts. Like their post bellum successors they were found at the crossroads, at central points in the more populous and older communities, along the rivers. There was, however, a fundamental difference between the ante bellum and postwar stores. Seldom if ever did these earlier businesses attract any considerable attention from the big wholesale houses outside the region. Likewise, they were without the advantage of legislative assistance which was granted the later stores by the reconstruction assemblies.

Never did the ante bellum country stores become a functional, part of southern agriculture and industry. Nor were they advance factors in the expanding of the rapidly growing commercial North. After the war the stores which survived became agents of adjustment for both the rural white yeoman and the Negro freedman.

Louisville was by no means alone in her anxiety for the southern trade. From the very beginning of the post bellum era in the South there existed the famous commercial conventions. These were schemes for selling merchandise by wholesale houses located in large cities on the fringe of the South. Likewise, they proved to mean weeks of general harmless debauchery for the wholesalers and their merchant guests.

The merchants' associations in the wholesale cities saw to it that their members made good impressions upon the rural visitors. If merchants went home and told their fellows in Mississippi, Alabama, Georgia and the Carolinas that the Belknap house in Louisville was hospitable to them, then this firm got a good share of future southern business.

In some instances telegraph facilities were made available

with the hope that merchants would wire home that they were having an exciting trip, and that these cheery messages would tempt other tradesmen to the city.

For the storekeeper these conventions served two purposes. If he were just beginning business, he could select his stock and form personal acquaintances which would be advantageous in the future. If he were well established, then he was able to see many new items before he bought them. Especially was this true of hardware. Hardware drummers were unable to carry samples around with them, and at best their unillustrated catalogue method of selling was a poor makeshift. If a merchant could actually see new types of plow stocks, mechanical planters, rakes, harrows, or improved harness, wagons, and buggies, he was much more apt to buy. The unimaginative country merchant was able to pick up many useful pointers on merchandising which would later yield him profits.

For a week a crossroads merchant could enjoy freely Louisville, Cincinnati, Richmond, Baltimore, Mobile, or Charleston. In some instances he was given free use of streetcars, hotels, restaurants, and theaters. Liquor flowed as freely as there was a desire for it. This was a season when a country merchant got away from home and enjoyed life at its fullest.

In the matter of entertaining the boys from the crossroads, Louisville and Cincinnati made themselves almost ridiculous. For the first twenty-five years after the war it was a fight to see which place was to get a lion's share of the rich southern trade. The Kentucky city enjoyed the strategic position of being astride the two main southern arteries of transportation. So definite was this stranglehold on both the railroad and the river that it led eventually to the construction, safely beyond the influence of Louisville, of a major competing railway line south. The cumbersome old-style invoice books are filled with records of this rivalry, and as better transportation facilities were developed, the flow of goods from the Ohio River towns was greater.

Southern newspapers after the war carried frequent commercial notices from these cities, and the cat and dog fight between them resulted in much good-natured fun at their expense. Occasionally an editor filled in at the end of a short column with a jocular reference to the two cities. "A Cincinnati girl eloped with a Louisville murderer," said an Alabama editor. "She was bound to do better than marry a Cincinnati man anyway."

In 1872, Louisville merchants advertised in the country papers an excursion throughout the South. They used Kentucky's famous Mammoth Cave as a major attraction. Merchants from Eufaula, Columbus, Macon, Savannah, Augusta, West Point, Opelika, Selma, Marion, Mobile, New Orleans, and Meridian were told that they could get special railway rates and it went without saying that their entertainment expenses would be kept to a minimum by the Louisville Merchants' Association.

In Baltimore merchants and manufacturers issued an elaborate cloth-bound directory and stamped on its cover the patronizing legend, "With compliments to the trade of North Carolina," or the trade of some other southern state. A folder from Lynchburg appealed to the small merchants in all of the southern states east of the Mississippi. If visitors purchased a thousand dollars' worth of goods, they were given free round-trip railway tickets. Frequently noncompeting wholesale houses co-operated in bringing country merchants to visit them where they could sell stock directly from their shelves.

For the crossroads merchant himself, there were few incidents in life so exciting as an annual buying journey. It gave him a personal sense of importance and it paid dividends in the good advertising it brought his stock in the community.

The larger cities came to depend upon the tiny outlets in the back country of the South. Their famous conventions were flirtatious gestures by which wholesale merchants wished to capitalize on these modest channels of trade. Thus it was that buried in bends of the rivers, hidden behind mountains, perched on rises of ground beside bayous, and strung along thousands of miles of virtually impassable roads grew hundreds of villages and towns, each one originally no more than a single store building. They were places such as Shoe Heel, Emmalena, White Oak, Sawdust Valley, Dewey Rose, Talno, Ball Ground, Cerro Gordo, Merrilton, Tyrus, Piney Woods, Yocna, Chorique, and Who'd-a-Thought-It known only to the natives, the drummers, Dun and Bradstreet, country politicians, and postal inspectors. But to the big-city wholesalers their influence as centers of trade was vital. They knew where these stores were and how good or how bad the credit of their owners was. They knew also of the millions of dollars' worth of goods which collectively they sold each year.

The stores of the southern countryside quickly became the the heartbeat and pulse of a good portion of American business. In their own communities they were centers of every sort of neighborhood activity. Everything of importance that ever happened either occurred at the store or was reported there immediately. If a man got shot, he somehow arranged to have the shooting take place at the store, or if he wished to give an enemy a first-class flailing, he usually found him on the store porch along with a highly appreciative audience. When he wished to "cuss" the government or to complain to the Lord because of the perfidy of politics and weather conditions, there was no place like the hitching ground around the store. No other place, not even excepting a country church ground, the polls, or a saloon, ever offered quite the same golden opportunity to get drunk. When a man's wife was about to give birth to a baby he bought from the country store twill or birdseye for diapers, flannel for gowns, bottles, black rubber nipples, scraps of unbleached domestic for "sugar teats," and plain goods for long dresses and caps. When his aged mother died he rushed a messenger off to the store with a note to buy her a shroud and metal fixtures for her homemade coffin.

As one old-timer boasted, his store was "where we put

clothes on anything that had a back to wear them between the cradle and the grave, crowded their feet into something to keep them off the ground, and rammed food down everything that had a gullet to swallow it."

2

BEHIND BATTERED FACES

PUTTING ON A FRONT became an important matter after the war. If a man had a small quantity of paint, he smeared it on the face of his house to give it the appearance, from the big road at least, of being painted. Even Negroes daubed a bit of whitewash on their cabin fronts and were satisfied with this single gesture at beautification. It was ever a matter in the South of keeping up a good appearance. So it was with the stores—a shabby little building sometimes had a face that would do credit to a store in Montgomery or Jackson. Somewhere some designer decreed that most store buildings should have square fronts. It was the mark of the trade from Chesapeak Bay to the Gulf and from Roanoke Island to Little Rock, just as a swinging boot pointed out a cobbler's shop and a tricolored spiral pole a barbershop.

Jutting out into the apexes of crossroads, perched on river bluffs, or standing at respectful distances from old-established church houses were the stores, solid, honestly built structures which reared proud, emblematic faces to cover the matter-of-fact meeting of their shingles and rafters. Although the square face was a badge of the trade, the universal porch which clung to the fronts of the buildings was a more practical necessity. It was the place of general preliminary community conferences in winter, and the scene of prolonged meetings in summer. There was no other place quite so well fitted for putting a heavy sack of goods on the back of a mule, or easing a basket of eggs down from a horse, and it was a fine place from which rheumatics and ladies could mount and dismount their horses. Before the porch was the eroded, bare hitching ground and the road where wagons crowded in on Saturdays to get weekly supplies.

Rambling back of the impressive square fronts were two-story buildings. Usually the structures were segmentary organs of progress and ambition. Their first units were built in hope of business, and two and three additions were, in time, made to cover up lack of foresight. Along one side feed or shed rooms leaned against the main buildings like architectural quotation marks. They served as whispering rooms for merchants and customers, and conveniently hid from view an occasional crooking of the elbow with a congenial drummer who brought along a little Bourbon to give a special bit of dash to his attractive line of goods. Women customers were always excluded because here off-color stories were told in their full ribald flavor.

A wide double door, flanked by heavily barred windows, broke the monotonous faces of the buildings. By day the doors were swung open, the heavy window shutters pulled aside and hooked to the corners of the houses. At night strong diagonal iron bars were pulled into place and securely bolted from the inside. More scarred than the veterans who hobbled home from Appomattox were the store doors and jambs. Every drummer pulled down competitive signs and tacked up his own; sheriffs, baliffs, auctioneers, and United States marshals nailed their notices to these informal bulletin boards. Between Garrett Snuff signs and auction notices were the invitational funeral handbills, once a part of southern burial customs. Announcements of all-day speakings, fiddling contests, singings, and camp meetings found their way to the store doors with seasonal regularity. Some store fronts were virtually covered with nails and tack heads. High-pressure American advertising pecked steadfastly at the very sinews of the buildings and like the rings on the body of an aged oak, the layers of nails and tacks divulged the life span of the store.

Some ingenious Yankee must have brought plans for a store south with him even before the war broke out. Even the big, awkward front-door keys bore evidence of being the standardized handiwork of some snowbound Connecticut locksmith who never quite mastered his calling. With the same combination of southern indifference and Yankee stubbornness these keys shoved back the rusty tumblers of crude front-door locks on the bayous in Louisiana, along the Tennessee River, and in the mountains of Virginia.

Above the inevitable porches were the bold white or red signet faces painted by medicine and milling companies which proudly displayed the name of the house. Occasionally an extra-officious metal sign dangled in the breeze to add further dignity to the fact that the building contained a United States Post Office.

There were other telltale elements of the age of postwar standardization. Almost precisely in the middle of the roof lines, stove flues jabbed their blunt and soot-stained noses upward. They were there ostensibly to draw off smoke from the stoves, but actually they performed the more important function of establishing the approximate geometrical center of the building. Many factors decreed that huge potbellied stoves should be in the middle of the long rambling buildings. They were located at the place where the greatest number of people could gather around them, and, too, there was a vain hope that they would heat both ends of the building with some degree of impartiality. Open spaces around the stoves, on the porches, and on the bare ground underneath the near-by shade trees were communal ground, where all neighborhood problems were aired and discussed. Here were the places where every religious doctrine was given the third degree, the weather was abused, and political parties taken to pieces. These were the neutral grounds where notional customers made up their minds to purchase goods or completed their idle "looking around."

During the four decades following the war, the square facets came to be as significant as steeples on churches and clocks on courthouses. In fact, the stores became a part of the trinity of best-known public buildings in the southern country. At Lavonia, Elbert County, Georgia, Colonel McAllister built a storehouse thirty feet wide and eighty feet long, with provisions to extend the building as he pleased. Hardly had he laid the foundation for his store before a competitor was constructing an exact counterpart across the road. Lavonia was growing before it was born. When Colonel McAllister began his store, it was nothing but a mudhole; now it was becoming a town, and idle dreamers began to take pride in the fact that they had a Masonic lodge in the making. They procured promises of a post office and were on the lookout for a doctor, a justice of the peace, and possibly a couple of lawyers. They were the seeds, they hoped, for planting a prosperous new Georgia town.

Above most of the long, rambling store buildings were Masonic lodges which shared their halls with Grangers, Woodmen of the World, and Junior Orders of Mechanics. They were convenient meeting places. Frequently a merchant entered into a peculiar arrangement whereby he would build the lower section of the store, the fraternities the upper, and they jointly financed the roof. So common was the arrangement of joint store and lodge halls that almost all the older houses had the Masonic emblem of the Square and Compass embracing the "big G" bolted securely to their gable ends.

Generally rooms overhead were rich assets for the storekeepers. They proved good trade-getters, and lucky was the merchant who had one. Sometimes, however, the overhead room involved him in impossible situations. Thespians found these rooms ideal places in which to cavort over improvised stages in melodramatic tragedies and comic blackface minstrels. Patrons of Husbandry and Grangers used the lodge hall to lambaste the merchant below for his impoverishing trade practices. Often these irate agrarian organizations adopted resolutions creating trading contracts which forced storekeepers to cut their profits and meet many of the cotton farmers' terms of credits.

But having a church overhead was even more complicating. On occasion, a congregation used these rooms until a church building could be constructed. Colonel Childs, in Elbert County, Georgia, magnanimously offered his overhead room to such an orphan congregation in the hope that it would yield tangible returns in business. The Colonel, however, acted too hastily. A church house was a sacred place of worship—and a place of worship, believed this particular minister, should be dedicated. This was a new and unhappy angle for the accommodating merchant. In the first place, Colonel Childs asked, how could he feel natural doing general-store business in a dedicated place of worship? Then, too, he was selling liquor, and certainly it would not look right to be selling and drinking whisky in a church. He had to withdraw his offer.

When trade expanded, upstairs rooms proved ideal places for keeping the newly introduced ready-made clothing. Men's clothing was lined up on one side and ladies' wear on the other. Occasionally a country milliner moved her sewing machine and bundles of gay-colored feathers and straw braid into these rooms and created top-heavy hats which would hardly pass down the staircase. Gradually other types of merchandise migrated up the steps. When cheap furniture and factory-made coffins came on the market in large quantities, they were stored out of sight in the big rooms; also some types of hardware were moved upstairs.

The external appearance of the average store was as superficial as the hull on a black walnut. It was the inside of the house that counted. Here again was standardization broken only by the degree of general confusion in the arrangement of stock. Near the door on the right hand, in the place of honor, was the United States Post Office with its official oak partition or its homemade bars and its dozen or so locked boxes. In the middle of the oak panel which hovered protectingly over the postmaster and his paper-rattling and string-breaking activities was the stamp and delivery window where customers approached the postal department of their government in a spirit of cautious supplication. Customers were kept well beyond the internal workings of this holy of holies largely because storekeepers themselves had a healthy respect for the postal laws.

Beyond the post office, to the right, a long, heavy, homemade sectional counter extended all the way to the door of the side room. The local carpenters were prodigal in the use of rich heart-pine paneling and molding, and they built counters to last for centuries. On the back sides were bins which either tilted in and out or were mounted on runners to be pulled back and forth as drawers. They were built to hold flour, rice, sugar, coffee, salt, garden seeds, and dried peas.

Rows of heavy drawers with stout knobs and finger pulls were used to hold all sorts of small or loose merchandise. In the early days brogan shoes, the principal item of men's footwear, came from the factory tied in pairs and without individual boxes. These were placed in drawers instead of on shelves. No attention was given to packaging because in most cases shoes were considered the coarsest sort of merchandise, and it made little difference if they were scratched and bruised in handling. Even today many of the old counter drawers are reservoirs of historical American footwear. Occasionally a pair of brogan shoes has been left in stock, or there are pairs of the famous red-top boots with copper toe-plates, or the heavy, stiff, child's "low cut" shoes to tell the sentimental story of childhood footwear for the years after the war.

Across the aisle in the approximate front half of the store, the improved glass showcase in time crowded out the sturdy wooden counter. These were filled with heterogeneous mixtures of fancy merchandise such as ribbons, buttons, needles, pens, collar buttons, knitting needles, hatpins, bow and self-tied four-in-hand ties, hairpins, corset stays, hair rats, pencils, garters, slate pencils, hooks and eyes, bottles of perfume, rings, earbobs, necklaces, dollar watches, scissors, and thimbles.

Aside from their heterogeneous stock of merchandise and their curious old buildings, the merchants were curators along with the country editors of informal museum collections. Large rattlesnakes, water moccasins, and hornets' nests were hung up on the porches for brief displays, or they were stuffed and placed on more permanent display on the inside. Deer-horns, eagle's feathers, owl's claws, queer-shaped eggs, extraordinary pieces of whittling or wire bending, Indian arrowheads and stone axes, Civil War relics, and newspapers, queer coins, strange root growths and weird knots from trees, first cotton blooms, and every other article of wonderment were left for the public to see. At Danielsville, Georgia, Doc Ferguson exhibited in 1878 a strange rooster which had two horns and no spurs.

In some other communities, storekeepers were either custodians of or they knew the whereabouts of those wonderful instruments of folk-medicine madstones. When a mad dog went on the rampage and bit someone, a messenger was sent in mad flight to fetch the stone and its owner to draw off the rabies infection.

There were showcases filled with an array of shirtwaists, paper collars, shirt fronts, bustles, false breasts, corsets, stocking holders, cloth, ladies' hats, shoes, trousers, suspenders, derby hats, stockings, and socks. Then there were the glass-top counters which were filled with bottles of herb tonics, dry herb mixtures, cans of pomade, fancy toilet and shaving soap, talcum powder, black rubber nursing nipples, fruit-jar rings, shoestrings, shoe polish, fishhooks, lead bars, balls of gum, opium, camphor, asafetida, and bottles of morphine. In a corner of these cases, well hidden from both the critical and the curious, were plain little cardboard boxes which contained the iniquitous devices of contraception which were called for in private conference behind the closed doors of the feed rooms, and which were smuggled to customers in the most adroit manner.

The back half of the store was devoted to heavy barreled goods and hardware. There were kept the barrels of whisky, molasses, lard, salt, coffee, rice, sugar, vinegar, kerosene, and engine oil. One grave offender in this mixed assortment of liquid merchandise was the kerosene barrel. The oil companies spent many thousands of dollars trying to perfect a barrel and pump which would prevent this highly absorbent product from ruining other goods. They failed, as many a country-store customer could have told you. Kerosene oil was forever getting into the sugar or the lard or the meat box, and sometimes it reached the liquor barrel. It had a sneaking way of creeping along the floor and contaminating everything it touched. Even the most casual merchant had to exercise special caution to keep kerosene away from its incompatible neighbors if he hoped to stay in business.

"Keep the cover on the barrel" was the golden text of storekeeping. One never knew when the strangest of foreign substances would get into the rice, peas, sugar, lard, and coffee. Rats and mice had a way of getting into bulk groceries, but most dreaded of all offenders was the docile store cat. The cat, of course, was a necessary fixture in every store, and, wisely, one standard requirement in the construction of every storehouse was an adequate "cathole" through which the feline guardsman could pass and repass without constant personal attention. Inevitably, however, careless persons placed obstacles in front of this passage and left the cat locked in the store. Thus many a barrel of loose groceries was ruined, and unholy wrath was brought down on the heads of clerks for their carelessness.

Clumsy racks kept whisky and molasses barrels off the floor at jug height so they could easily be emptied into the passing parade of receptacles which came to their spouts. More than convenience, however, necessitated keeping the whisky barrel above the floor. If barrels were not high enough, or were too near the wall, there was a reasonably good chance that they would be emptied at night by use of a brace and bit and a short length of pipe. Sometimes these casks were set on iron plates to protect them. North Carolina thieves once bored a series of holes diagonally across the floor of a building in search of a barrel of liquor. In south Georgia a thief fastened a spigot to a barrel underneath the floor and for a time enjoyed an abundant supply of free liquor.

There were prohibitionists among the merchants, but even the most pious were tempted by the easy profits and they ordered whisky by the barrel. Invoice books contain frequent orders. From Kentucky came the early brands—Wildcat Family Whisky, Old Taylor, Old Pepper, Lexington Club House, Harrison County and Bonnie Brothers' Bourbon—and from Maryland came the old southern favorite, Maryland Club. The records of the personal accounts show that many a pious toper bought whisky in the name of his wife, or on the flimsy excuse that he was having a special affair and needed a little liquor to help things along. Perhaps none ever thought up a more elaborate and hypocritical manner of ordering liquor than did George Washington Spinks of Alabama, who asked J. C. Brown to send him "a pint of good whisky for my wife and a small bottle of good paregoric. Tell Strudrick that the bottle of paregoric that I got from him turned out to be whisky certain as I have made toddies for my wife."

As a matter of ritual each fall, the farmer brought his cotton to the merchant's gin, sold it at the store and paid his year's account if he had enough money. The merchant in turn rallied the farmers around the barrel and gave them powerful drinks of the raw stuff by the tin dipperful. This was expected by the cotton farmers as a part of their business, and if they got a little rowdy each fall, no one thought anything of it. Cotton wagons bumping long miles over Georgia, Mississippi, and South Carolina hill roads carried brown-stone liquor jugs buried in seed cotton, "to get a little liquor," said the drivers, "for the old ladies." Late in the afternoon of the fall months many a gaunt pair of cotton mules made their way home with their masters sprawled drunk as lords on the spring seats. They had paid their debts, and they were coming home free and drunk to prove it.

At Society Hill, Virginia, J. M. Waddell and Company did a general merchandise business, but their liquor trade was of such magnitude that they advertised North Carolina corn whisky on their letterhead. In 1882, Mr. Waddell wrote the distillers in North Carolina that he expected a big fall business and that he wanted a good supply of corn whisky to serve the trade. Always the reformers were upbraiding the country-store liquor trade by citing the fact that cuttings and rows of all sorts occurred around the stores because they sold liquor. There were many who embarrassed the merchants in the early seventies by saying that the reason the Negroes were drunkards was the fact that they sold them liquor.

Beyond the liquor and molasses barrels off in one corner was a long, greasy counter which sat directly in front of one of the grocery shelves. Lined up in solid phalanx on the counter top were bottles of pepper sauce, catsup, and vinegar. There were the inevitable boxes of salt and red and black pepper. Piles of cracked bowls and assortments of tarnished knives, forks, and tablespoons were permanent fixtures. At one end stood the lords of the counter, the mechanical cheese cutters equipped with broad knives. One stroke of the handle moved the golden yellow disc of cream around a "nickel's worth." Selling cheese at the lunch counter was never a matter of fractions of pounds, but rather the "clicking" of the levers. Flanking the cheese cutters were the twenty-four-pound boxes of crackers from which clerks dipped crackers on the irregular price basis of "one handful, one nickel."

Eating dinner from a country-store counter was an experience which brought joy of variety and spiciness which rural southerners could get nowhere else. Southern fried chicken and hot biscuits were commonplace when compared with the fare of the counter. It was here that more than half of the South's population was introduced for the first time to "bought" prepared foods. The oyster fishermen of the southern Gulf and Atlantic coastal waters, the Norwegian and Maine canners, and Gustavius Swift and the Armours and Cudahy of the Middle West earned handsome profits from their cove oysters, sardines, and link sausages. No statistician has even seen fit to investigate the importance of this outlet in the fishing and packing industries, but certainly its influence was considerable.

On Saturdays hungry cotton and tobacco farmers consumed literally thousands of cases of oysters, sardines, salmon, and link sausages. Most popular of all, however, was the sardine packed in cottonseed oil, seasoned with pepper sauce, and eaten with salty crackers. So popular was this combination that it was recognized as a popular characteristic of the entire country-store trade.

The cove oyster was a powerful competitor of the sardine. At many places along the southern coast line, canneries packed oysters during the fall and winter seasons and distributed them to their big inland market through the wholesale houses. This product was a bit fancier than the sardine and it appealed to a little more delicate taste than did any other of the canned sea foods, but nevertheless it had its enthusiastic partisans. A can of cove oysters served in one of the store's cracked bowls with a handful of crackers, a bottle of pepper sauce, and a nickel's worth of cheese was a Christmas dinner in July for a customer who was fagged out on "steady" rations.

Both walls of the store were lined with shelves. On the dry-goods side were bolts of cloth and oilcloth. Across the way there was an assortment of schoolbooks, pencil tablets, canned goods, medicine, hardware, spices, castor oil, turpentine, pills, chewing tobacco, snuff, cigars, vanilla extract, laundry soap, baking powder, soda, and epsom salts.

Along the top of the counter were the J. and P. Coats cabinets. Every store had an assortment of these small walnut, maple, and cherry cases filled with thread and trinkets. There were the smaller ones with two, three, and five sliding drawers, and then there were the larger golden-oak ones built like desks which most of the merchants used as top-of-the-counter catchalls.

These thread cases had back of them a long story of Scotch-American enterprise. J. and P. Coats started business in Paisley, Scotland, in 1826, and in 1870 a branch of the company was operating in America in connection with the Conant Thread Company. This latter organization had its beginning along with that of the New South itself. Hezekiah Conant and a group of associates started in the thread business in Pawtucket, Rhode Island, in 1868, with a capital stock of $30,000, but the thread business in America promised to be a prosperous one, and Conant persuaded the Scotch company to come to America. The first J. and P. Coats thread was wound in the Pawtucket plant in April, 1870, and the American demand for it brought about the construction of three additional plants within four years.

Actually the black and gold label bearing the legend J. AND P. COATS BEST SIX CORD was introduced first in America in 1840, but it did not become a universally familiar product until the American factories were built. The ingenious Scotch thread winders had an eye for the country trade, and they printed from the beginning a six-inch ruler on their boxes which became an important household tool.

The thread business in postwar America was a prosperous one, and advertising men for the highly competitive companies had to devise clever methods for keeping their goods before the public. By a lucky circumstance, the J. and P. Coats Company hit upon the idea of utilizing the by-products of their spool factory to make cases which could be placed on counters in stores. Their names were placed in bold letters on the fronts of the drawers, first on brass strips and later behind glass panels. In 1887 a special box factory was erected in Pawtucket to turn out thousands of boxes for country-store counters. Merchants bought thread and received the box free. These thread cases became as standard in the southern stores as the lunch counters and Arm and Hammer baking soda.

But "Best Six Cord Thread" was not to enjoy its popular market unchallenged. Other thread winders sensed the rich possibilities and entered the fight by giving away paper dolls, jingle books, calendars, thimbles, songbooks, and fancy miniature boxes. The eighties were sentimental years, years when making scrapbooks was a joyous female pastime, and the thread manufacturers were quick to take commercial advantage of this spirit of sentimentality by giving away serialized pictures and cards. A formalized domestic scene or a bit of Poor Richard moralizing came with so many spools of thread, and, with true Yankee foresight, a considerable capital outlay on the part of the customer was necessary to acquire the whole series. These devices of advertising became big business within themselves, and soon the companies were spending millions of dollars annually to promote their lines. Women made nearly all of the clothes worn by the family, and every purchase of cloth included several spools of thread. So common, in fact, was the thread trade that many lazy bookkeepers made the simple entry "1 spool $.05."

Dividing the front aisle into two passageways were rows of tables on which were displayed pants, overalls, jumpers, socks, stockings, dishes, caps, hats, pitchers, bowls, and shoes. Back of these were the racks loaded with cheap ready-made clothing.

A generous circular space was left about the stove, for this was customers' ground. Kegs of nails and horseshoes, rickety chairs, soft-pine boxes, and knife-scarred benches were pulled up within easy spitting distance of the bulging stove. This was the scene of gabbling, whittling, yarn spinning, chewing, dipping, and sly nipping at the bottle. From the very beginning merchants resigned themselves to the inevitable fact that their stoves were going to be spat upon. Customers looked upon this practice as their inalienable right, and no power short of death could deny it to them. Most merchants made only one attempt to curb this traditional right and that was by putting spacious sandboxes around the bases of the stoves.

When spring arrived and the weather once again permitted the philosophers to move outside, the average stove in a country store gave the appearance of having been at sea among the barnacles for several years. Likewise, every break in the counters was fair territory and came in for a constant bombardment from less fastidious customers. There was no place in country stores for "nice" men as merchants. Before they could have finished their first week, they would have given up in disgust and gone back to Alsace, Connecticut, or to life on a farm.

Counterpart to the constant chewing and dipping was the beloved pastime of whittling. The country store was the only place in the South where a man could find a piece of soft northern box pine on which to use his razor-sharp barlow knife. Whittling was an exact and delicate art. Some exponents of the knife whittled for a purpose; they cut out forms and faces and then whittled them away to begin all over again. Then there were those who stuck to making long smooth surfaces or making angles and ovals. The sensation of keen knife blade gliding smoothly along a piece of pine board was a satisfying one. The less artistic whittled for no other purpose than that of making long thin shavings and of keeping their hands busy. They were the ones who idly cut holes in the nail kegs or rendered in twain bench slats. Then, too, whittling was a fine decoy. One never had to look his associates in the eye and give away the purpose or complete lack of purpose in his conversation.

Down the center aisle past the public circle were racks loaded with meal and flour in bags, salt, and feed. Piled up behind these were odd lots of hardware. No space was wasted; plows, wagon spokes, buggy shafts, coils of rope, plowshares, axes, wedges, sledge hammers, rolls of bagging, and ties were on open display where not too much effort was required to point them out to customers. Shopping for many goods became a matter of craning the neck around the whole store. Hanging from the ceiling were many crude but necessary utensils and tools of the everyday life in the rural South. There were the well buckets of Samuel Woodworth's sentimental song, stocky wooden kegs heavily bound in brass and "swung" with sturdy iron bails, which were a vital part of the long era of the "dug" well. Securing a water supply in the country was a major physical undertaking. Surely the poetic

Woodworth never had to draw enough water from a dug well with one of these heavy, three-gallon, keglike buckets to quench the thirst of a lot full of livestock, or to supply a large family. Their inevitable loose staves spouted water all over the drawee, their rough, wet chains had an unhappy way of getting themselves covered with sand, and the rickety, rusty pulleys were always suspended from flimsy crossbars. Nothing tested the fortitude of a southerner just home from the spiritually revitalizing influences of a camp meeting so much as drawing water barehanded for a herd of thirsty cows. It was by the side of the back-country wells that much of southern womanhood lost both beauty and health. There was none of the Old Testament romance connected with these shallow sources of water below the Mason and Dixon line.

The red-cedar stave water buckets also to be seen swinging from store ceilings completed a vicious cycle of unprogressiveness. Every self-respecting household had a water shelf on the back porch which was crowned with a cedar bucket, a gray enameled washpan, and a gourd or tin dipper. Water from a cedar bucket, thought the countrymen, always tasted better and was healthier. Tin and enamel buckets poisoned drinking water that was allowed to remain standing in them, so wooden pails were universally used. There was a fine point in the mores of the back-porch shelves: Careless, sloven persons put the dipper back in the bucket after they had finished drinking, but the well-bred put it down beside the bucket or hung it on a nail driven in a near-by post. This was not primarily a point of sanitation, but rather a principle of rural chivalry. A large portion of these back-porch fountains was made in Fayetteville, North Carolina, by the Fayetteville Wood Ware Company, and they were as necessary in the stock of country stores as were J. and P. Coats thread and hoops of cheese.

Related to the buckets only because of a common position on the store ceilings was that other emblem of polite southern home life, the chamber pot. These earthen and enamel receptacles alternated between discreet places in the sun just inside garden gates in the daytime and underneath the guest-room beds at night. Ordinarily they were not designed for members of the family, who knew the lay of the land and could find their way around in the dark, but rather for guests, the sick, and the occasional ministerial callers. As a matter of fact, earthenware chambers became as much a part of the tradition of the minister's visit as feather beds and fried chicken. Large numbers of invoices among store records tell the vivid story of the fragility of these simple masterpieces of the potters' wheels. Baltimore was a great distributing center of these homely articles. D. F. Hayne and Company and Frank M. Baker and Company sold them at wholesale for as little as $1.75 per dozen.

Keeping store was a game of guessing just where something might be found, and always involved hazy directions of looking under something or behind something else. A western Kentuckian once ordered a shipment of "buckheads" for steel beam plows and put them in the accustomed place where buckheads were kept, but when a customer wanted one, he could not find it. His whole psychological system of locating buckheads was unaccountably upset. He wrote the wholesale house asking that a new supply be sent at once. Not until he had gone through the regular procedure of putting the new ones away did he discover the ones he already had.

There is another old anecdote told on storekeepers everywhere that illustrates their indifference to orderly stock-keeping. It's the old pump-handle story. A merchant ordered a pump, and when all of the crating and excelsior padding was pulled apart, the handle was missing. After a diligent search the storekeeper decided that the wholesale house had maliciously left him in the lurch, and in an impassioned letter he bemeaned the shipper for his willful duplicity. But before he could seal the letter, a boy came in to say he had found the handle. Instead of destroying the letter and forgetting the matter, the storekeeper added the mildly apologetic postscript. "Never mind what I have said. We have found the damned thing," and sent it on.

As the architecture of country stores was standardized, so was their odor. It seldom varied from one store to the next, and it was as impossible to define as an institutional odor could ever be. It had, however, a great fascination. Perhaps it was because the smell was a vital part of the exciting confusion which prevailed everywhere. Like the casual mixture of hardware and groceries, dry goods and notions, tobacco, onions, whisky, and soap, the scent was of nothing in particular and everything in general. It was in reality an odoriferous inventory of the entire stock. It was of the glaze on the calicoes and the starch in the checks, rotting cabbages and potatoes, spring-onion sets, cheese, neat's-foot oil, leather polish on new shoes, oil and wax on saddles, horse collars, and buggy harness, kerosene, sardines, salmon, the stove, tobacco, the cat, the customers, asafetida, peppermint and wintergreen candy, and engine oil. It was a blend of salt meat, rats and mice, paint on plow tools, cottonseed oil, bananas, tar on steel cotton ties, jute bagging, mixed "sweet" feed, and naphtha soap.

Thus it was that the store became more than a market for produce and a place in which to buy supplies. Its stove in cold weather and its porch and shade trees in spring, summer, and fall were places of general assembly. Merchants were busy long hours each day with the affairs of the community. Inside their little latticework doors and beside the tall breast-high shelflike desks, they worked at their books and held whispered conversations with their debtors. Trading followed a ritualistic procedure. A boy rushed in with a note and handed it to a clerk, and the clerk in turn consulted with the merchant *sotto voce*. The order was either approved or disapproved and the boy was sent on his way. Timid customers led storekeepers away from curious ears to talk over crop prospects and credit situations. In this way business went on from day to day in one whispering conference after another.

Country storekeeping was one-half orthodox merchandising and the other half sizing up the capabilities and honesty of customers. It was a highly personal sort of enterprise which required a generous amount of giving and taking and a keen sense of humor and understanding of all the frailties of mankind.

Few country merchants ever heard of statistics, but they were always well informed about the crop every customer had planted and about its general state of cultivation from week to week. They knew the approximate size of shoes, the length of legs, chest measures, and girths of most of their customers. From week to week they took mental notes of goods which they showed, knowing full well that most customers would go home and debate the matter before making a purchase, and would then send a note. They were philosophers who weighed five pounds of sugar, cut off huge pieces of fat meat, pumped five gallons of kerosene, or dished up buckets of lard while they kept up a steady flow of advice or lamentation. Working hard, living closely, and paying all debts was ever a cardinal rule of economy with them. Their whole philosophy of the credit system was one of strict control and constant retrenchment for the debtor. Paying one's debts was ever a virtue which gave customers high standing at the stores.

In the words of the editor of the Fayetteville (North Carolina) *Eagle* in 1872, the merchants often advised their customers to "plant cotton this year, make your own meat and bread at home, *but always have a pile of cotton bales to bring in clear money at the end of the year.*" The editor found near his office the pleasantest sight of all to the general merchant. Stacked in irregular rows were "fifty odd bales of cotton—big heavy bales of five hundred pounds each, and it is sold for $.20; one hundred dollars in cash for each bale. . . ." Here was the one-crop system of agriculture of the New South being born and wrapped in swaddling clothes. Behind the swinging lattice gate to his little office, the storekeeper read illiterate order notes and recorded charges against the credit of his customers. He was a puppet master who made his community go through its peculiar economic dance.

Typical country stores: The stock of stores like these was practically inexhaustible. (Photographs courtesy J. Winston Coleman, Jr.)

Fox races, tobacco, cotton, horses, women, politics, religion—no subject is barred from the most serious or light-hearted consideration. *Above*: At the storeside. *Opposite*: In good weather, the porch provides a forum and meeting place. (Photograph above courtesy J. Winston Coleman, Jr.)

DRINK
ROYAL CROWN
COLA
Take Home a Carton
POST-OFFICE.
LINWOOD KY.

Scenes of rural enterprise in bygone days.

3

STOVE OR SHADY PORCH

"RIDE UP and get down and look at your saddle!" was a southern countryman's favorite greeting. When a smart-aleck stranger rode up to a store in Bowman, Georgia, and asked of a crowd of loafers if there were any fools about, a sharp one answered in a flash, "I do not think so—are you lonely?"

The average southern farmer would have been bored mightily if he had not known that when the weather was bad he could always mingle with kindred souls at the store. He fabricated the flimsiest of excuses to get away from home when it was raining or the weather was too cold for outside work. A wag in 1876 said that when one of the members of the "Flatwoods Gentlemen's Leisure Club swaggers up to a store and pulls off his hat, slaps his leg, and says 'Whew! I've done the biggest day's work today I ever did in my life' the other members know he has been in a shady nook while his wife cut stove wood and blacked his brogans."

Often families drove to the nearest village and spent the day visiting with their neighbors and buying their supplies. Sometimes they brought their dinners and ate them in their wagons or combined the contents of their baskets with those of other customers and made a picnic of the meal. Morning was spent in selling produce and looking around, and at least half of the afternoon was spent in gossiping. By midafternoon both white and black customers got in a hurry to buy their supplies, load their wagons, and get home in time to feed the stock. Merchants became accustomed to this type of spasmodic trading, so they never made an effort to spread their business over the entire day, but spent their idle time gathering in the news and passing along advice.

Through the week most stores were deserted except for the habitual loafers who hung around to pitch dollars or to use the checkerboards, or for customers who came to get spare parts for farm tools and extra tobacco to tide them over until Saturday. Long drowsy afternoons found faithful checker players stooped over their grimy boards. The assortment of checkers which slid heavily back and forth under indecisive fingers traveled hundreds of miles in their history of moving from one tiny square to the next. Neighborhood checker fiends spent much of their time each year pondering the momentous question of the "next move." Some of them reached such a lethargic state that the only signs of life was an occasional shifting of the head to one side to spit out tobacco juice or occasionally to slap a thigh when some strategic move bottled up an opponent. A storekeeper, in idle moments, often fell victim to checkerboards and card playing and allowed these frivolities to interfere seriously with the conduct of his business. It was not unusual for a merchant to deny that he had certain articles in stock when a pestiferous customer insisted that he leave a game to wait upon him.

Hand in glove with the constant checker playing and the profound discussions which enlivened the company of loafers and customers were the merry yarn-spinning fests. Heads were bowed close together and voices toned down to practically an inaudible droning, and one salacious yarn after another was told and applauded. In stores where all the clerking was done by men, women usually kept well back out of these charmed circles. They stood near the front door with embarrassed grins on their faces showing clearly mixed feelings of eager curiosity and shocked modesty. They were caught in the unhappy situation of not knowing whether to stay until someone came to serve them or to leave the store.

There were some merchants, like the Cohn Brothers of Lorman, Mississippi, who forbade customers the privilege of loafing about their stove or of playing checkers in the house. And occasionally a pietistic reformer put the indolent and sinful ones to shame. Such a person was Mr. Boggs of Selma, Alabama, who placed an exceedingly high premium on rural morals. Generously he offered "five shares of stock in the Central Agricultural and Mechanical Association valued at fifty dollars to the young man between the ages of seventeen and twenty-one, a native of Alabama, who can show the best record of *industry* and morality, who has not taken a chew of tobacco, nor smoked a cigar, nor taken a drink of whisky, nor used any profane language, and who has engaged in some honorable business for the last twelve months." This pious challenge must have caused a considerable number of chuckles in the Selman and Columbiana countryside. Certainly the self-righteous Brother Boggs was safe. There could hardly be a seventeen-year-old country boy growing up around a country store who could say truthfully that he had never chewed tobacco or "cussed."

Between 1915 and 1930 much of this social element withered away and died. No longer did men sit and swing bony legs down from these porches and shout simple witty quips at their neighbors, and the communities were indeed poorer for this loss.

The boys of the earlier days always had an answer. There was no wiser spot on earth than the porches which jutted out from the long shotgun buildings or the whittling circles about their stoves—places of the telling of thousands of yarns, the production of bumper dream crops, the exchange of all the news and community gossip, and heated discussions of every religious philosophy known to southerners. The porches were literal platforms for delivery of the rampant speeches of hundreds of flannel-mouthed demagogues who sought every office from constable to United States senator.

Poor roads and generally ineffective means of communication had brought the stores into existence and then helped them to prosper. The roads were a prime topic of discussion in store forums from the time big front doors were opened in the morning until they were locked at night. Throughout the long period of ante bellum history an army of garrulous politicians and impractical visionaries poured forth eloquent words on "internal improvements," but somehow they made little headway with actual accomplishments.

The South came out of the Civil War without a plan for the future of her highways. In winter a traveler was buried in mud, and in summer he was smothered by dust. Building and maintaining country roads was an unsolved riddle, and few local politicians were brave enough to institute a system of taxation sufficient to finance road building. Instead the responsibility fell directly upon the citizens themselves. Road supervisors and commissioners "warned" the male population out for so many days each year, and every man over twenty-one years of age was required either to give work or to contribute an equivalent in money, unless he was otherwise excused. Among the records of the country merchants are occasional reports of commissioners showing the names of citizens either checked off or penalized.

If a commissioner was reasonably patient, every man in his district would in time come walking up to the store and save him many long horseback rides.

A highway, before the advent of the automobile, was a narrow winding, mud-choked streak across the landscape. With careful maneuvering, two cotton wagons could pass each other at most places. Bridges across streams and creeks were designed primarily to aid a wagon to pass over them without getting the team drowned.

Back of this whole problem was the faulty assumption that the higher soft dirt was piled in the middle of the road the quicker it would drain. Road machinery was unknown. Victims caught in the "warnings" came equipped with axes, shovels and hoes. One and two-horse turning plows were used for opening ditches, and soft dirt was piled with flimsy "A-frame" drags. Where sticky hills and long stretches of miry bottom lands became impassable, short split pine poles were laid down in long panels of corduroy and then buried beneath a slushy covering of mud. Elsewhere shovel and axe gangs filled the deeper holes with pine tops and again heaped on mounds of loose soil.

Here was one fundamental weakness of the New South. While her officials made eloquent speeches from store porches, at community picnics and from balconies of court-houses, and while they bowed and scraped to the "fairest of all times," their mules and horses floundered in mud up to their bellies and the axles of their vehicles dragged ground.

Discussion of bad roads was a point of departure for the lengthy communal forums. A half-frozen, mud-splattered individual rode a partially drowned mule up to a hitching rack at a store and then made his way to the fire. In language in keeping with his appearance, the countryman described his ordeal in getting to the store.

Rescuing a wagon loaded with cotton from a quagmire of soft pipe clay and quicksand was an accomplishment of strategy and execution equal to that of many a general who fought victoriously against similar odds in the Civil War. Merchants knew their customers spoke the truth. Most of their stock was dragged in from distant railway stations. Barrels of sugar, meal, whisky, flour, and sacks of coffee and rice had arrived covered with mud from having been rolled off wagons in the middle of mudholes. Scores of ledger entries indicate money paid out for hauling. It required two long days to go sixteen treacherous miles and return. These wagon trips would have been monotonous had the drivers not been devil-may-care rowdies who took the mud as a part of their life. The less adventursome customers listened to stories of drinking liquor by the gallon to keep warm, catching chickens on fishhooks baited with corn and dragged behind wagons, and stealing hogs to cook at the campfires. Once when two drunken Mississippi drivers became bored with riding their wagon, they stole a buggy, hooked it on behind the wagon, and plodded home in grand style!

Few issues were so hotly debated as that of fence laws. For more than two centuries most southerners had done about as they pleased, and one of the best proofs of this was the habit of grazing their cows at large. Now this issue moved like the boll weevil across the country from one county to the next. The stores were centers of the conflict, and many rampant arguments which began by the stoves were finished in fist fights on the outside. Elections were held to decide the question, but more often than not, no results were forthcoming.

The problem of cattle grazing was not only one of an open or closed range, but also of how long a range should be closed. Some farmers judged the proper length of the "closed" season by the minimum time it took them to grow and pull the last nubbin of corn, and pick the final shriveled lock of cotton. When they had the last of their cotton and corn on a wagon, they opened wide the gates and turned their livestock out to pester laggard neighbors, excusing themselves with the explanation that "they didn't have nothing out that a cow could hurt, and their neighbors oughtn't to." From Winchester, Virginia, to Shreveport, and from Somerset, Kentucky, to Mobile, store forums roared with arguments over the range question. On the part of the voters, the issue was always clear: did they want to fence in their pastures or their fields?

The Scriptures were another favorite subject for dispute. Negroes were permitted in these discussions provided they did not call the white man a liar and confined their remarks to the Hebrew children or the confusing figures of Revelation. Uncle Will Graham for many years rode his ramshackle old crosstie wagon to Tom and Louis Massey's store in Winston County, Mississippi, to set the boys straight on the Bible. Uncle Will's favorite theme was the spiritual whereabouts of the Savior, and when with a voice as stern as that of William Harrison as "De Lawd" he puffed out his shriveled old chest and pounded it with a bony black hand, shouting, "Boys, Jesus is right hyar!" they believed him. Years later, in Fair

Brothers' big general store in the cotton town of Louisville, Uncle Will was still having the loafers feel of his chest and of a thumping heart which was right.

In regions where Methodists, Presbyterians, Disciples of Christ, and Baptists were predominant faiths, there were eternal arguments over church organization—deacons versus elders and stewards. But the hottest of all was over baptism. Methodists and Presbyterians aligned themselves against the Disciples of Christ and the Baptists. One side believed in infant baptism and the other did not. Two of them sprinkled and the other two immersed, and their members argued back and forth on long summer afternoons. Perhaps no one was ever convinced, but at least he found the discussions delightfully infuriating.

All of the stores had Bibles, either as stock or as standard argument-settlers, and those which have survived show signs of rough service. One old South Carolina merchant in a solid Protestant community owns a huge Vulgate Bible which is practically torn to pieces. It has not only settled arguments, but it has started many new ones because of its variations with the King James version. Perhaps as a result of these forums the South remained far more tolerant than it might have otherwise.

There was scarcely a dividing line between religion and politics in the southern country stores. Here was a public assembly where southerners could strike back at their political oppressors without too much fear of revenge. As the stores became more numerous, their influence as public political stamping grounds increased rapidly. Surely many of the major southern political movements grew out of these discussions. Certainly the Ku Klux Klan movement was given active support through the merchants who procured new types of guns and ammunition to be used in the nocturnal raids against Negro and carpetbag rule.

When General Wade Hampton was campaigning for the governorship in upper South Carolina around Lexington,

Edgefield, and Abbeville, there was a considerable show of Red Shirt, or Hampton Partisan, strength. At Abbeville a procession of knights three miles long galloped into town to honor their chief. Old merchants in this region still recall this period.

In McCormack County, at one store which antedated the war, the Red Shirts met in the lodge hall and secured arms through the store downstairs. The Ruff store in Ridgeway bought rifles and cartridges for Hampton's men, and its basement became a veritable arsenal. The near-by modern Ruff store still has samples of the old cartridges. By the time General Hampton's Red Shirts were terrorizing the countryside of South Carolina and were forming clubs at every crossroads, country stores were buying the newly improved and more effective Winchester and Henry rifles which had come on the market that year.

Occasionally brazen paragraphs appeared in the columns of county papers which gave evidence of the gun trade. As early as 1868, the editor of the Fayetteville (North Carolina) *Eagle* was whooping up the arms trade. He informed his southern friends that "George L. Johnson, untiring and energetic agent for the celebrated house of Yale, McFarland, and Company of New York is now in town. We are pleased to learn of his trip here and further South. . . . Friend George is a good drummer, and is building up a good trade, but from the great number of guns he has sold South, we are inclined to think he is somewhat disloyal, and may be in sympathy with the Ku Kluxes. Our local has tried him twice and has ever been entirely satisfied with goods and prices."

That arms salesmen were successful farther south is vouched for by the testimony of Attorney General D. H. Chamberlain of South Carolina. General Chamberlain told the "Joint Select Committee to Enquire into the Condition of Affairs in the Late Insurrectionary States" on June 10, 1871, that Hope Brothers in Columbia shipped large quantities of arms out into the state and that the Democrats were arming themselves with Winchesters and Henry rifles. Elsewhere through the numerous volumes of testimony gathered by the committee, witnesses gave an indication of the gun trade in the state, and there is little doubt but that this testimony was generally truthful. Stored away in store basements and attics, the new rifles were businesslike instruments of death. Their heavy blunt-nosed, rim-fire 45-70-caliber bullets enabled politically oppressed white Democrats to carry the war to their enemies.

When one unit of Wade Hampton's Red Shirts rode to Edgefield to attend a political meeting, they ran amuck of colored sharpshooters hidden in the top of a pine tree. Knight John Gilmore was shot by Negroes from ambush, and as a result one of the store clubs in the adjoining county of McCormack went into action. For several days a local state of civil war prevailed. Alfred B. Williams has left a good account of the complete movement in the state in his posthumous book, *Hampton and His Red Shirts*. Many old-timers can yet be warmed up to the subject around the stoves. Newspaper accounts are often graphic. The *Carolina Review* requested its readers to "Rally around the Red Shirts. Are you going to Monroe [North Carolina] soon? When you go up be sure to call at the store of Messrs. Stevens Brothers and English, general merchandise. They are the noblest work of God, honest men. South Carolina is represented in this house by two true and gallant knights of the Red Shirted brotherhood. They delight in donning the old garment."

Since South Carolina became more deeply involved in the slough of reconstruction than most of the other southern states, the political activities around the country stores were more dramatic. At old Mathias Singly's store at Jolly Street in Newberry County, the white voters took a decisive hand in controlling the elections. In 1876 the Democrats voted tickets four inches long and two inches wide, while Republicans used ballots twelve by three. When the votes were counted, it was discovered that there were far more ballots cast than there were voters registered. Of course, some means had to be found by which this error could be corrected. G. M.

Singly proposed that a Democrat be blindfolded and allowed to withdraw ballots until the excess votes were drawn off. The drawing, according to the Democrats, was to be above suspicion. Everyone wanted a fair election, but it was an interesting fact that the blindfolded Democrat could feel only the large Republican ballots.

Of greater importance in the South Carolina election of 1876, however, was the part played by Wade Hampton's knights of white home rule. At Longshores' store a Red Shirt club was organized, and it became immediately a decisive factor in local politics. Across Newberry County another club was organized at Jolly Street around the store owned by the Singlys. Uncle Mat Singly was a colorful Rebel who had spent months in a federal prison and had cultivated a profound respect for Yankee discipline. When the boys asked the illiterate old man to join the Red Shirt Club, he balked. "You might as well let alone, you might as well let alone," stormed the former soldier, "when he [I] takes a compendium he is hard to consequence." So hard was the crusty reprobate to "consequence" that he refused to have anything to do with the Hampton crusade so long as there were Union troops left on South Carolina soil.

By 1878 the menace of radical reconstruction was ended in Georgia. Once again native sons sought election to office without the aggravation of federal soldiers, Republicans, and Negroes in control of the polling places. Old Confederate favorites offered their names for election on the Democratic ticket. "Little Aleck" Stephens continued in politics, but in this contest William M. Reese, a local candidate, opposed him. The campaign grew warm between the loyal men "in gray" and those who would put the former vice-president of of the Confederacy on the shelf. William Reese's supporters advertised in the papers that they were leaving tickets at the stores with the name of the Honorable William Reese printed on them. But Alexander H. Stephens' supporters were equally active, and they distributed handbills to the voters across the counters, and in the election their man won.

Store porches were choice "stumps" from which bellowing politicians roared promises of faithfulness after election; hitching grounds were ideal places for shaking hands. Weather-beaten, red-necked farmers in faded chambray shirts and denim overalls bleached by too many dippings in lye soap spat tobacco juice in the sand and greeted every candidate in sight. Candidates cornered certain of these black-crowned patriachs of the wool-hat fraternity and persuaded them to "go down the line" in their neighborhoods. When the crowd grew restless and began milling about, bighearted office seekers chipped in and bought treats from the storehouse barrels of Bourbon. Free cans of sardines, oysters, salmon, and crackers were political factors by which many candidates were able to curry favor.

In South Carolina most of the rural white democratic clubs were organized around the stores, and storekeepers were made custodians of the roll books. Until the present day this custom prevails, and much of the vote registry is still in the charge of merchants. Historically, this has played into the hands of the storekeepers, and they have been known to determine the outcome of close primary elections by liberally adding "safe" names to electoral rolls. In other southern states, even though roll books were left in the custody of circuit clerks, the country stores remained the polling places.

Storekeepers, appreciative of the commercial value of political gatherings, helped to organize picnics on their grounds and stocked up with knickknacks for a a rushing business. Jolly Street and Singly's store had its annual barbecue and, in election years, a whole day of political speakings. Candidates nailed handbills to the store fronts, and either distributed their cards to customers or left them lying around to be picked up at will. Some of these stray cards and handbills filtered down into boxes of papers, and in this way many merchants have unintentionally preserved records of these early practices.

Since 1876 the South has been regarded as a land of one political party. It is a one-party region only in the same sense that it is religiously a land with a single God. Around the stoves and sprawled out on the shady porches political factionists have argued their views by the hour. Often these discussions were comedies of rare flavor in civil affairs, but at other times they led to vicious "fist and skull" fighting on the wagon grounds. Points of argument were emphasized by the ejection of long, spattering streams of tobacco juice. Always the southern farmer was in hard luck; if it was not the panic, it was malaria, grass, freight rates, and taxes. His political reactions were the result of the weather, the panics, the price of cotton and tobacco. Rural southerners dealt in personalities. In religion it was a matter of a personal savior, and in politics personal economic salvation and advantage. A Mississippian became enraged at the unhappy turn of a political argument, arose from his nail-keg seat, slung a sack of flour over one shoulder, placed a chunk of fat meat under the other arm, picked up a bucket of lard, and started toward the door. He was not going home, however, a licked man; with a snort of triumph he stopped in the door and snarled back over his shoulder that James Kimball Vardaman was the only friend the poor people had. This was a characteristic southern attitude toward the army of demagogic office seekers and their endless promises of economic deliverance.

Ben Tillman, South Carolina governor and United States senator, pitched his first campaign in a lusty attack against the discriminations in prices and interest rates charged farmers. In reality he was charging the country stores of South Carolina with the failure of the farmers. Tillman supporters were predominantly rural and were steady customers of the stores, and his platform was discussed hundreds of times in the circles before their counters. Literally scores of debates followed each of his truculent assaults against the usurious bankers, guano dealers, and merchants. Country Democratic clubs were overwhelmingly for this fiery leader of the hill country, and the elections around the country stores were veritable Tillman love feasts.

Across the line in Georgia, country-store customers were

struck by the exciting stories of the little man from Crawfordville who had a genius' head but an invalid's legs. The name of Alexander H. Stephens was one that carried great weight for many years in state politics, but by 1878 there were those who wished to see the "Lion of Liberty Hall" bearded, and they set out to do it by organizing support in favor of William M. Reese. Later Tom Watson took the boys on the porch by storm with his roaring denunciation of the myriad oppressors whose heavy loins rested figuratively upon the shoulders of the tattered Georgia cotton farmers.

If it had not been for the farmers' support, there never would have been the agrarian liberal from Thomson, nor would his reactionary successors have settled down upon the state like the seventeen-year locust. Gene Talmadge, of more recent years, would have remained an unknown local politician if he had not secured the support of several hundred thousand voters whose reactions were governed largely by what they heard on the country church grounds and around the country stores.

Perhaps one of the most colorful campaigns ever conducted in the South was that one in Alabama in 1894 between Captain Reuben F. Kolb, champion watermelon grower, and the one-armed hero of Henry County, Colonel William C. Oates. This race was a perfect one for the crossroads discussions. Colonel Oates, a Cleveland supporter, represented the Black Belt, and his followers called themselves the "True Blues." Kolb supporters, however, were the people whose yearly accounts were carried on the store books. These accounts, when totaled at the end of the year, amounted to less than a hundred dollars each, but they were seldom paid because of a lack of both cotton and cash. It was these victims of all the ills of Alabama during the Cleveland panic who sat on the store porches on Saturdays whittling and spitting, or squatted about hitching racks digging tiny trenches with their sharp-pointed knives as if they were plowing their scrawny acres with bull-tongue plows.

By some unfathomable manner southerners believed politics was back of much of the rural South's trouble, and if the Alabama farmers could only get one of their kind in the governor's chair at Montgomery, then they could expect relief. They were the people who sought higher prices for cotton and cheaper prices for meat, overalls, implements, freight, guano, and interest rates. Punctuating arguments with sharp, thin spurts of tobacco juice, they made positive declarations of their personal beliefs and choices."Kolb, the immortal Kolb," said one idolator. "His name will go down with Washington's." Others believed him an Alabama Patrick Henry, and their eyes brightened hopefully when his name was mentioned.

For Kolb the stores as community meeting places were useful centers of influence. He profited in votes by the numerous discussions, but so did his opponent, Captain Oates. Kolb men drove up to the hitching grounds in their wagons and broken-down buggies decorated with corncobs. They smoked cob pipes, twirled corncob walking canes, and wore festoons of cobs on their wide-brimmed wool hats. Oates' men, not to be outdone, put sprays of oats in their lapels, in their hatbands, and festooned their horses and buggies with bundles of oats. Even women and children aligned themselves in this battle of the cobs and oats and were loud in their praise and condemnation.

On the day of the election there was a great commotion around the stores. At Coleman's in the village of Pinckneyville a generous amount of box stuffing went on, and the Coleman ledger showed a goodly quantity of liquor sold that day. "Jack Peeples," a "True Blue," was registered as having cast a ballot, and when the excitement of the election was over, curious citizens wondered who citizen "Jack Peeples" could be. A casual investigation revealed that he was Bill Peeples' well-known bird dog. All over Alabama there were stories of every imaginable sort of irregularity in this election. Oates won, but there followed a hot post-election contest which Kolb wound up by having himself sworn in as governor on the streets of Montgomery in a mock inaugural ceremony. Then he disappeared from the political scene.

Everywhere in the South it was much the same story. Alabama had Kolb and Oates, Mississippi had Vardaman, Percy, Russell, and Bilbo; Louisiana had Huey P. Long; Arkansas had Jeff Davis; and Tennessee had the Taylor brothers and their colorful "War of Roses." At every crossroads political talk went on incessantly, and tattered fragments of election-year propaganda appear in country merchants' papers. An Alabama customer in 1894 informed J. C. Brown that his "beat would be lost" unless he "came down and put in some good licks" in behalf of their ticket. Poll-tax receipts which appear frequently among "cash orders" tell their own story of political interest on the part of storekeepers. Seldom did a merchant enter actively into discussions unless he was certain of the views of his hearers. His influence as steersmen for politicians of his choice was more subtle. Dabbing in politics openly was dangerous for merchants who depended upon the trade of rampant partisan customers, but nevertheless most of them played a decisive hand in each election. Many a debtor was apprised of the way he should vote in subtle feed-room conferences.

In Mississippi, James K. Vardaman had his biggest bloc of supporters among the small farmers, and on more than one occasion that long-haired proponent of white supremacy pulled up at a crossroads to bellow vituperation upon the heads of trusts, aristocrats and Negroes. Before him stood crowds in overalls, faded denim jackets, brogan shoes, and big black wool hats. With tobacco-stained mouths agape, they drank in the thundering tirade of their patron saint.

Huey P. Long found the Louisiana country stores excellent places for taking political soundings. As a drummer selling Cottalene, a patented shortening, and later flour and patent medicines, he served a useful apprenticeship for getting votes in rural Louisiana. Riding about the country spinning yarns, joking with housekeepers, and giving rapid-fire sales talks, he formed personal associations which helped him get elected to office and secured backing for his policies as a public official. Huey never forgot the value of these forums of lazy farmers. When he wished to stir up public opinion, he had only to get the boys about the stores through the Red River Valley and in the hill country talking in his favor. Likewise, the memory of the Kingfish has remained green about the stores of the Teche country. He made them exciting places during his administration as governor and later as United States senator by bringing the world to their doors. His good roads improved conditions of the backward communities, and his tax program was not without its benefits to both merchants and customers. For many he was making good his slogan, "Every man a King."

Of course political discussions were seasonal, but the query, "How's crops?" was heard every day. Through the winter and early spring, farmers planned what they were going to plant, and they loved nothing better than discussing their hopes for a good crop season. In fact, much of the economy of the country-store trade was based upon this perennial optimism. Both merchants and farmers clung to the belief that next year they might hit it lucky, pay off their debts, and get back on the road to financial independence.

Good crops were as important for merchants as they were for farmers, and the long stoveside farming sessions were always valuable sources of information about the condition of soil, crops planned, and the next year's credit prospects. If every bale of cotton, bushel of corn and wheat, gallon of molasses and hogshead of tobacco planned for and talked about had reached the market, the South would have become a land of fabulous wealth.

Some hillside farmers grew eloquent for the only times in their monotonous lives in descriptions of plans and methods of farming. For instance, such a fundamental question as ripping up cotton stalks with a bull-tongue plow or not ripping them up at all was good any time for an hour's talking. There were those who favored planting corn at the bottom of a furrow, while there were steadfast contenders that it should be planted atop soft beds. Some growers preferred a variety of corn which produced one large ear to the stalk, while others liked another variety producing several small ears. So it was with the discussion of cotton yields. Arguments waxed long and fierce over the virtues and shortcomings of Simpkin's "Little Seed," Cleveland "Big Boll," "Half and Half," "Double-Jointed," and Peterkin's. In South Carolina there was feuding in the latter years over the improvements made by David L. Coker and Peterkin. Letters from Clemson College Experiment Station now packed away in country-store records indicate how news of improved varieties of cotton was passed around. Storekeepers were given samples of seed which they distributed to farmers to be tried and reported upon.

The harvesting of cash crops created the most excitement because of the variable range of production and price. Many years wishful farmers actually saw before them poor crops, but they hoped by some miraculous process that they would be enabled to gather more produce than they had any reason to expect. There were always incurable braggarts who rushed over their cotton crops and picked out a light bale of half-opened cotton and then drove a pair of mules nearly to death getting it to the gin so as to claim the ephemeral honor of being the first to gin and sell. For the next three months these triumphant farmers crowed over their fellows and regarded their accomplishment as a kind of heaven-sent reward for good farming.

Cotton-picking time was a season of anxiety for country-store customers because it was the period when they learned whether they could pay for their last year's supplies, or would again have to sign a note and carry over portions of their accounts to another year.

Many a fox ran figuratively round and round a country store, and the baying of long-eared, gaunt-bellied potlicker hounds was the most musical thing in the county. In rehashing all-night races, enthusiastic participants jumped up and down in wild pantomime from one gully bank to another, ran through brier patches, scrambled over rail fences, and ran up every old field hillside for miles around. In discussing this subject, owners of dogs were not only privileged, but expected, to lie freely. It was not normal for a man who had entered a dog in a fox race to observe even the most elementary principles of truth-telling. There was something magical in the mournful barking of a hound close on the trail of a fox which lulled the moral sensibilities of the average man. A post-mortem the next day at the store was even more absorbing to many southerners than taking sides in a primary election.

There were always other matters of importance which found their way to the community gatherings at the stores. Every serious illness was reported, and daily news of the progress of the patient was made available by most of the casual passers-by. Deaths and births were likewise publicized around the stoves. Shootings, scrapes, and cuttings were reported, and all of their details discussed. Actually many justices of the peace held their courts in the stores, and sometimes these hearings resulted in miscarriages of law and justice because they became a part of the informal everyday discussions of the loafers. At least these courts had the benefit of spontaneous testimony from many opinionated bystanders.

Courtings, marryings, and separations were ever matters of great interest. Three-fourths of the southern country courtships were threshed over at the stores long before the brides and grooms ever reached the marriage altars. If, by chance, there happened to be a little element of the shotgun mixed up in an unexpected and sudden taking of the marriage vows, the news was far more exciting and got around faster.

Humorless bachelors spent uncomfortable hours about the stoves as butts of ribald jokes. A store reporter for the Greensboro (Georgia) *Herald* sought a wife for a bashful neighbor. "Wanted," he wrote, "a wife. A young man of our acquaintance who is very timid, wants to get married. He says that the first girl between the age of fifteen and twenty-two, who is pretty, intelligent, and industrious with a good medium size, and is ready to change names and will keep house for him, he will be ready to say 'yes.' P. S. If you know of such a girl send her around. Address 'Caro' care of C. C. Pennington's store."

When the topic of store conversations was matrimony, there were always varied opinions on the subject. More conservative loungers rendered judgments on the subject which were as staid as were the lithographed wedding certificates hanging from rural parlor walls. At one of the stores where the conversation had dwelt an unreasonable length of time on matrimony, an irritated bachelor rose, stretched his arms high over his head, and rendered the profound statement that there were three things he would not do so long as he remained in Georgia—"dig wells, top trees, and get married."

Next to a country churchyard, the stores were perhaps the best places for courting. Many of them were located at strategic places for holding barbecues, picnics, all day singings, and general community gatherings. "There will be a picnic at Powell's store 4th Sunday. Music will be that of the violin, and will be rendered by some of as good performers as the county affords," proclaimed a newspaper notice in 1883.

These gatherings around the stores were "blowing-off" places for the oppressed, or they were places for the jocularly minded to exercise their wit. Waggish country reporters have embalmed many of these debate subjects in their gossipy local columns—"Which Is More Beneficial to A Country Store, Fice [*sic*] Dogs or Popcorn?" "Is the Conscience A Correct Moral Guide?" "Do the Learned Professions Offer A More Promising Opening to A Young Man Than Mercantile Life?" "Should the Negro be Colonized?" and "Which Is Better for the Laboring Man—to Work for Wages or Part of Crops?" It was said of the last proposition that one ancient gentleman of color resolved that "bof is best." Some of these were actually vital questions in the lives of the people, and many of the more serious discussions were effective in bringing their problems out into the open.

Almost every community had its aged counterpart of Uncle Remus whose keen sense of humor and aptness of homely phraseology endeared himself to the country-store clientele. There were others, both white and black, who were colorful only because they lacked completely the elements of respectability, and some had the distinction of being pointed out as the biggest chicken thieves in their respective states.

The Negro and his antics formed topics for many light conversations. Sometimes he got himself into trouble because of the easy availability of merchandise. A former slave stole a piece of meat in a Georgia store and got caught in the act. While the merchant was preparing a warrant to have him sent to jail, the thief stripped off his coat and asked to be whipped then and there. The merchant laid on fifty lashes and let the shame-faced culprit go free. A luckier colored brother strolled into a North Carolina store with a two-dollar bill marked with Roman numerals, bought a quarter's worth of goods and strolled out again with ten dollars and seventy-five cents in his pocket in change. Life around the stores, to the observant and aged philosophers, was "always one damned thing right after another."

4

THE WALLS GROW LONG PAPER TAILS

On February 10, 1892, a clerk in J. C. Brown's general store at Faunsdale, Alabama, struggled to remove from the wall a long tail of wire strung with paper. He wanted to add a brown-and-green-striped piece of coarse tablet paper to the ever-lengthening file. There was just a hint of urgency in the request for the articles listed. Laboriously scribbled, with hands which were obviously more accustomed to the plow and hoe than to the pencil, were instructions to "pleas let Rarlph Callwell [have] 1 pint of whiskey & 25 cent of sugar and 40 flour and a small Bottle of turpentine for his wife. She is veary sick at this time in child Burth Let Him have them and Charge the same to me. Yoas, Nathan Long." It was a typical store order for that section of the South. Before the clerk strung this order on the long wire strand, he made a careful notation in the ledger: "whiskey .25, sugar 1¼ pounds, flour .25, and bottle of turpentine .10." He had reduced the pitifully small flour order from forty to twenty-five cents.

Buying by store orders was a universal practice. For an hour every Saturday morning a farm owner's time was taken up with writing orders to the storekeeper for a tenant who wanted a new pair of brogan shoes, or for a smiling Negro girl who came up to the back door and asked if she could buy five yards of calico and a batch of bright red ribbon to make a new spring dress.

On Saturdays the roads were literally filled with customers

bearing tiny little slips of paper. These orders are fascinating studies of the availability of paper in the average household and likewise of the general education level of the rural southerner. Every conceivable type of paper eventually found its way to the store in the form of an order. One barely literate landlord must have searched the place over for a piece of paper and finally brought his hunt to an abrupt end by snatching a piece of wallpaper off the wall and scribbling on its blank side. John A. Bratton of White Oak, South Carolina, formerly a general in the Confederate Army, gave store orders to his field hands as meticulously as he had given commands to his troops at Chattanooga and at Richmond. Less sedate southerners tore blank margins off newspapers, ripped open used envelopes, or pulled pages out of their patent-medicine pocket notebooks. The more fastidious wrote neat little orders on slender pieces of polite "slick ink" tablet paper. So prevalent was this custom of ordering goods by note that many of the larger furnishings merchants had special printed forms.

One can picture an Alabama Negro boy sliding from the bare back of the mule he had ridden several miles. In his pocket he carried an important note from his "bossman." Wave Fitts was out of tobacco, and life had reached a low ebb. He wanted, at once, a pound of Missing Link chewing tobacco, a half-pound of smoking tobacco, and a package of cigarette leaves. The boy eased through the side door of the store, fumbled in his overalls pocket, and then produced his paper without uttering a sound. While the clerk cut the chewing tobacco and wrapped it into a tight bundle with the pipe tobacco and cigarette papers, the boy stood rolling his eyes, vicariously enjoying the heterogeneous collection of merchandise tumbled along the floor, piled on the counters and shelves, and hanging down from the ceiling.

Literally hundreds of Wave Fittses waited anxiously at home while boys galloped off to stores. A large portion of the tobacco distributed through the country stores was taken out by orders.

There is an old folk story told about the circuit rider who drove up to a steward's place to spend the night. The good brother was plowing near by, and suddenly there came a thunderous outbreak of profanity and shouting. Everything seemed to be wrong. The mule was guilty of all the misdemeanors of his stubborn hybrid predecessors. It was downright embarrassing for his wife that the parson could hear his profane tirade. She called one of the children around to the rear of the house and sent him to the store for some chewing tobacco. Within a few moments after the boy's return there came from the field the joyful sounds of a happy Methodist husbandman who found the business of farming a happy one.

This practice of merchandising was the vital element of the whole lien and mortgage system. Time after time anxious purchasers were told that they had already overordered their monthly credit allotment. On the records of the accounts many merchants wrote statements of the extent of yearly credit, and this in turn was divided into equal monthly portions. In this way the merchant exercised a specific check on the amount of goods purchased, and, likewise, through the acceptance of lien notes he controlled his competition. Evidence of this monopoly frequently crept into the orders. In 1893 an Alabama customer wished to pay a hired hand $2.50 by issuing him a store order. The laborer demurred. In a spirit of supplication the employer wrote, "Please let Frank trade two and one half dollars and let him have things the best you can as he complains of your charging too high prices. I owe him money and have asked him to accept this order instead of money, so do your best for him."

During the busy crop season farmers kept orders pouring in for money with which to pay wage hands. One planter faced with the problem of paying his field hands on the night before a big Negro picnic, had to get the money from the store or have downright mutiny on his place. Cotton-chopping season came just at the time of year when few farmers had any cash; and every night a weary cotton chopper spent his wages at the store in the form of an order for goods, on which he paid a profit and a credit price, and the farmer paid an interest charge for good measure.

Many merchants served their communities as semi-bankers. A farmer brought in his crop of cotton, tobacco, or other produce and sold it, but seldom received cash in payment. There was always a genuine fear on the part of the countryman that he would lose his money out of his pocket or be robbed of it. Then, too, many persons were doubtful of the security of banks. One backwoods cotton farmer sold his cotton crop for cash and had the merchant sew it securely in his pocket. He then commanded a faithful Negro to follow in his footsteps to see that he didn't drop it. Since the merchant was to get most or all of the returns from a crop anyway, it was much simpler just to take a credit allowance on the merchant's book and do away with the worry of losing the money. Long before the next crop season closed, the debit side of the ledger had consumed the credit surplus funds. Few rural southerners went beyond their communities to purchase goods, and store orders were for them a counterpart of cash.

Each week an army of wagons was deployed around the stores and their hitching racks waiting to receive their weekly loads of "rations." Carloads of northern flour and meat were carted away on Saturday afternoons. In the long strings of paper orders there is a monotonous succession of these standard ingredients for southern diet of the eighties, nineties, and first decades of this century.

The orders which arrived at the stores contain the whole picture of the rural southern diet. One customer ordered a bushel of meal and hinted that the merchant's integrity was not quite exemplary by the admonition that he "give me good measure." Another humble request on a ragged piece of brown paper for ten pounds of dry salt meat wound up with the earnest plea, "Get me a piece with as much lean as you can." A patron sold a final bale of cotton in early spring and left the money at the store. Late in April he wrote, "I think there is about $12 between I and you, and if you can send a barrel of flour and can of lard by surry, you will oblige, A. Lowry."

At best much of the merchandise was of questionable value. That emphasis was placed upon quantity rather than quality was clearly indicated in the cash orders. A farmer ordered a barrel of flour and underscored whether it was for family use or for his field hands. A conservative farmer ordered a pouch of tobacco and a shirt "good enough for a darkey to wear." Occasionally a one-crop cotton farmer ordered a dozen eggs and later wrote that every one of the eggs he received was spoiled. A jug of molasses caused a minor culinary disruption in one fastidious household. "My wife," wrote the husband, "complains that the molasses is so *unreal* that it will not make ginger cakes. Please Mr. Brown see that something genuine is sent."

Not always could the grinning couriers be trusted to perform their errands. They rode homeward with watering mouths at the thought of the white meat slung across the backs of their bony mounts. Many a piece of meat found its way to roadside bushes to be recovered later and cooked over a cabin stove. Such deceptions were discovered, however, and these undernourished brigands often became victims of squeeze plays between the merchant and his customers. This was a bit comical when the illiterate errand boys delivered orders for meat, herring, sugar, flour, and nutmegs with emphatic instructions *"to send the number of pieces of meat."*

In late February an industrious Alabama farmer sent a boy to get half a bushel of seed potatoes and a piece of meat. By long experience he knew the holding powers of the store and asked the merchant to cut short the bearer's loitering and start him home in time to plant the potatoes before night. Illiterate though many of the messengers were, they soon learned the possibilities of the written word and got in their gazing and loafing before divulging the secrets of their messages.

Buying clothes by note was a business of approximation at best. Styles and sizes were of secondary importance and color was only a question of vague generalization. A dutiful son and husband ordered ten pounds of meat for his mother and a pair of gaiters for his wife. Stonewall Scott, a second-generation Confederate, wished to buy a hat for his wife—"a neat one but in these hard times [1892] not too high priced." The whole issue was to get off, in this time of the approaching Cleveland panic, as cheaply as possible.

A storekeeper had to be a catalogue of his community's tastes. He had to know the approximate pants size of every man in the neighborhood so that when he received an order for pants or drawers or shirts, he could fill it with some degree of satisfaction. If there was doubt in his mind, he could usually pick out a loafer of the right build from the line-up on the porch and check the length of his legs and the circumference of his waist. Even so dignified a purchaser as General John A. Bratton ordered a suit of clothes from the Patrick store at White Oak, South Carolina, without giving specific measurements.

Until about 1915 buying and fitting shoes was a little-understood art. In the mind of the average southerner of the seventies, eighties, and nineties, a shoe had only one fundamental dimension—length. If it was long enough, then the width was a matter of being in the right proportion. In the fall of the year, at cotton-selling time, a landlord lined up his hands and their families and measured their feet from heel to toe on pieces of string. In the same way he measured his own family's feet and then carried the bundle of strings to the store to secure shoes. No allowance was made for atmospheric changes which might shrink the string or for the inability of the clerk to get a string into a shoe without kinking. Unfortunately therefore many a southern boy hobbled through the first four months of a new pair of shoes because "pa" had erred in tying the knot at the right place. It became a matter of family debate when a boy's shoes hurt as to whether the trouble was in the size of the shoe or in the spreading influence of going barefooted for eight months out of the year.

From the end of the Civil War down to the middle of the second decade of this century it was a custom for the head of the household to choose his family's footwear, specify color and whether the shoes were to be lace or button, coarse or Sunday, or, in the case of boys, shoes or red-top boots. Only the long seasons of warm weather rescued many southerners from the ill-conceived and poorly made brogans of fiendish Massachusetts shoemakers.

Occasionally a discriminating customer turned up with a complaint. A patron of Reed's store at Flat Creek, Tennessee, wished to have sent "little child shuse fore a sunday shue and apair off blacke wostid hose and three yd of callico sutibul for a childe." The selection made by the merchant was entirely unsatisfactory, and a later note had an element of impatience in it. "Those shues," wrote this phonetic speller, "dont sute at tall I want some like thies aire with springe heels and I dont want eny that aire any color than thies aire. I want no 5. These hose dont sute either." But perhaps it was not too exasperating to have received a pair of shoes and hose which "dont sute" for in the same letter the writer took another shot in the dark and ordered "a nice sundy good shirt if you please."

Running a country store was always a matter of remembering the preferences of customers. "If you have on hand a no 38 alpaca coat," wrote a local dignitary, "that you had when I was there send it by Dick—I mean those best ones." In this matter of taste not all notional shopping was a sin of the female. Files of store orders abound with stories of men who debated the wisdom of their meager purchases and with notes asking that a pair of shoes or a suit of clothes which the writer had inspected several days before be delivered for examination on the home ground. Then there were orders for goods like those purchased several days before or like those sold to some neighbor. A benevolent relative ordered "a shirt of the same kind I got yesterday. One that will fit Uncle Lish."

Buying new clothes was an unusual occurrence for many southerners, and lack of experience often prevented their getting entirely satisfactory results. Again, price governed the purchase. "Let Bennie have a suit of clothes $5.00," wrote Thomas H. Ladd, "a hat .65 and shirt .55. He dont case [*sic*] to have the pants alike the coat and vest a cheaper pants will suit him." One mother said to select for her Jim "a good pair of trousers—the best you have for fifty cents and if you have some good ones for less than that—it will do." Then, looking forward to the first washing, she admonished, "Be sure and have them large enough."

Sometimes following a haphazard purchase a frantic note came to the store saying that a customer had been swallowed alive by the coat and that he had been forced to call in outside help to extricate him from the constrictive hold of the pants. Coats were expected to meet around a man's chest, and the sleeves were required to reach some conservative point between the elbow and the wrist; otherwise, little attention was given to style, for generally the coat to a nine-dollar suit was without form. Pants were made for two purposes only: protection from the weather and prevention of an indecent exposure of knotty limbs. Most often they were made of jean or coarse worsted and had about as much shape as a forked stovepipe. It was these formless combinations of coats and pants which characterized the southern countryman both on foot and in jest.

Naturally the more frequent orders for dry goods were tiny paper missives bearing samples, and again the matching was purely a matter of gross approximation, of availability rather than of quality and general appearance. It was much more important that the average woman, anxious to attend church in a new dress, get ten yards of cretonne immediately and at thirteen cents a yard than that she get exactly what she wanted at some indefinite date and price.

As the spring and summer approached, every southerner bought some sort of an outfit to see him through the rounds of picnics, political gatherings, and protracted meetings. Sometimes a storekeeper closed out his stock of dry goods by supplying the "big meeting" trade alone. Brief stories of these great events in the southern way of life found their way into scratch-paper notes. A father looked forward to the salvation of his two sons, Ben and Buster. He ordered knee pants, hats, shoes, enough cloth for two sheets for the preacher's bed, four pounds of lard—enough to fry several chickens—and a baptismal gown for Buster. Here was a customer who was in the midst of an exciting summer!

A landlord asked a merchant to sell William Henry, a bachelor of color, five dollars' worth of unspecified merchandise. "William Henry," he wrote, "expects to take unto himself a wife." Occasionally similar orders appeared which could easily be identified as a modest trousseau for a "hoe handle" belle who wished to marry in as much glory as her credit and the stock of the nearest store would permit.

A timid and precise young Tennessee schoolteacher anticipated the opening of school. Writing in the vein of a Mother Goose tale, she addressed herself to her local merchant: "Kind Sir, please send me a black top skirt if you have any not over $2.00. I guess I can get a very nice one for that and also a cheap trunk if you have it and if not get it from Mr. Melford, and send them by the first wagon or peddling wagon. For I have to go off to teach Monday and I will need them." A black top skirt was the finishing touch for a "schoolmarm." She had spent all summer making poplin underskirts, pleated shirtwaists, and flannel gowns. Immediately behind the schoolteacher's request came a complicated order for two four-inch strips of velvet, one of rich brown and one of dark red, and a strip of "figured or solid light or dark silk," also several spools of thread in bright colors. The ladies of the near-by Methodist church were engaged in making Brother Ogle's quilt, winter cover for their underpaid circuit rider.

The storekeeper had to serve as both adviser and confidant of a family's secrets and distributor of goods. A woman, frankly bedeviled by that greatest of all social blights, bedbugs, sought relief from her nightly attacks by using a mixture of quicksilver and corrosive sublimate. This formula was high-sounding for a country store, but actually it was almost as common as castor oil. Most drug orders, however, were for Gray's Ointment, pills, chill tonics, bitter herb mixtures, and linseed oil. One customer wanted turpentine, bluestone, soda, and enough asafetida "to mix with the other ingredients." This was medicine making of a high order. Other compounders of folk cures ordered rock candy, quinine, sugar, and turpentine, from which they produced a concoction only slightly less revolting than those made by neighborhood "conjure doctors."

There were rank hypocrites in the South. A note from a toddy-drinking deacon asked for a long list of innocuous ingredients and a gallon of "medicinal whisky." Biliousness was ever a convenient excuse. When a customer asked for half a dozen lemons on a hot July day, he knew only too well that nothing short of the great summertime complaint would insure his getting such a fautous luxury.

Clerks in country stores never dry-rotted from lack of variety in demands. One note bearer wanted a fly minder. Before the days of screen doors and windows, a patent fly shaker gave a family just a little more dignity than did the ordinary peach-tree branch or a homemade minder bespangled with long newspaper fringes. It cost only $2.50. Another customer wanted a gallon of "cearcene" oil, one "pencil with a rubber," and a pound of buckshot. Another note reported a major tragedy to Cesor Drake [*sic*]. "Please to let me have some spoke for hine weel. my wagon broke down." This indeed was misfortune. Cesor's wagon was the most important of all his farm implements, and to break one of its dish-faced and weathered rear wheels was calamitous.

If it wasn't an order for spokes for a "hine weel," it was for a new supply of shuck collars for plow mules. These clumsy pieces of harness were home-manufactured throughout the South during the winter months, sold to the stores, and then distributed among the cotton farmers when plowing time came. Made of corn shucks, these antiquated pieces of harness at once marked the backwardness of a farmer. It was a common occurrence to torture a pair of gaunt mules by leaving them at a store hitching post all day Saturday without food and water until they had eaten the collars off each other. These impractical circles had to be put over a mule's head, and they caused much rearing and pitching around stable doors at harnessing time.

Of a more businesslike nature was a note from a community sport who wanted to know if his pistol had arrived. A somewhat less militant blood wanted a pair of black studs for his shirt and promised to pay for them when he "arrived in the city." Inquiries about pistols and studs were not numerous, but requests for knives were. V. C. Bailey asked that his bearer be given "a good Rodgers (barlow) or Wostenholm knife, and I wish you would please pick me out a good one and send it by boy. I want a good stout knife." Nothing pleased the rural southerner more than a good, serviceable pocketknife. This was a fact well known among manufacturers, and barlow knives were as much standard stock in the country store as were fat meat, calico, and brogan shoes. Older men yet recall with a joyful gleam in their eyes ownership of one of those famous double-bladed steel wonders with their characteristic brown bone handles and long holsters bearing the sterling mark of an arrow piercing the letter R. For the southerner, ownership of a knife was as necessary as keeping the body decently covered with clothes.

Not all of the grimy slips of papers were orders for merchandise. Down in Alabama, Willie Kerrington, in a hurry to get Dr. McCants, sent his boy galloping to the store with this note: "Aunt Sarah is bad off. She is got the *colre mobus!*" A less frantic customer asked the storekeeper to "back" a stamped envelope to a kinsman in Mississippi and charge it to his account. A local politician in one of the outlying beats hastened a note off to the storekeeper to come at once and help do some fence mending at the polls. Another had to meet his gambling obligations. "Send me a pound of *nice* fancy candy," he wrote. "I need this candy to pay a bet that I lost on the rain yesterday."

Rural psychology and community life of the New South stand revealed in the so-called "cash order notes." In these clumsy files lies the story of an effort to supply a rural neighborhood's economic needs with limited cash and credit resources, of keeping face with just as little cost as possible, and of one man controlling the tastes and desires of his neighbors. When a woman needed a piece of dress goods, but was undecided as to color, the merchant made a selection for her. A man needed a pair of shoes or a suit, and the merchant guessed at the size and sent them along. Once delivered, the articles were seldom returned. A family made arrangements for limited credit on a yearly basis, and generally the storekeeper and the landlord restricted buying to that by orders. In this way a customer's desires were checked carefully by at least two creditors before any purchases were allowed. The little order slips enabled the country store to hold on to its trade, and for the most part were tokens of an endless process of credit business.

Only the notes where requests were granted are found among the files of the stores. However, there is a long-buried story of pathos in notes which were not honored. A half-starved customer requested meat and meal for his family and a sack of feed for his ill-fed team, but behind him at home was a cotton crop which had been rained out or that had been caught hopelessly in the grass. He was a poor credit risk, and his request for goods was refused. It was indeed a long, weary road home in an empty wagon, and his return was as cheerless as the march of destruction itself. His wife could have easily greeted him with that doleful southern ditty, sung to the tune of "The Bonnie Blue Flag":

My husband came from town last night
As sad as man could be,
His wagon empty, cotton gone,
And not a dime had he.

Huzzah! Huzzah!
'Tis queer, I do declare!
We make the clothes for all the world,
But few we have to wear.

[illegible] Sept 10th 1897

Mr. J. C. Brown
I send 2 bales cotton
try & send you 2 more by
first week in October

Please send me
1 barrel good flour [illegible]
can diamond bright [illegible]
can [illegible], sardines [illegible]
sack salt [illegible]
if not the other will do
1 box soda crackers 24 # [illegible]
1 can lard [illegible]
1 case 1 oz snuff [illegible]
Will settle above bill in
[illegible] days. Yours [illegible]
J. H. Bledsoe

$50.47

Mr T. C. Patrick
Dr sir
I want to get you to pay the taxes for the parties on the inclosed list. I believe tomorrow will be the last day. I expected to get some cotton ready this week, but cant get it ready now before next week. You can send a check to Davis for the amount and inclose the list, I got the amounts when he was at Woodwards
Yours truly
R. L. Miller

[illegible] may I trouble
[illegible] to put a stamp
[illegible] this for me.
Jerusha Mitchell

74 Ashepoo Phosphate Co's

Mr Patrick please
let Benjamin Richard
have a $60 lien and
take a morgige
on all his crops
and I will try
and secure you
oblige yours
J. Y. Stewart
Adgers
March 2nd
1887

You need not believe us, but try the goods and be convinced.

Mr. Brown I send
you two (2) bales cotton
Receipt me by Frank
Send Three rations [illegible]
pounds each — [illegible]
you can with the cotton
for [illegible] — J. H. A.

"Long Paper Tails." These are the notes which poured in daily asking for everything in stock, including the merchant's most human consideration.

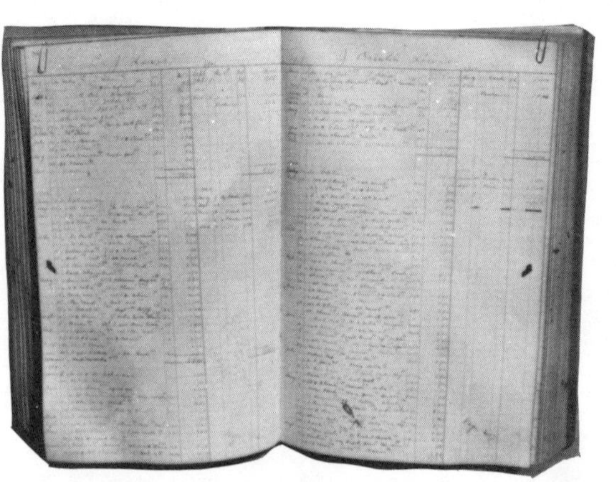

LEDGER
D M CO

5
12
19
26

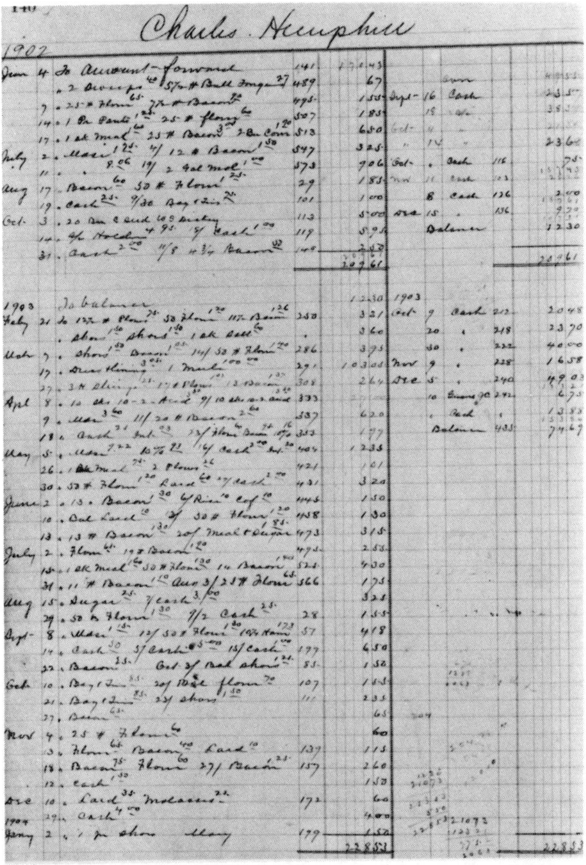
Charles Hemphill

1902

Ledger books, accounts, and bookkeeping were the merchant's lot. The goods went out in terms of money, but the payments might be in other terms—bushels of corn, bales of cotton, or other media of exchange.

Victims of "progress."

5

SOCIAL CORRESPONDENTS

Love in the cotton fields of the South was a throbbing thing which required vigorous expression. An enraptured but heavy-handed swain laboriously scribbled a note of passionate devotion on the back of a greasy store order. "miss susie haris," he driveled, "i love you my dear girl you are the lark you are the stalk you are the derling of my hart. i like to get a sweet kiss tonight." This was getting down to business in a land where paper was scarce and writing was a tedious undertaking. That a love letter got to the point without subtlety, inuendo, or superficiality was the main requirement.

Storekeepers served as intermediaries for love. A gallant but unschooled beau sauntered into the secluded post-office corner of the Reed Store at Flat Creek, Tennessee, and dictated a letter to his best girl. His is a Victorian Tennessee classic generously larded with misspelled words. "Deare friend," he began, "will you allow me to Correspond with you, not at all will I blush to say that I am in love with you so mutch. it will brake my hart for you to go back on me, I hope you will grant me the privildge of Esscorting you to the X centennial at Nashville May 1—1897. I am glad to say that your complements are actcepted with many thanks, returned for your past favorites to express my self before going too far, if you were only mine I would be the hapest man in the world. Oh you are so so fine it makes me cry to here you when u tell me will you only be mine." There was more. In the end this patient Tennessee Jacob asked his "sweet," "how long do you wish me to wait [this] is the 8 yeare I have waited for you."

Courting couples appreciated the possibilities of the written word, but for many of them the art remained a profound mystery. They learned, however, the knack of keeping the complete story of their affairs well obscured. In many instances one merchant wrote letters and another read the answers. In this way only half the story was ever revealed to a single individual.

More numerous than love letters were those to relatives and friends in other parts of the country. During the first three decades after the Civil War, numerous families moved to Texas and the other western states. Literate immigrants wrote long letters back to the home folks, and it was a common sight to see a customer sitting by the stove listening anxiously while the merchant or a neighbor read a letter from a relative. There were descriptions of the new part of the country, of agriculture, of land values, and of sickness, deaths, and births.

In characteristic "I take my pen in hand" style, home folks answered with long, rambling accounts of family affairs and then launched into detailed descriptions of community misfortunes. Letters were limited news vehicles, and to a majority of writers the stories which had the greatest news value were the sensational ones. A good case of shouting, rheumatism, or pneumonia was a first-class sensation. In a halting manner, one after another illiterate correspondent poured out tales of delicious woe to their merchant scribes. From the beginning, however, merchants adapted a brief stereotyped style of writing letters. Paradoxically they closed their gloomy tales of calamity and sickness with the stock nineteenth-century ending, "that this leaves us well and I hope it finds you the same."

From writing love letters and producing annals of joyful affliction to answering requests for specific information about heaving jackasses was a long step, but for storekeepers it was just another of life's brutal incongruities. A righteously indignant farmer in Godlettsville, Tennessee, wrote Ed Williams, storekeeper at Eagleville, "Please pardon me for taking this privilege without an introduction. Under the circumstances, however, you will I believe, do so, and farther more give me information that I desire. I bought a jack from J. S. Bell in the summer. I find that through the cold spells in winter, that he would take something like the heaves or bellowses. I would like for you to see the parties who had fed him, and groomed him; and find out if he had trouble when sold to me. I paid sound money for him and could not sell him for such, without misrepresentation.

"Please do me this favor & I will keep it masonically without troubling you in the future. P.S. This jack ("Long Tom") was formerly owned by R. S. Brown.

"His age was very repeatedly misrepresented but I have no proof. I would like also to know the number of colts a year and his breeding."

Every day the storekeeper was called upon to give information of all sorts and to write recommendations for his neighbors. A customer wished to buy a sewing machine or a graphophone on the installment plan, or he wished to boost his income by becoming a peddler for some "fly-by-night" product and gave a merchant's name as a reference. A customer's son wished to go away to school or to get a job, and the school or prospective employer wrote back for information. Sometimes a young neighbor was on the verge of matrimony to a girl away from home and her parents wrote to the storekeeper for their prospective son-in-law's family background and character.

The chore of writing recommendations was not without its compensation, for it gave a storekeeper a powerful whip hand over his neighbors. Behind his word was the vital matter of granting credit, and it had far more weight than that of a local preacher or schoolteacher. It was generally believed that the preacher could speak no evil of a parishioner and that schoolteachers too often were here today and gone tomorrow. The merchant was a permanent factor in a community, and no one else had quite such efficient means of gathering inside information.

A Hamilton County, Georgia, editor noted in a local column in November, 1875, that "three or four families migrated from Whitakers district leaving several disconsolate creditors to mourn their departure. It is supposed they went to Texas." Nearly always, however, when a man pulled up stakes and went, figuratively at least, "to Texas," he stood in need of a good word from back home. So many people from the Lower South poured into Texas and the West before 1900 because of unsatisfactory conditions in their home neighborhoods that there was an element of suspicion of these newcomers among the old settlers. One such Texas immigrant of questionable origin was W. Alvah Cooksey of Eagleville, Tennessee. Alvah had in his personality a touch of the adventurer seasoned with a sobering element of evangelism. On June 24, 1891, he executed a note to the Williams Store in Tennessee for $100.69, and then struck out for Texas. In 1894 it became necessary for Brother Cooksey to start a vigorous campaign to secure his letter from the Eagleville Baptist Church. He was out in Texas running a combination summer normal and church school. He had talked too much about his church connections in Tennessee, and he had to have a church letter so as to operate within the law of his denomination. He wrote one letter after another back to the members of the Tennessee church board without receiving a reply. Each succeeding note became more anxious and pleading. "Trouble, misfortunes, and disappointments from other parties" stood in his way, he wrote the neighbors. High interest charges on his note were piling up at the Williams Store, and so far he had showed no signs of paying it.

In terms of close fraternal endearment the involved Texas debtor cajoled the merchant to forward his church letter, but no letter went forth. Instead the unctuous Cooksey was beset with constables, bill collectors, and neighbors, put upon his trail by the Eagleville church board. The deacons of the church where he attended in Texas began to accuse him of being an imposter and a hypocrite. Thus, for four years the one-sided church-letter argument raged. In the end, the financially delinquent brother became enraged at the inhumane way the church clerk-merchant was treating him, and in a strong letter he threatened to put off final payment of his note until an indefinite judgment day. As an alternative to this rather extended time of final execution, the sporting Cooksey offered to send the clerk of the Eagleville board a hundred dollars only when he had a church letter in hand. The bill was finally paid on Brother Cooksey's terms, and he became once again a church member in good standing.

Frequently letters and accounts appear among merchants' papers to show how influential they were in running church affairs. In 1893 one Tennessee storekeeper wrote another asking about a preacher. "Dear Brother, have received 2 or three messages from you regarding your preacher would you do us the favor to write all about his preaching whether a young or old man and just what you think about his preaching for us. . . ."

At Faunsdale, Alabama, J. C. Brown was in charge of building and equipping a new church house for the Methodists. After close bidding, a contract was awarded a company in Meridian, Mississippi, and because of a careless blunder in its estimate the storekeeper was able to get the church constructed at less than cost. When the contractor begged for an adjustment of the bid, he found the stewards, under Brown's leadership, determined to stick by their original agreement.

Not only did the shrewd Brown get the church house built at less than cost and according to exact plans, but he also secured a bell for the tower practically without cost to the congregation. He put the proposition of making substantial contributions up to the wholesale houses with which he did business, and many of them responded generously. The Moore and Handley Hardware Company of Birmingham allowed a 50 per cent reduction in its list price of the bell.

In only two instances wholesalers refused contributions. A New Orleans grocery house wrote, "The demands for donations have been so numerous that we have been compelled to adopt the line of declining to assist churches and other institutions, and to limit our donations to actual suffering or relieving actual distress only." Tapp, Leathers and Company of Louisville, makers of "Kentucky jeans," made the patronizing response that "we appreciate your appeal for the cause of Methodism and are only sorry we are not able to respond to every call which is made to us along this line, but our whole firm belongs to a Methodist Church which is now in the midst of a struggle to pay off an indebtedness of ten thousand dollars."

Subscription lists to building funds or for the hiring and support of ministers were circulated through the stores, and frequently merchants became more important in religious-financial leadership than were the preachers themselves. Accounts for church supplies appear in their books along with the monthly salary of the janitor. Every year at protracted-meeting time there appear charges for kerosene, lamp chimneys, and brooms.

Leadership in church and school affairs paid dividends in additional business, but likewise a hot row and factional division of a church membership and patrons of a school could play havoc with business. Perhaps merchants dabbled in these institutions more for the sake of the prestige and feeling of self-importance which it gave them.

Being a country postmaster, however, was a different matter. There were both dignity and certain financial return attached to the office. The United States Post Office Department gave a large academic-appearing certificate of appointment which made its owner as proud as if he had a University of Virginia diploma displayed on his wall. Most post offices paid only cancellations, which amounted to very small sums of money, but the post-office windows were excellent places for keeping a check on customers who occasionally ordered goods from mail-order houses. In such cases it was possible for alert clerks to suggest that better goods could be secured from the store or from the catalogue of another house if they were ordered through the store. Especially was this true of jewelry and ready-made clothing.

Account books carry frequent entries for three-cent stamps.

Messengers came riding in bringing letters without envelopes but with notes instructing postmasters to back, stamp, and charge them to individual accounts. "May I trouble you to put a stamp on these [letters] and get them off on up train this eve," asked one customer. Another requested, "Please put stamps on three letters for me and send me one dozen lemons and 1 lb of soder crackers and one hot pickel and one can tomatoes, if you have not got them please [go] to the other store and get them for me as I am sick and can't eat."

Many of the unsealed letters involved money orders, and merchants were asked to supply the money and pay the carriage of the letter at the same time. An anxious customer asked an Alabama merchant to "please send by registered letter today three dollars in cash to Mrs. Mollie A. Banks, Toomsooba, Mississippi." Another asked, "Will you please put the money order for five dollars in the letter I send to you for Willie please have the money order made to Willie. I am anxious for the letter to go tonight." "Will you please send Clair Ten Dollars by first mail and charge to Ormond place. Kindly inclose this letter or one stating that I have granted his request," wrote another.

One of the most difficult requests for the merchant to meet was that of supplying cash. Notes came in asking for money with which to buy a money order to pay for goods bought from Sears, Roebuck or one of the other mail-order houses. As postmaster, the merchant received a nominal fee for the money order. The fee, however, hardly ever made up for the profits which he lost. Sometimes a customer was brought under control by the merchant's refusal to order goods until he had paid his bill.

Newspapers were filled with advertisements of goods which would be sent without money to be given a brief trial or to be paid for immediately upon their receipt. All a prospective customer had to do was to fill out a simple coupon or write his address on a postal card, and the goods would be sent C.O.D., an abbreviation which had little or no meaning to the average patron. It was an easy opportunity to get mail, and getting mail was an event in the drab lives of rural people. Receiving an official notice was a matter of dignity and an assurance of self-sufficiency. It put a man in the position of having some official business to take care of, even if it was no more than that of looking longingly at the package and then instructing the postmaster to return it because he had no money.

Merchants were bedeviled by the constant arrival of cash-on-delivery packages which had to be returned and for which they did much work but collected no fees. Many a mail-starved victim got his name on the rolls of those understanding list makers who seduced their victims with the simple inquiry, "Do you wish to receive a lot of important mail?" When the innocent countryman sent in his affirmative answer from an obscure post office, he was soon showered with "bargain offers—C.O.D.," and his country-store post office was jammed with shoes, lamps, "art" objects, and medicine which he had checked as wanting on a slick "postage free" card.

Always there was money to be paid. In 1893 an Alabama customer was notified by the Planters and Merchants Bank of Uniontown that he owed a note to the Singer Sewing Machine Company; he asked his neighborhood merchant to meet the bill for him. Henry Jackson, a neighbor, was in a similar predicament. He was a victim of garnishment proceedings with J. W. McCarthy at the store–post office of Coatopa, Alabama, and he asked J. C. Brown for a money order with which to settle the pressing obligation. In writing a note to the merchant, Henry Jackson's landlord, asked that he likewise be "credited" for stamps and registry fee.

At White Oak, South Carolina, General John Bratton asked T. G. Patrick and Company to send a draft of one thousand dollars to his son in San Francisco. The draft was honored, and the money was dispatched by mail. News of the successful negotiation of the loan was sent on ahead by telegraph and the charge placed on the General's account. General Bratton said in his letter requesting the loan, "Don't let it take your breath." Few stores could have met such a demand, but hundreds of them did finance money orders for much smaller sums every week. They not only got a profit from making out money orders and from cancellation for stamps, but they received good interest returns on the cash spent for the mail-order goods. In this way many of the mail orders shipped south by Sears, Roebuck, Montgomery Ward and Company, J. Linn, Charles Williams, and other popular houses yielded a profit to the country stores. Literally thousands of entries appear in account books for "cash" which was expended outside the stores, but which yielded the merchant a return.

Taxes, lodge dues, church contributions, doctors' bills, express and freight charges, and many other small bills came due during the season when customers were without money, and they looked to merchants for small loans. Doctors' bills and taxes were high enough, but often they became much higher when a merchant placed a stiff interest charge upon them. "Please pay Mr. Hopper my dues for this month," wrote a delinquent brother. "Will return it in a day or two. I would not ask you this favor, but I am sick in bed, and not able to attend to it just now." A progressive stock farmer in the South, caught in a busy spell of work, asked a storekeeper in South Carolina to "send seven dollars to C. M. Winslow, Brandon, Vermont. It is to pay for registering calves. If not done it will cost me double. . . ." Another customer asked a merchant to stamp and register a letter addressed to J. F. Davis' Racket Store, and the clerk noted a charge of twelve cents for the transaction. "Please enquire if there is an express package in the Depot. If so *Pay* for it & send out by Careful hand passing." And, finally, an abused patient writing on a tattered half-page of a Simmons' Liver Regulator memorandum book instructed, "Please dont pay no Doctor Bill for me untill i see you. George Shields."

When a man needed money to pay small outside charges, it never occurred to him to get the money from a bank at perhaps a lower rate of interest. He could think in terms of only one central crediting agency, and that was the merchant. Even the most casual glance at any account book from a country store in the South during the last seventy-five years would beveal how informal banker-merchants were.

In the beginning the monetary system of the rural South was so badly disorganized that stores were practically the only places where money or credit could be had. Later, when banks in greater numbers appeared, the habit of depending on the stores had already been established. Likewise, there was much hesitancy and fear connected with dealings in a bank. Its business was run on a more impersonal basis. Seldom, if ever, would it honor a request written out on a piece of scratch paper and delivered by a sweaty Negro. Banks were largely for the merchants and other businessmen to patronize.

Frequently the first telephones in rural communities were those located in the stores. Today, either nailed to the back walls of storehouses or strewn through dirty attics are the remains of these fascinating instruments with single-wire connections and their long-necked transmitters and bulky battery boxes. These clumsy and inefficient phones were the first steps toward giving isolated communities instantaneous connection with the world outside.

To the loafers sitting around the stove, Dr. Alexander Graham Bell's invention was beyond understanding. Over and over the question was repeated, "How can the sound of a man's voice be carried through a solid wire?" For the nail-keg scientists every fact had a logical conclusion, but no one could find a hole in the wire. To the less curious the telephone was nothing short of a miracle of God. But one thing was certain—it was an instrument of practicality. Day and night perspiring messengers galloped up to store doors astride foaming mounts. They came to get storekeepers to call the doctor. Scores of rural tragedies kept merchants busy rendering aid. A barefoot boy was snake-bitten, an aged citizen was stricken with apoplexy, an ax glanced off a piece of stovewood and gashed a leg, a mule caused a brain concussion with a close and well-aimed kick, or a baby was smothering to death with hives or croup. Farmers generally put off calling the doctor until late in the afternoon or late at night and then rode to stores to get merchants and their families out of bed to use the phone. To put a check on this practice, some merchants permitted free use of their phones in the daytime but made twenty-five- and fifty-cent charges at night.

For doctors and storekeepers Alexander Graham Bell was a cross between a saint and a devil. For the merchant the telephone was a source of new business of an exceedingly unsound character. When a man asked a merchant to call a doctor for him, the doctor nearly always attempted to secure the merchant's endorsement of the visit, and in this way many a sleepy storekeeper faced by an anxious, perspiring father with a grassy cotton crop and a sick child agreed to stand good for a bill which in other and less appealing circumstances he would have refused. Because of it, neighbors were forever asking favors. In 1899 a customer wrote an Alabama merchant, "Owen Allen has a child in Selma and she wants to come home will you please telephone for her to meet him and arrange it with the Depot Agent to pay for her railroad fair [*sic*] I wish you would attend to it for me and pay for her ticket and obliged." Merchants time and again supplied money for railroad tickets. They were sources of information about train schedules, and frequently they were called upon to make arrangements for shipping livestock, carloads of lumber, and other types of freight.

An extreme case of calling upon a merchant to render service because of his nearness to the railroad was that of a South Carolinian who craved apples and oranges. He wrote a merchant to go aboard the afternoon train and secure these things from the butcher boy. In the same spirit merchants were called upon to meet trains and take care of children and aged relatives until someone could get to the station to take them home.

In communities where there were no railroads, storekeepers were called upon to sell stagecoach tickets on credit. In many instances they were agents and sold tickets on the same basis of credit as they did fat meat, molasses, and snuff. Frequently customers along the rivers had to cross ferries and didn't have enough money to pay their ferriage charges; neighboring merchants supplied the necessary funds. At Northport, Alabama, across the river from Tuscaloosa, the T. J. Christian Company provided ferriage every Saturday for patrons who wished to go over the Black Warrior River to see the sights in Tuscaloosa after they had finished their trading in Northport.

There was a general feeling that when something unusual happened, the news should be sent immediately to the store. In the same manner that supplies were ordered, customers sent messengers with notes publicizing the latest news and excitement. A white customer in South Carolina, following a minor tragedy on his place, sent an order to the Patrick store saying, "One of the colored children has gotten burnt. Send me a little linseed oil if you have any." In Tennessee a neighbor sent a request to the store to know if an old lady had died. In another community a farmer could endure the suspense no longer and dispatched a Negro boy to get the election returns from the storekeeper. These were services which merchants rendered as a necessary part of their business. They were more or less obligated to glean news from those who passed through their stores and to pass it on. The technique of news gathering was subtle. Usually it was initiated by a merchant's saying, "Old Man Bryce is down with his back. He sent a boy up here today to get a porous plaster," or "Lem Wilson is getting married Saturday." Lem had just requested, in a note, that his friends behind the counters advertise the fact for him. A restless patron waited for a neighbor to come by and pick him up, and he got tired of waiting and went on. He "left word" at the store, however, of his departure. When a man went away for a day and found that he could not get home, he sent word to the storekeeper to inform his family.

Not only were stores places where messages could be cleared, but also were places where packages could be left to be picked up. If a woman wished to send a dress to her daughter who lived some distance away, she sent it to the store to be delivered by the first passer-by. Often stores took on the appearance of baggage rooms.

There were frequent requests for goods which were never carried in stock, like the request of a customer in Eagleville, Tennessee, who wished to buy "sulphate strychnine, mallo-pepsin, four ounces of nitro muriatic acid, half ounce of podo phylum, one ounce of iodide potassium, one tube morphine tablet gr. ½." It was necessary to send such an order to a drugstore in town. There were literally hundreds of such requests which became an obligatory part of the business of keeping the public good will.

A barn was struck by lightning, and the farmer's feed and livestock were lost. The loss of his property threatened to bankrupt him. A subscription list was started, and as customers came to the store, they were asked to sign it and state how much they would give toward restoring the barn and livestock. In another instance a child was dangerously ill and its only hope of life was to get to a hospital, but hospitals in the earlier decades of the postwar South were located only in larger centers. To pay railroad fare for the child, a member of the family, and the doctor required more money than the entire annual cash income of the father. The family needed help, and the only source of relief was from people in the community. A committee prepared a petition and passed it around at the store to secure assistance. Every subscriber signed the list, and it was turned over to the receiver as a sort of receipt and reminder of community generosity. One of the finest features of rural southern social relationship was its willingness to give aid to a neighbor in need of help. Mississippians alone gave away hundreds of thousands of dollars to help faltering neighbors regain their feet after spells of bad luck.

A group of persons became interested in the organization of a new church and left agreements on store counters to be signed as supporters came along. A community wanted a new road opened or a bridge built to take the place of a dangerous ford or an expensive ferry, and a petition was circulated to be signed and turned over to the board of supervisors. Occasionally a band of supporters wished to secure the nomination and election of a hand-picked candidate, and they took a census of voters by asking them to sign a request begging the candidate to make the race.

A group of Tennessee petitioners sought the attention of the second assistant postmaster general to change the star route from Franklin to Bethesda, Arno, and Harpeth. Their mail was coming through Reed's Store post office on Flat Creek only three times a week, and they felt that the Post Office Department could give them daily services if only the second assistant postmaster general would listen to reason. They were specific in their statement of views, but politely they informed the official, "Not that we wish to dictate for you we give our views in the matter & of course leave the verdict to your better judgment."

The petition was written out in longhand by J. B. Reed, and the language was that of a backwoods horse trader who was able to set forth the essential facts of an argument with more clarity than grammar.

Reed's experience was comparable to experiences of all southern merchants. Hardly a week went by when they were not called upon to draft notes, mortgages, deeds of trust, liens, rental contracts, bills of sale, and numerous other papers. A common type of legal paper was the rental contract, of which this is an illustrative sample: "On the 15th of October, 1896—after date, I promise to pay Mr. Seeden on order the sum of thirty dollars—for 10 acres land on Ingleside Plantation." Frequently when notes and mortgages were properly signed, they were left in custody of merchants. Most merchants had old-fashioned iron safes, and they assumed responsibility for giving such important records safekeeping. Likewise, they were experienced in collecting notes, so they were entrusted with the task of seeing that the terms inscribed in an agreement were properly observed.

Often it could be said that a merchant's safe was the financial depository of his community. Important to him was the knowledge of what liabilities were registered against each farmer in his territory. This gave a storekeeper a certain basis on which to gauge the amount of credit which could be safely granted individual farmers from year to year.

A Confederate veteran found himself in a financial pinch, and he sought a pension from the county and state organization. Before he could get the pension, however, he had to fill out a form with the assistance of the postmaster-merchant. When finally the money was available in small monthly payments, the checks were endorsed and left at the store to be drawn upon for supplies. A poverty-stricken customer needed help from the county, and a merchant secured permission to get him admitted to the poorhouse, or a demented individual was finally sent away to an insane asylum after he was committed according to law.

On the business side there were frequent calls from advertising agencies seeking professional information. Most common were numerous blanks which came in the mail requesting names for mailing lists. Sometimes slight rewards were offered for the submission of a certain number of names of good prospects. Distributors of a new product nearly always sought prospective agents to sell it in the locality of a store, and they wrote the merchant for his recommendations. Patent-medicine makers every month sought lists of customers so that they might bombard them with circulars and frugal samples of comsumption and cancer cures.

Politicians seeking state and important district offices sometimes wanted the names of patrons of a post office, and other times they asked for only one or two names of individuals who would make active representatives of their candidacies in the neighborhood.

Dun and Bradstreet regularly sought information which would keep up to date their useful financial ratings. Much of Dun and Bradstreet's work was done in personal interviews, but often blanks were mailed to storekeepers, who were asked to make a confidential estimate of a neighboring merchant's capabilities to meet obligation.

It was not uncommon for life-insurance companies to enlist country storekeepers as confidential advisers about prospective policyholders. They were always anxious to establish connections with the larger merchants because of their eternal vigilance in granting credit, though perhaps few policyholders ever knew that their applications had first been approved by a local storekeeper. If they had ever been ill, the merchant would report the fact, and if in any way they had falsified their application, he would know it. Many merchants could recall what everybody in the community had died with, and they passed this valuable information on to the insurance companies. Likewise, they knew who in a community was able to buy insurance.

The theory that every crossroads store in the postwar South was a sort of community clearinghouse has an early beginning. In 1869 an unscrupulous scoundrel using a fetching Wall Street address and signing himself J. Noyes and Company was ready to prey upon the financially stricken southern trade with a slick proposition. He claimed that he had on hand "a large stock of exact copies of the genuine United States Treasury notes which we desire to dispose of on the following very liberal terms——" His terms were $200.00 for $15.00, $500.00 for $30.00, $1,000.00 for $50.00, and $2,000.00 for $80.00. If a merchant ordered at least fifty dollars' worth of the Noyes "paper," he was assured the exclusive privilege of paving his way into the federal penitentiary in his village. For $80.00 he was given a monopolistic right of slipping fictitious bills to his customers at cotton-selling time.

Shrewdly the J. Noyes Company encouraged customers, for good business reasons and expedition, to send money first. As a final and finishing touch of irony, the offer concluded, "We place reliance in you as far as offering this opportunity & confide in your ability to keep the whole thing a profound secret, these notes by the knowing ones are pronounced perfect copies of the genuine and we claim the right to make our own terms in disposing of them. If we sent samples it would make our business much too public as disinterested parties would send for such therefore in justice to ourselves we positively refuse to send *samples* or sell in any less quantities than above stated to anyone or on any other terms." Parenthetically the letter explained that the bills were things of artistic and financial beauty executed "by the most skilled men in the art outside of the state's prison."

This swindler distributed his letters among the country stores, and only on careful examination was it revealed that they were printed rather than handwritten. Temptation to meet the urgent need for money in the South was too great for some merchants. A North Carolinian near Salisbury fell for the seductive bait of J. Noyes and ordered a quantity of money, cash-on-delivery by express. When the package arrived and the charges were paid, the purchaser found that he had paid a dear price for a box of shavings. A conciliatory note packed in the top of the box said that the money-makers were unhappily under annoying surveillance by New York police and that shipment of the money would be held up for an indefinite time.

Even this type of swindling saw in the country store a fine opportunity to get at the people. Fortunately for the people, however, few merchants did business with such crooks.

6

TEN GROSS JUNE BUGS, ASSORTED

Next to Frankie and Johnnie the great American dramatis personae are the "Traveling Salesman and the Farmer's Daughter." These two characters have lived long and happy lives in which they have given flavor to a multitude of slightly off-color accounts of the excessive amatory tendencies of the commercial traveler. The drummer involved in the story wore away his life traveling in a two-horse buggy calling on country storekeepers, and spent his nights wherever he could. One particular night he found himself before the proverbial farmhouse seeking food and lodging. The hospitable farmer was willing to take the drummer in, but explained that he would either have to sleep with the baby or spend the night in the hayloft. Visualizing a restless infant with erratic social habits, the exhausted drummer chose the barn. The next morning when he came down with his touseled hair filled with straw, he saw a buxom redhead of twenty at the well, who upon inquiry explained that she was the baby.

This fanciful story scarcely describes that important agent of merchandising in the period following the war. When the Boston *Advertiser's* reporter, Sidney Andrews, came south in 1866, he was impressed with the commercial activities of the region. Eastern and western Georgia, he related, "I found full of 'runners' from Louisville and Cincinnati. They represented all branches of trade, and pretty generally reported that they were getting many orders. In this section I find more representatives of eastern houses. I believe the delivery of goods already ordered will give a stock in the state sufficient for the coming year. Everybody seems to have a passion for keeping store, and hundreds of men who are going into trade should go into agriculture. If the coming season brings a 'smash' in many lines, the prophecies of numerous business men will not be unfulfilled."

While carpetbaggers, scalawags, and military governors were causing political havoc in the South, agents of the expanding national wholesale business were bumping over country roads selling goods and organizing new store outlets. They came from houses located in the big northern, coastal, and border towns. Their trunks bulged with an astounding assortment of articles. Dry-goods salesmen's trunks were filled with bolts of goods and shoes.

Hardware salesmen brought no cumbersome trunks filled with samples. Theirs was not so much a task of displaying new patterns and designs of goods as it was of selling old standards. They were selling the very same implements with which pap and grandpap had turned the red soils of Virginia, the Carolinas, Georgia, and Alabama: pony turning plows, dow law and Louisville cotton planters, Georgia scooter stocks, side harrows, grass rods, and scores of other articles. These were things which storekeepers could visualize, and the salesmen needed only lists, catalogues, and order books to serve their customers. When descriptions were vague, drummers turned amateur commercial artists and drew pictures of the articles which they offered.

To Hardware drummers the consistency of the land, the condition of the roads, the types of houses along the road, and the kinds of little industries which flourished were all factors governing the sale of goods. Seasonal changes and crops shaped the hardware and notions trade, and neither salesmen nor the firms they represented could afford to ignore these surface manifestations.

Cast in the traditional role of high-pressure salesmen were the medicine drummers. Slick-talking, flashily dressed dandies representing Dr. Bull of Louisville, Dr. Shoop of Racine,

Lydia Pinkham of Lynn, Peruna of Columbus, Ohio, the Chattanooga Medicine Company, Dr. McClean of St. Louis, and Spurlock, Neal and Company of Nashville drifted over the South with their "lines." Like the effusive claims of health smeared on the backs of almanacs, calendars and memorandum books, or stuffed into the "patent pages" of country newspapers underneath zinc etchings of their cadaverous victims, these salesmen were aggressive. The morals and futures of their jobs were governed solely by their belief in the validity of the medicines which they sold. If they believed they were good, then their efforts were directed toward standardizing them in the stores. If the goods were trashy, merchants were high-pressured into buying as many cases as possible for cash or on short-term credit, and then left to get their money back as best they could. Sometimes a drummer even carried his product with him and delivered it at the moment of the sale. Some of the St. Louis medicine companies sent out drummers on small paddle-wheel boats, and they sold their goods to the stores located along the navigable streams.

Selling was not the drummer's sole task. He was the "ear to the ground" for both his house and his city. In many instances he helped to establish stores in places where there were reasonably good trading prospects. He selected the locations, designed the buildings, bought stock, set up systems of bookkeeping, and gave advice on general business procedure.

For merchants who were already in business, drummers served as advisers on such matters as credit, prices, rates of interest, stocks, and lines of goods which would boost trade. A storekeeper nearly always had one or two dependable drummers who advised him on the amount of stock he should buy. They also helped him to arrange counter displays, special bargains, and gave him advice on the produce-buying end of the business. In short, the more reliable drummers were often as much economic advisers as salesmen.

While representatives of the wholesale houses were looking out for the interest of the local stores, they kept track of such matters as credit rating, personal eccentricities, and business enterprise of their customers. Although Dun and Bradstreet began reporting on the credit rating of country stores at an early date, it was the drummers who really established for their houses a highly personalized system of credit ratings.

For merchants the periodic calls of the drummers were looked upon as happy events. Traveling men in the rural South came with the romantic glamour of having been in faraway places. The dust of cities and coal smoke of trains were still upon them. They were generous chroniclers who knew the news and gossip with which to enliven the barren lives of the people. They spent considerable time around the stores "gassing" about things which were happening over the country. They were up on the current and sensational news, the standing of baseball teams, outcome of prize fights, the big national crimes, the weather, politics, and scandal. But most important of all for their army of hearers, they knew what the folks just up the road were doing, and how their crops were progressing. They knew the extent of the local thundershowers, the muddy roads, the schedules of stages, steamboats, and trains, and the results of the latest election.

News-bearing was a useful and informative service cheerfully rendered by the drummers, and it was not without compensation. Talk around the stove was the most subtle kind of salesmanship, which had for its purpose the checking up on the nature of the community, crop projections and prospects, credit risks, and the general taste of customers. They were informal business surveys. At the same time a jovial salesman could turn these stoveside chats to good advertising advantage for his line. If customers never asked for a product, there was no reason why a merchant should stock it, and the drummers kept this fact uppermost in mind in their neighborly conversations.

Thus while drummers served their houses as salesmen and fact gatherers, they likewise performed the duties of advertising agents. Riding behind a slow team, they had much idle time on their hands. It was a simple matter for them to take boxes of samples, folders, memorandum books, and tin pie plates along and pitch them out at crossroads, on church and school grounds, at farm gates, and around mailboxes. This was an excellent way to advertise medicines, needles, soda and baking powder, flour, and farm machinery. For goods which could not be advertised by the sampling method it was necessary to nail and paint signs on trees, fences, and barns. At stores one of the regular duties of a drummer was to nail signs to doors and walls, and accidentally to cover or tear down as many of those of competitors as could be done without making his actions too obvious.

Many drummers were former Confederate soldiers who, to hear them tell it, had fought all over the region, and they sat for hours reminiscing and bragging about the exploits of the army at Fort Donelson, Shiloh, Vicksburg, Chancellorsville, Richmond, and, with voices lowered in reverence, at Appomattox. It was a great selling point to be able to talk with familiarity about "Old Bed" Forrest, Morgan and his men, "Fighting" Joe Wheeler, or of Generals Lee, Jackson, Bragg, and Stuart.

While the bullets were flying thick and fast at Chickamauga, or at the moment when the Yankee line was falling back at Fredricksburg, many a frugal merchant made up his mind to order a bill of goods which under less exciting circumstances he would not have bought at all. If a drummer lacked the technique of maneuvering the Confederate Army and his line of goods into a strategic position to mow down a cornfield full of Yankees and stubborn sales resistance, then he resorted to another method. Often a good hot political discussion with a salesman taking the storekeeper's side was as clever a method of lowering sales resistance as could be used. If not politics, then religion served as an excellent topic for vigorous discussion. A salesman born and brought up on the farm could engage his hearers in a "practical" discussion of farming methods and the merits of one variety of cotton over another. Seldom did the early drummers make an immediate and direct sales talk for their lines. The South was not far enough away from the personalized attitudes of the frontier to tolerate the workaday methods of the present-day "shelf runners."

There was Colonel W. H. Bradley of Kentucky, who discovered a nonpartisan device which completely disarmed merchants and stirred the curiosity of store loafers to the point of exasperation. The *New South,* of Elberton, Georgia, announced on September 3, 1884, that the Kentuckian "was in town a few days since and exhibited a curiosity in the way of a bean which he called the 'Mexican Electric Bean.' He and his bean are a terror to the superstitious colored population." Truthfully Colonel Bradley's bean was a terror to all, particularly merchants who found two weeks later when dry goods began to arrive from the Kentucky wholesale house which he represented that the wonderful curiosity was the means of throwing them off guard.

Sizing up a customer was an everyday job for a drummer. To offer a teetotaling deacon and community pillar a drink was to ruin prospects of business for "the house" for a long time to come. Yet to fail to offer a tippling merchant a drink was to do serious harm. If a merchant drank, it was necessary for a drummer to exercise extreme caution. The object was to create a comfortable rosy glow in a customer but not to get him drunk. Too much liquor would make a moderate credit risk buy enough goods to load a Louisville and Nashville freight train, or there was danger of selling a big order of goods and then having it canceled.

An old-timer recalls that he tried without success to sell a bill of goods to a gruff storekeeper. His sales talk had made no impression whatsoever. That night in a country hotel a fellow salesman informed him that a quart of liquor would make a new and generous man of the merchant and that it was the old man's long-standing practice never to buy from a drummer until he had been "liquored." The next day the drummer returned and after a short session in the shed room in which the storekeeper took several hefty swigs from the bottle, he turned and asked, "What was that you said you was selling? Write out an order for any amount and I'll sign it."

Liquor and fancy off-color stories were stocks in trade. Generally drummers were purveyors of all the lively yarns afloat in America from 1865 to 1920. Being a masterful storyteller was every bit as good as being a ripsnorting Confederate veteran. Women customers hardly dared venture into a store when they saw a drummer's rig drawn up at the hitching rack. They knew there would most likely be a ring of men and boys gathered around the stranger listening intently to his flow of wit and color. Here were the stories of the cities being passed on to the bumpkins of the crossroads, and they loved the new yarns. Not all of them were vulgar; many drummers developed the art of telling Negro and Irish dialect stories which always found listeners.

After a revival meeting or some other local reform and spiritual rejuvenation, merchants and their customers changed momentarily their philosophical outlook on life. In 1885 the editor of the Elberton (Georgia) *Gazette* remarked that "We heard a tobacco drummer say the other day that one of his best customers in Hartwell had recently professed holines and quit chewing and smoking and refused to handle tobacco."

That drummers were well informed about their business is reflected in the thoroughness with which they did their work. Night after night they gathered in the rooms of county-seat hotels to play poker, drink, and spin yarns. But actually they spent much of their time exchanging practical information. They discussed every merchant in the territory, and passed on tips about their eccentricities of character and buying habits. It was an unwritten rule, except among their most active competitors, that drummers gave their fellows full benefit of their experiences around the circuit. One merchant had to be "liquored and yarned" before he would buy, but another would not permit liquor or racy stories in his store. From these evenings in the hotels drummers gathered an enormous amount of useful detailed information on the resources and moral temper of the New South which was to influence the whole process of distributing merchandise in the region.

Often friendships grew up between drummers and they co-operated in covering their territories. A hardware merchant would take along an order book of a packing-house salesman, or a dry-goods drummer would keep at hand an order book for a shoe salesman and would sell bills of goods for his friends. But where there was close co-operation among many drummers, there were "soreheads" who were worn and tired by years of difficult traveling. They were crochety in the evenings in the hotels and were shut-mouth about their experiences with merchants in the territory. Because of their unco-operative attitudes they were often the butts of rude jokes. Sometimes they would get caught at a store and would have to spend the night with a farmer or with the merchant's family. Occasionally one of the jocular boys from the poker table was caught along with an embittered old knight and the two were forced to sleep together, to the amusement of the host and his family.

Grocery, meat, and feed salesmen called as often as every month or six weeks. Medicine drummers came along at irregular intervals ranging from six months to a year. Dry-goods, shoe, notion, and hardware salesmen came regularly every six months to keep up with the change in demand for seasonal goods. They arrived in the winter to sell spring goods, and in midsummer to sell fall lines. Likewise, hardware drummers came in the fall to sell stock for the spring planting and in late spring to sell supplies for the harvest season.

Selling dry goods and shoes were complicated jobs. Salesmen came with small bolts of samples packed away in huge trunks. Merchants learned early that careful selection of goods determined their volume of sale later. For this reason they had to see the goods spread out in fairly large pieces in order to visualize their appearance on a customer's back. Too, they had difinite notions about the taste of the people in their communities, and they could tell with some accuracy beforehand what patterns would sell. Generally wives and daughters and women clerks were called upon to select piece goods, and drummers would stay for two and three days at a time. They unpacked their trunks and wound off hundreds of yards of checks, calicoes, plaids, and muslins. In fact they spent much of their lives unpacking and packing trunks. There was one compensation—they enjoyed the friendship of the merchants, and they were around long enough to gauge the volume of their business and to remove barriers of formality which often existed for salesmen of other lines. Many times they were invited to stay with the storekeeper's family and close ties of affection grew up between them.

Shoe drummers, like representatives from dry-goods houses, brought trunks filled with actual goods as samples. For two and three days at a time they dug into trays and dragged out new numbers of Sunday shoes for men made on the congress and side-button lasts, or the newest creation in women's shoes. The latter underwent just enough changes each year to satisfy feminine whims, and this involved the greatest risk in the shoe business. Buying men's work shoes and brass-toed footwear for children was a simple matter of deciding the number of pairs needed and the range of sizes most in demand. But the business of stocking a full line of fancy shoes was one of the most expensive trial-and-error experiments in the business of merchandising. In many cases drummers were relied upon to put in stock what they thought would adequately supply a season's trade. Thus it was that many a merchant in years to come laid much of his hard luck upon the optimism of a drummer who overstocked him with shoes to the permanent injury of his business.

Some of the more imaginative salesmen utilized the sample rooms of the country hotels in which to display their wares and wrote their customers in advance to come in and visit with them. This required only one showing, and put the drummer in a position to extend certain hospitalities to his guests, thus building up a slight obligation which was a factor in selling his goods. Certainly it lessened the necessity for travel and the tedium of unpacking and packing trunks at each store. Filed away in store records are frequent notices written by drummers that their lines would be displayed on certain dates in neighboring sample rooms.

Salesmen who made regular circuits became almost as much a part of the store business as were the cat and stove. They were constantly giving advice on good methods of organization, prices, and credits. They gave their steady customers advantageous information about their competitors, gave them tips on the trend of styles, improvements in types of merchandise, and economic conditions in general. Merchants in need of money often got from them information about where it could be borrowed on the most favorable terms. Likewise, many of the drummers were able to visualize a large portion of the regional economic pattern and could make pretty accurate guesses concerning which way the fickle economic scales would tip. When the boll weevil began its devastating march across the South, some of the drummers kept up with its progress and guessed for their customers the effect it would have when it invaded neighboring cotton fields. They knew the trend of the general market and were able to bring about a slowing up, or increased business activities, as the occasion warranted.

Their methods of selling were subtle. Sometimes high-pressure sales methods were necessary, and they talked gullible storekeepers into buying more goods than could be sold at a profit. This was especially true when a merchant was just beginning business and depended upon drummers to select his stock of goods. A mistake of this kind lost the drummer a patron and caused many a sad but wiser storekeeper to close his doors in bankruptcy on an overstock of shoes, clothing, and notions. Yet many drummers started their most successful customers on the road to success by selecting stock and giving them periodic advice on the best business methods to employ.

Occasionally the antics of a clownish salesman enlivened the whole calling. Among the boys of the derby hat and two-horse buggies who could always be counted upon to do the unusual in making a sale was "Red" Meadors of Kentucky. He had a reputation of being able to sell Red Ox chewing tobacco even to a session of the Ladies' Missionary Society. He distinguished himself, however, by selling his largest order to a dead man.

On his rounds the jocular Meadors learned of the death of one of the most cautious merchants in his territory. By clever manipulation he got into the old man's store at the time of the funeral and placed an antedated carbon copy of an enormous order for chewing tobacco on the wire file. Immediately after the burial, a daughter took over the business, and scarcely had she reopened the doors of the store before the large shipment of Red Ox arrived. She accepted it and filled the shelves along one side of the store with tobacco and waited for buyers to appear. But Red Ox was an extremely slow seller and the bereaved daughter sat day after day for months staring at her father's last great mistake until Meadors again appeared at the store. When he suggested that the daughter make a reorder, she almost went into hysterics, shouting, "Heavens, no! Father must have thought your company was going broke from the order he gave you just before he died. My shelves are now breaking down with Red Ox tobacco and no one wants it."

After salesmen traveled through a territory for several years, they built up a trade which was theirs for the trouble of writing orders. They knew all of the storekeepers; they knew whom to trust for a year to pay their bills, and whom not to risk even for ten days. If a salesman of long standing either died or was removed from his old territory, trade for his line fell off immediately. His was a highly personal business which only secondarily depended upon the quality of the line which he was selling. Frank C. Rand, president of the board of directors of the International Shoe Company, said that he followed John C. and Eugene Roberts on the road in two of the southern states selling shoes. Both of these men had been popular with their customers. Gene Roberts made only one trip on the road selling Star Brand shoes before he died. "Gene died in September, 1898," said Mr. Rand, "having made one season's trip for Roberts, Johnson and Rand; but on that memorable trip Gene sold Star Brand shoes to every one of his old customers—not missing a man.

"After Gene's death I was given his territory, southeast Missouri and northeast Arkansas. When I started out on my first trip, twenty-two years of age, with no business experience and little knowledge of shoes, I had a list of the customers whom Gene had sold. As I called on them one after another and introduced myself they expressed keen regret and genuine sorrow in Gene's passing; but indicated that their first order for Star Brand shoes had been placed out of loyalty to and friendship for Gene. They felt that, since he had gone, their best interest lay in a return to Hamilton-Brown and the shoes they had handled for years."

Faithful drummers made a sentimental appeal to both the storekeepers and their daughters. An infatuated maiden who twice a year saw the dry-goods salesmen come around with their battered trunks wrote for the *Drummer* a sentimental defense of their reputations. She thought, "Of all the men living, the commercial man is one whose life is a long list of romantic incidents, some extremely sad, indeed, and some infinite mirth. No wonder he is a man of resources, and great of heart. He obtains the experiences of more people than any other man on the face of the earth. His own experience is the cream of all those poured into his eager listening ear, or snatched by his watchful eye. His nimble wit is at the command of every man he meets. Are you heartsick and burdened with troubles? His tongue is tipped with humorous philosophy that drives away sorrow and disarms troubles of all their stings. Are you in financial difficulty? His hand flies to his pocket and relieves your monetary distress as easily and as heartily as he does your mental woes. To sum up, he is everything that goes to make up a good and splendid manhood. Of course, there are some bad ones, but they only serve to enhance and bring out in greater prominence the virtues of the majority. He is a walking encyclopedia of practical everyday knowledge and you can get more real, solid, satisfactory information on any subject, be it business or pleasure, from one commercial man than you can from ten ordinary men. He is a moving, breathing, hustling edition of Rand and McNally, and his brain is one seething mass of facts, fun, and figures. He has been accused of living rapidly. He eats, drinks and sleeps on the run, and his brain and all ideas move at the same rapid gait. Truly our commercial friend lives a 'fast life' never too fast to give up his seat to that aged lady (for the drummer has a mother somewhere). Never too fast to amuse that fretful child, and give its poor, weak mother a few moments to rest and quiet. Never, in fact, too fast to do the needful. The commercial man may be fast in a way but he is a dandy and I am in love with him."

From a drummer's standpoint he did live a life of rushing around, if driving hundreds of miles over impossible roads in a buggy and riding through all hours of the day and night on ill-equipped and inefficient local trains could be called rushing. Many drummers were heroic in their ability to get from one store to another and still be in a good enough humor to solicit orders for their goods. They ate poor, starchy food in many of the hotels, and in others they were given the richest victuals of all to eat. Perhaps this latter-type food accounts for the extraordinary sexual promiscuity which was characteristic of the trade, or perhaps it grew out of the anxiety of their lonesome wives at home. Nevertheless, they kept at their business. In 1881 the Greensboro (Georgia) *Herald* carried a line saying that the "drought didn't seem to affect the crop of drummers—well they are all clever boys and we are glad to see them." Editors of local papers everywhere recorded the appearance of the salesmen, and they wrote of them in tones of high regard.

Occasionally, driving along the winding stretches of monotonous roads lined with dense growths of pines, the drummers turned their thoughts to devilment. An Atlanta salesman went down to Lakeland, Georgia, to demonstrate to the clerks of the Patton store the technique of trimming and lining factory-made coffins. Arriving at the railway village of Naylor, the drummer hired two colored draymen to haul his samples over to Lakeland. As they crept along the hot, dry road through the "sawgrass" bottoms, the Atlanta salesman began explaining to the Negroes that while he talked to the storekeeper he wanted them to get the coffins upstairs, brush them off, and then get in two of them as models. Immediately the prankish drummer found himself sitting alone with a pair of mules, a wagon, and three coffins. His helpers had taken to the woods, where there was no immediate chance of their having to model caskets for an aggressive Atlanta factory. There were hundreds of similar occasions when drummers relieved the tedium of life with comical antics involving the ignorant natives who bought their goods at the stores.

Sometimes the going got too tough, and the drummer found himself hopelessly befuddled. Liquor, rich food, too much poker playing and muddy roads threw his mind into a terrifying dilemma, and his reports to the "house" became unintelligible. There was that New York traveling man who ran amuck in Georgia and wired his house an urgent request for "one barrel of condensed beef, thirteen steamboats, one medium white elephant and ten gross June bugs, assorted."

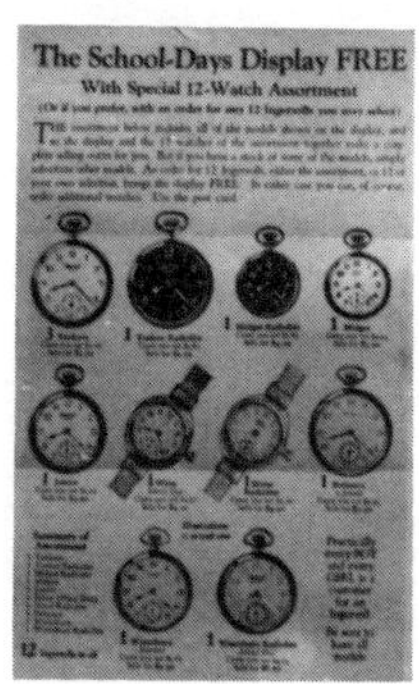

7

A LITTLE BIT OF SANTA CLAUS

ONCE EACH YEAR the southern country store took on a delightfully new appearance and a fresh, exciting aroma. New boxes, bales, barrels, and sacks obstructed the passageways and overflowed onto the shelves and counters. This seasonal addition of new stock was even permitted to break into the holy circle about the stove. A general assortment of holiday goods was superimposed over and around the regular stock. Barrels and boxes of candy were rolled in between the sugar, coffee, meal, and flour or put down on the counter tops among the thread and knife cases. Bags of coconuts were ripped open and the tops of the sacks rolled down displaying their fuzzy brown wares awaiting purchase by the cake makers. Boxes of oranges were opened and leaned end-up against the counters. Barrels of apples were distributed among the nail kegs and benches about the stove circle. Toys were suspended from the ceiling among the lanterns, water buckets, horse collars, buggy whips, and lard cans, or they were mixed in with the everyday merchandise of the glass cases. On top of the counters were small wooden boxes lined with red paper and filled with sawdust and shavings, and the contents were ruffled into a seductive state of confusion. These contained the firecrackers, torpedoes, and Roman candles.

Above the commonplace everyday odors of the stores there was a change. There was a much stronger overtone of cheese. Oranges and apples gave a richness; burned powder from fireworks added an acrid flavor, and above all of this was the fragrant bouquet of Bourbon or the raw tang of corn whisky. Newly opened tubs of corned mackerel sat well back out of range of careless tobacco chewers. Here was an assortment of merchandise and rich smells which made indelible impressions on several generations of southerners and which are to many, even yet, a reminder of Christmas. Clarence Nixon wrote of his father's store in his understanding book, *Possum Trot,* "We stocked up with fruit in December, and I still think of Christmas when I smell oranges in the country."

The South was a land of deep sentimentality. Family ties were close, and the hard years following the war tended to knit them even more securely. Christmas was a time of family rededication, and a season of erasing old and irritating scars of discord. It was a period for visiting and feasting. Celebration of the holiday was the one institution which came through the war unchanged except for the matter of simplification. Until 1915 rural observance was uncontaminated by commercialization. Simple gifts were passed around, and these, as a matter of course, came from the country store.

Much of the masculine taste in celebration ran to boisterous forms of expression. For more than fifty years the liquor barrel furnished ample cheer for all customers who could rake together enough cash or "stretch" their credit to buy a quart of Kentucky or Maryland Bourbon, or a half-gallon of North Carolina corn. A quart of whisky was admittedly a vigorous start toward a glorious Christmas season. For the temperate, however, a package of firecrackers was enough holiday amusement. One little nickel package of Chinese firecrackers provided plenty of Christmas joking and pranking. A favorite stunt was to explode the tiny cylinders at the heel of some humorless deacon, with the hope of starting him into "cussing." Another was setting them off near a pair of mules in a storehouse yard. The number of runaways made many a good celebrant regret that there was such a thing as Christmas. But there was the more pleasant aspect to this form of amusement.

Thousands of country children were happier waking up in a cold farmhouse on Christmas morning because Santa Claus had not forgotten the firecrackers and Roman candles.

There were also torpedoes which exploded with thunderous repercussions when dashed on the floor underneath girls' feet, and Roman candles gave great gusto to the Christmas celebration. They lifted the holiday spirit high into the air in sputtering balls of varicolored fire followed by sulphurous tails which outdid Halley's comet in the eyes of backwoods cotton farmers. Sometimes they were used in sham battles which generally wound up unhappily. But all in all, there was something in the violent cracking of fireworks that gave zest to Christmas week, and which marked the completion of one crop year and the beginning of another.

Unlike their Yankee brethren, southerners saved their fireworks for Christmas instead of the Fourth of July. There seems to be little fundamental reason for this traditional difference between the sections. Some have explained that because the siege of Vicksburg was ended on the Fourth of July, southerners refused to celebrate the day in any other way than that of going to fish fries and political picnics. This is hardly true. Perhaps the weather conditions were a more vital factor, but whatever the reason, the stores did not stock firecrackers for the July trade. It has always seemed that for a southerner to shoot firecrackers and Roman candles in the summertime was just about as incongruous as killing hogs in August.

The louder the noise the country-store customers could make, the happier they were. When the last firecracker fizzled out, the more adventuresome resorted to the use of black powder and anvils for noisemaking. Powder was packed tightly into the round and square holes of one anvil, and a second one was placed securely on top of the charge so that when the powder was ignited both anvils rang out in loud metallic tones which could be heard for miles around. Traditionally, anvil shooting was a part of every Christmas affair. Country stores, school and church grounds boomed with thunderous impacts of these black-powder charges, and evidence of this primitive custom has lingered in many farmyards. Few of the half-drunken celebrants who fired their steely blasts realized that they would dehorn their anvils in the explosion, and many a "muley-headed" block of steel was carried home to tell its mute tale for years to come of a hilarious country Christmas.

All of the stores kept black powder during the years 1865 to 1900. One entry after another is for the inseparable combination of powder, shot, caps, and sheets of wadding, and it is a remarkable fact that with all of the storekeeper's harum-scarum methods of keeping stock there is no record of powder kegs exploding. Yet many powder barrels and kegs were left as carelessly exposed inside store buildings as were barrels of sugar and coffee.

The Winchester Arms Company along with all the other manufacturers of guns and ammunition were quick to shift manufacturing practices after 1865 to that of supplying ready-prepared ammunition which could be used in the new-type breech-loading guns. But the muzzle-loader remained popular in the South for forty years after Appomattox. The typical reluctant rural southern attitude toward a change in plow tools and implements prevailed toward guns. A muzzle-loader would shoot, and a man could hit birds, rabbits, and squirrels with it; it took time to load, but time was cheap. Because of this unprogressive attitude the powder, shot, and cap trade remained constant in the stores. Not only did merchants sell supplies for ammunition, but they made some profit from the sale of detachable tubes which were screwed into the base of powder chambers and on which percussion caps were exploded. Literally thousands of entries were made in account books for these outmoded hunting supplies. The muzzle-loading gun was an institution, and if not an entirely safe and certain one, at least most people had learned its weak points. They were slow to accept new and improved arms which involved such a fundamental change as that of loading prepared ammunition into the breech.

When at last the primitive weapon of the ante bellum South was outmoded, orders for shot and powder were changed to demands for boxes of shells, and the South quickly became a land of the single-barrel breech-loading shotgun. Remington, Stevens, Winchester, Iver-Johnson, L. C. Smith, Sears, Roebuck, and Montgomery and Ward distributed thousands of these cheap weapons throughout the South. Rabbit hunters much preferred the light choke-bore, single-barrel twelve- and sixteen-gauge guns. When they were loaded with their characteristic yellow hulls charged with three drams of black powder and one and one-eighth ounces of number-six shot, they became bush cutters and rabbit killers of a high order.

By December crops were gathered, and it was safe to set the woods and fields afire. For a whole week during the Christmas season hillbilly and cane-cutter rabbits lived in misery. Christmas Day was the big day of this season of hunting. Sedge fields and heavily wooded bottomlands rang out with the constant firing of hard-kicking breech-loaders. Scarcely a southern community got through the season without some type of casualty. Occasionally accidents were slight; sometimes they were the result of an irresponsible prankster's forgetting that shot and powder were wholly devoid of a sense of humor. There were, however, unhappy tragedies which caused many southern families to bemoan Christmas Day for many years. Persons were killed or maimed with unhappy regularity in the big hunting sprees. Livestock was killed and fences and buildings destroyed. Yet these big hunting parties were as characteristic of the holiday season as were coconut cakes, apples, oranges, and raisins.

Of a more doubtful virtue was the considerable country-store trade in pistols. These instruments of rowdy community life were seldom if ever displayed in the stores in open cases, but they could be had either by immediate private purchase or on special order. Cartridges, however, were always openly available. Many southerners, both white and colored, desired to make big noises and sporting impressions. They bought pistols which they shot at random into the open air, and sometimes they emptied them without discrimination into both enemies and friends with the same deadly results. There was a spirit of rowdiness and irresponsibility which was handed down from the frontier ante bellum South to the younger southerners of the postwar period. Young bloods had a love for lethal weapons. Knife cases in country stores had their share of constant admirers flocking around and gazing at the long-bladed wares, and almost always knives were adjudged on the basis of their length of blade and potential powers of destruction. This respect and admiration for knives was carried over to a fondness for guns. Perhaps not all of this attitude was of southern origin. At the time when postwar stores were being organized and the general business scale was upward, colorful stories of life on the Great Plains were finding their way back across the Mississippi River to the South, and doubtless these stories of quick-shooting had much to do with keeping alive the love for pistols. It was a day when many make-believe southern Billy-the-Kids with sharp-pointed handle-bar mustaches posed for formal photographs with a brace of pistols across their vest fronts. Certainly, in general appearance, they were fierce men. Along with the unhappy influence of the Great Plains, the excitement of courting, Christmas, crap shooting, and liquor, all seemed to encourage "gun toting." Notes in private papers of merchants and items listed in wholesalers' lists are indicative of this popular gun trade.

Generally pistols sold through the country stores or listed in the "silent drummers" were exceedingly poor weapons. There was the popular Harrington and Richardson "double-acting, full nickel plated, rubber stocked" model which sold in the nineties at wholesale for $2.98. This gun was popularly known to the trade as a "nigger killer," and it was said that it fired a standard short thirty-two-caliber bullet sidewise. Competing with the "nigger killer" was the well-known Iver-Johnson "owl head" which was a double-acting piece of unreliable rubber-stocked artillery. Perhaps this gun was found on more people in the South when they were arrested for one sort of public disturbance or another than all other types of hip-pocket guns put together. There was a third popular brand of "short artillery" which was sold extensively throughout the cotton states. This was the cheap, short-barreled pistol called the American Bulldog, which was bought in dozen lots for the individual unit wholesale price of $1.25.

Seldom was there a public Christmas entertainment in the rural South at which there were no altercations and where cheap country-store pistols did not play an insidious part. Under the laws of all of the states it was illegal to carry concealed weapons, but these laws were universally ignored. In fact, in the whole irregular pistol trade there was an excellent commentary of general regional attitude toward laws and community conduct.

Southern backwoodsmen galloped home from their best girls' houses at Christmas firing pistols with wild abandon. So common was this practice in some southern communities that the erratic firing of a pistol by a single man was a sure sign of two things: He had either broken up with his girl, or he was going to get married right away.

Firecrackers, guns, and ammunition were only a small part of the country stores' Christmas trade. During the period of reconstruction, buying holiday goods because of inflated prices was actually a matter of expending a considerable amount of money without getting a satisfactory return in goods. For the first time rural stores were introducing items which were to characterize the yuletide season in the rural South for the next three-quarters of a century. E. F. Nunn and Company of Shuqulak, Mississippi, sold oranges at a dollar a dozen, apples at sixty cents, dolls at twenty cents apiece, and whisky at two dollars a gallon. E. F. Nunn, the bachelor proprietor, charged to his account the purchase of skyrockets, two candy trunks, four kisses, five candy rolls, one bunch of torpedoes, three packages of firecrackers, three dozen eggs, three pounds of candy, two Jew's harps, and two rattlers. In this benevolent merchant's Santa Claus account was nearly the whole story of the more temperate southern Christmas. Self-explanatory were the eggs and whisky. Even the most temperate southerner could be prevailed upon to break over and sip a little eggnog at Christmas time. At Raymond, Mississippi, a solvent countryman in 1869 bought of the newly established house of Drane and Dupree a bottle of perfume, a photographic album, a pound of candy, two pounds of nuts, half a dozen oranges, a dozen nutmegs, a bottle of lemon extract, a toy wagon, four dozen apples, a gallon of whisky, six bananas, a toy drum, one Roman candle, and a coconut. Here were all the ingredients except two for a joyous southern Christmas. Missing were fire-crackers, shot, and powder.

Twenty years later another rural Mississippian at Black-hawk was buying a dozen apples, four dozen eggs, two pounds of mackerel, a box of salmon, seven pounds of cheese, fifteen pounds of onions, a toy work box, four pounds of nuts, six dozen oysters, a box of raisins, and a dime's worth of nutmegs. About the same time merchants in Alabama were stocking oranges, raisins, nuts, oyster crackers, mincemeat, premium chocolates, citron, currants, sardines, toys, glassware, picture albums, coconuts, and bananas.

Fruits and nuts were items of real luxury for the southerner, and they were purchased only in the spending orgies of Christ-mas time. Oranges and apples in the extreme southern states were rarities, yet they were both produced on the periphery of the region. Oranges at some time or other became an insep-arable part of the general history of Christmas, and especially was this true in the South. By the seventies the account books showed that oranges were bought generally, but it is doubtful that many people knew anything about the history of their production. They, perhaps, believed that oranges could be bought only at Christmastime because merchants never dis-played them at any other season.

Families bought a dozen oranges and felt that they were well supplied. Children waked up on Christmas morning to find a golden ball in each stocking, and to discover that Santa Claus, in a generous mood, had left an additional half-dozen by the fireside. Although for the most part anything which went into a stocking was, by a type of domestic common law, the individual property of the child receiving it, oranges were an exception. These were common property and were eaten by the family, in many instances, one at a time. Mothers usually stripped off the peeling and passed the fruit around in segments. Every part of the orange was saved. Peelings were carefully preserved to be used throughout the year as flavoring for cakes, custards, and puddings.

Apples, in the extreme southern states, were as rare in December as were oranges. Crossroads merchants bought them from distributors in Maryland, Virginia, Pennsylvania, and sometimes North Carolina. They were bought by the barrel and were retailed by the dozen, and seldom did the wholesale and retail prices bear any relationship. A barrel of apples cost from three to six dollars, and they retailed by the dozen at from twenty to sixty cents. In many merchants' papers the letters of Henry Wright of Aberdeen, Maryland, appear in the November and December files. He advertised himself as "giving special attention to the southern trade." Certainly he was an important dealer, and his garrulous patronizing letters are long stories within themselves of this aspect of Christmas in the country stores. He well understood that buying apples was for many customers a bit of sentimental extravagance. As with oranges, few members of some families had ever been so profligate as to eat a whole apple at a time. Occasionally pitiful entries in individual accounts show that a dozen apples was the lone recognition which many impoverished customers of country stores could give to Christmas.

Nuts, raisins, and striped peppermint stick candy were common items listed in a great majority of the December accounts. Raisins had a special appeal, and many a farm child pulled brown bunches of these delicacies out of his stocking with more excitement than he showed for new toys. Love for stick candy and nuts came through the war unchanged. Stores bought candy by the barrel and sold it pound by pound at a very good profit. By the end of the century when the days of McKinley prosperity had changed somewhat the financial situation of the country, confectioners began placing a varied assortment of fancy piece candy on the country-store market which sold at a higher price and for a fancier profit.

There were many other Christmas purchases mixed in with the standard entries. Coconuts formed a vital part of Christmas cooking. A ten-cent coconut placed a distinct emphasis upon Christmas feasting. In fact, next to fresh oysters, it gave real distinction to the Christmas dinner. Mrs. M. H. Jennings ordered six coconuts, two boxes of gelatin, and a bottle of lemon extract from an Alabama merchant. She was preparing a rich Christmas dinner for a houseful of company. Six coconuts were sufficient to make enough cakes to last all of Christmas week and well into the new year. Mrs. Jennings' generous order was an example of much of the southern attitude toward food. If one coconut cake was good, then six would be that much better.

Opening coconuts was a real adventure for rural southerners. First there was the sport of punching in the soft eyes in order to drain off the richly flavored milk which was a much better drink than spring water. Then there was the business of cracking the hull and extracting the crust of meat. Often great care was taken not to smash the hull into bits when sawing open the nuts. The lower half of the shell made an excellent bowl for a dipper, and many families of limited resources went through the year drinking water from a dipper made by mounting half of a coconut shell on the end of a strong wooden handle.

Long hours were spent rubbing hunks of the meat of coconut over coarse homemade graters. The results, however, were nearly always satisfying. It was with a spirit of genuine triumph that southern women placed before their families thick rich coconut cakes. This was almost sufficient achievement to make a full Christmas celebration within itself. There were rivals of the huge cakes which were heavily frosted with the meat of the coconut. Frequent orders for citron, currants, and other types of dried fruits and spices indicated the extent to which fruitcakes were considered a part of every holiday meal.

Along with foods that were bought at the stores or prepared at home was the game brought in during Christmas week. Birds, squirrels, and rabbits suffered tremendous casualties when every man and boy in the neighborhood turned hunter for ten days. Rabbit meat became commonplace, and great platters of bird and squirrel went begging after the first few days. Before World War I southerners failed to appreciate with any degree of intelligence their sinful extravagance. Rabbits and birds were thrown away because no one cared to eat them. Shooting a gun was an exciting sport, but shooting it aimlessly at an inanimate target was a senseless waste of money. With the smoke of their valuable woodlands in their eyes, southerners exterminated game and rich natural resources at the same stroke. Yet the pleasantness of all memories for many generations of rural southerners were the exciting Christmas hunts and the taste of fresh-killed wild meat.

Southerners generally liked oysters, both canned and fresh, and many of the store books contain records of numerous purchases of this highly perishable food. It is a matter of amazement that a store so thoroughly isolated as was Ike Jones' at Blackhawk, Mississippi, could get oysters through the New Orleans market and keep them fresh for several days. Every box of freight which reached this place had to be hauled many miles over muddy roads on a wagon, yet Christmas always found a stock of oysters on hand. Where transportation facilities were poor and the sale of perishable merchandise was an impossibility, merchants relied upon salt herring and mackerel for a change of diet at Christmas. It was a genuine treat for most families to get a kit of mackerel to sandwich in between salt meat, rabbit, and quail. Cheese enjoyed a position of favoritism on the list of standard yuletide purchases. Where cash resources were limited, one- and two-pound orders were common, but customers who wound up the crop year by breaking even or with a little clear money were satisfied with nothing short of a hoop of cheese. So popular was cheese that even Santa Claus sometimes left wedges of it by hearth sides or crammed into wide-mouthed stockings. He even carried his whim of practicality to a greater extreme and left salt mackerel and coconuts along with meager offerings of firecrackers and fruit. This was the simplest way for a man without funds to ease himself out of an unhappy predicament with his family and keep up the spirit of Christmas.

The Christmas trade was not alone a matter of doing a profitable business in fancy groceries, toys, and gifts, but it was also a matter of buying a large variety of farm produce. Womenfolk saved eggs for weeks to provide funds for holiday shopping. Sometimes frugal customers started in September packing down thirty or forty dozen eggs in cottonseed awaiting the seasonal rise in price. Among the Christmas orders are notes which tell in their simple eloquent way a sorrowful story of poverty. A South Carolina mother scribbled on a rough fragment of scratch paper, "Willie, I send 5 dozen eggs give just what you can and Sammie will trade it out in something for the children times are so hard that is all I want to give them for Christmas."

A strange assortment of produce found its way to the feed rooms during November and December of each year. There were sweet potatoes, butter molded in all designs and in numerous stages of preservation, tallow, home-cured meat, shelled corn, cottonseed, dried herbs, mink, 'possum, skunk, and coon skins, kindling, black walnuts, cowhides, and peanuts. Everything that would bring a little extra cash and could be spared was hauled away to be sold for Christmas money. Crossties and cordwood for gin furnaces supplied a meager income, and many a wagon loaded with crossties was dragged over almost impassable roads by a pair of ill-fed mules to stores along the railroads. The last of cotton and tobacco crops was sold, and ramshackle farm wagons jolted home with their precious boxes, bags, and cans of merchandise. Children listened for the clucking of these wagons over the rough roads, and they rushed out to climb aboard as soon as they came in sight. It was with adroitness indeed that many of the drivers were able to keep their Santa Claus supplies safely out of sight when their vehicles were boarded by a band of expectant children.

Closely associated with the celebration of Christmas in southern farmhouses were the community Christmas trees and parties. These were given primarily for courting couples, but they afforded equally as much pleasure for children and older people. School yards and church grounds were crowded with buggies, wagons, and saddle horses while, inside, half-drunken community wits, dressed in flimsy red suits and shabby cotton whiskers, carried on a stream of humorous banter as they handed down presents from bespangled holly and cedar trees.

Gifts off a country Christmas tree were curiosities indeed. A favorite present for girls was plush-bound photograph albums and memory books. Sentimental females loved these cheap artistic atrocities, and they filled them with family photographs, bits of hair, stray pieces of cloth, pressed leaves, poetic clippings from newspapers and magazines, and personal notes. For the merchants these items yielded a good profit, and many times generous orders for them appeared in the invoices.

Merchants also stocked special assortments of fancy china and glass bric-a-brac to lend color and grace to the useless whatnots and shelves which lined parlor walls. Plates with fancy fruit and floral designs, bowls with berries, fruits, and vegetables burned into them were good sellers. So were the long platters adorned with sad-eyed bass which gave a lasting impression that every hot piece of meat lying on their backs was burning their very souls out. There were platters with luscious halves of watermelons, clusters of rich purple grapes, or bunches of small game. Those with rabbits suspended from a wall made an appetizing scene indeed; it was truly stimulating to a ravenous southerner to be able to scoop up spoonfuls of gravy from the furry backs of lithographed rabbits firmly glazed in the bottom of meat dishes.

From the end of the war, lamps had a continuous patronage. There were the tiny little brass lamps with stubborn round wicks which had a constant habit of sticking in the ratchets and refusing to go either up or down. Then there were those of a later period which stood on heavy glass and metal pedestals. These used the improved flat wicks and boasted safety air tubes permitting kerosene to flow freely upward without danger of exploding the glass bowls. But these were commonplace household utensils and were never regarded as things of art. It was not until the era of heavy chandeliers with their gaudy trappings and curlicues which hung in pretentious homes in the cities that colored lamps became a part of the rural merchants' stock. This was an era when church lamps were heavy and ornate monstrosities hanging from sturdy beams at the ends of bronzed log chains. Big-bellied tinted lamps became necessary fixtures all over the South. They were at once indicative of a certain amount of dignity and social well-being. There was always considerable room for doubting that their lighting functions were adequate, but just standing by in their very stuffiness upon center tables they performed a mute service of art. This service actually was that of epitomizing the lowest ebb of a degenerating Victorian taste in the nineties for a South which was trying hard to keep abreast the vulgar artistic fads of the rest of the country.

Even the "silent drummer" descriptions of parlor lamps were staid bits of formalized commercial prose. One model that bulged voluptuously in exactly the same places and proportions as well-fed matrons of the day was described by the wholesaler as "a Parisian shaped body parlor lamp with a ten inch globe, tinted and shaded in fine enamel finish, beautiful hand-painted flowers, best center draft burner, solid brass oil fount, gold plated foot, twenty inches high to top of globe." These Parisian beauties sold, packed three in a barrel, for $8.29. There were others which had less gold on their feet, and less bulge in their bellies and bosoms which could be retailed for not more than two dollars.

Country merchants stocked fancy cups bearing the highly imaginative legends, "A Present," "Lucky Dogs," "Baby," "Father," "A Souvenir," and "Think of Me." There were quart-sized mustache cups with their built-in china retaining walls. These were adorned with lurid sprays of flowers or lodge emblems and saucy legends designed for the dominating male of the age. The china dashers fought back the unruly ends of handle-bar mustaches from the coffee and helped partly to dispense with the indelicate business of sucking one's whiskers, or having them drip coffee on false shirt fronts.

Companion pieces to the rotund mustache cups were the big-bellied shaving mugs with their heavy, round, looping handles, and cavernous mouths opening through their side with as much grace as gaping sensuous lips. They, more than mustache cups, symbolized the sternness of manhood in the nineties. Potters were little influenced by the gaudy art of their day in the manufacture of these mugs. Their primary concern was that of making a receptacle which would hold a cake of soap with reasonable firmness while an irate male dragged his whiskers off with a dull straight razor.

Of a distinctly feminine nature were the delicately tinted, flower-decked toilet sets which were composed of from three to six pieces. These contained toilet bottles with globe stoppers, comb and brush trays, manicure trays, hairpin boxes, and powder-puff boxes. They were customary gifts for sweethearts and were sold for one to six dollars a set. Scarcely a rural parlor dresser went without these milk-glass or colored-glass adornments, and nearly always they were displayed as signs of a girl's popularity rather than as necessary fixtures of her dressing table.

A long list of cut and molded glassware was sold to the Christmas trade. Most common of all the vases were the glass flower holders and vases called Bohemian and alabaster. They were delicately colored, but were trimmed in gaudy fins and flounces, which, like pompon lamps, gave them the appearance of a female who had on entirely too many petticoats. There were butter dishes with quaint glass covers, glass hats, slippers, compotes, pickle dishes, and large, round-cut glass berry bowls. These pieces were sold by the barrelful, and scarcely a household, including the humblest cabin, was without some of them. Most practical of all was the covered butter dish which helped in a day of patent fly-minders and peach-tree limb-shakers to insure some degree of momentary sanitation for the huge cakes of hand-molded butter.

Standard among the utilitarian sets were the water pitchers and glasses. By accident these were made in attractive designs. Even today along modern southern highways, myriad antique shops are reselling hundreds of pieces of this once cheap country-store Christmas glassware. Along with Bohemian and alabaster toilet sets and vases and the big mugs and mustache cups, the bulging, ugly old floral lamps have found their way to the antique stands. Cheap water pitchers which once sold for as little as a dollar a dozen now bring twice that much apiece. Colored-glass hats, or "toothpick" stands, sold for twenty-eight cents a dozen, and were retailed at ten cents apiece. Now some of them sell for the original price of a gross.

Santa Claus not only brought cheer to the juvenile country South, but he was likewise an agent of cultural taste. In a lefthanded way he was in at the kill of Victorianism on the store shelves, although it was not so gruesome a murder after all. For three generations rural southerners have found their tenderest memories to be of the crossroads stores and their completely disorganized stocks of Christmas goods. Sentimentality for Christmas historically spilled over into affection for the stores themselves. For the countryman the store at Christmas time was literally a meeting place of stark everyday reality with a fantastic world of temporary but pleasant escape.

8

UNDER THE SIGN OF THE STUD HORSE

THE YEAR 1870 was a trying time in South Carolina, if one is to judge from the number of lien notes and orders for piles cures recorded by William Carrigan's general store at Cheraw. One customer after another gave a lien on a crop not yet planted, saw a charge of $1.30 made against him for registration fees, then drowned his feelings of frustration with liquor.

Among this disillusioned army of moneyless customers was Moses Strickland, whose purchases are typical. For the first six months of that year he bought horse powders, trace chains, shuck collars, fifty-six plugs of tobacco, six gallons of whisky and brandy, five pairs of shoes, a blind bridle, two tin pans, lead pencils, many yards of homespun, five bottles of Quick Cure piles remedy, and a bottle of Hoyt's cologne. With the last Moses was paying homage to spring and hot weather in a favorite southern manner.

A thirty-five-cent bottle of "imported" perfumery seems indeed a cheap gesture in a land so often proclaimed the home of the Cape jessamine, the magnolia, and the crepe myrtle. Yet it was a part of the artificiality of the age, a subtle apology for the difficulty of frequent bathing.

Thousands of tiny round bottles of Hoyt's famous German perfume were distributed by merchants. Spring and summer accounts testify that it was as much a harbinger of warm weather as were asafetida, sulphur, onion sets, and plow lines.

Colognes, like other types of merchandise, were sold under many trade names, all selected with an eye for the little business. There were Hoyt's, Little Tot, American Girl, Boudoir, Bridal Bouquet, Duchess Ladies, Sensible, Home Sweet Home, Bow Wow, and Happy Family, and these brands retailed at prices from 25 cents to $83.75 a dozen. Most popular was the common counter brand, "Hoyt's 5-center." All had a faint aroma of the rose and the honeysuckle, but usually the carrying agent was stronger than the fragrance.

Despite its lowly associations, there was ever a touch of romance hovering about the cologne trade. In the files of orders for humble sardines and crackers, tobacco and postage stamps, it stands out like the proud daughter of a noble family to tell its exciting story of social distinction. Just as moonlight and roses, camp meetings, and safe buggy horses were attributes of courting, so was Hoyt's cologne. One would like to think that its sly "come hither" effect spurred many a tongue-tied heavy-handed rural beau on to more vigorous conquests. With a thirty-five-cent vial of "imported" perfume a timid Lothario could impress a neighboring daughter more effectively than he could on a ten-mile buggy ride in the moonlight.

In lean years after the war, there was a smell universally characteristic of public gatherings. Even where "poor and downtrodden" farmers and their wives attended the speeches of the perennial political saviors, there reeked the spirit of far-away cologne. It gave the assemblies a sort of "lavender and lace" effect. reminiscent of a bygone age and suggesting the dream of one to be.

As years went by the demand for cheap perfume tended to boost quantity with a disregard for quality. In 1876 it cost polite southern women thirty-five cents to smell like a Black Forest spring, but in 1912 belles of the cotton fields enjoyed this social advantage for a nickel.

Everywhere in the South dusky maidens who labored with sack and hoe splurged their hard-earned wages for this luxury. In time, Hoyt's tiny bottles ceased to indicate a sort of gentility and became the great odor of the common people. Its fulsome bouquet, however, was always to have a nostalgic appeal similar to that of oranges and apples at Christmas time.

Although cologne admittedly was a subterfuge, there were certain workaday social demands which could be satisfied only with water and scrubbing. Fancy-goods catalogues and circulars listed brands of soap by the yard. There was a good profit in soap, and it was one of the first commodities to exploit high-pressure modern methods of advertising. Imaginative displays, cardboard cases, and glass containers, "hand-colored" cards, special assortments, and gaudy premiums were offered as inducements to merchants to favor one brand over another. Sets of pewter spoons, knives, and forks by the gross were given with each purchase, and in some instances storekeepers who bought as much as fifty dollars' worth almost had to build a warehouse to take care of the free goods.

For a time Blackwell's Durham Tobacco Company gave a twenty-five-pound box of soap with each box of Bull Durham smoking tobacco. "Send by the bearer," wrote an army of anxious purchasers, "a bar of soap and a plug of tobacco."

At first the general use of toilet soap was looked upon as a thing for women and children who had extremely tender skins, or for polite visitors such as preachers and young men who came courting eligible daughters. Tougher citizens used stronger stuff than the perfumed goods from Montgomery, Savannah, Philadelphia, Buffalo, Cincinnati, and Chicago. There was something incongruous about the smell of toilet soap on a plow hand.

During the years when the South was regaining its balance, most soap was manufactured at home from the ash hopper and the soap kettle. It was strong, and the soft man got his hands and face burned, but for the hard-calloused sons of the plow it was the only thing which would penetrate stubborn grime. The use of this homemade product explains the frequent appearance in order notes and on ledgers of the strange entry, "1 ball of potash," and, later, boxes of concentrated lye.

Occasionally a hard-bitten male smeared his face with the mahogany-colored soap of the kettle and shaved off his whiskers. This, however, was an experience which not even the hardiest could endure without some sober reflection on the potential torments of hell.

In the passing years when southern rural society began to be aware of the influence of the great era of *laissez faire* enterprise, soap became a more commonplace factor in everyday living. From the Montgomery Soap Works and the factories above the Ohio River came cases of varicolored cakes of highly perfumed and gentle glycerin products. There were romantic brands such as Venus, Rosadora, Fairy, Wild Rose, Lenox, King Cotton, El Capitan, Pale Olive, Petroleum Joe, Madame Ayer, Dandelion, Dandy, Oakley's Glycerin, Pear's, and P. and G. Blue, Jap Bang, and White Clover.

Prior to World War I, Pear's was rapidly monopolizing the market. Its characteristic advertising consisted of an "Aunt Polly" type of woman gouging at the ears of a reluctant "Tom Sawyer." A cessation of advertising activities during the national emergency changed the public taste, and this popular soap was never able to reclaim its market.

When peace came, ingenious advertising directed the popular demand toward Woodbury, Lifebuoy, Palmolive, Sweetheart, and Ivory, or merchants pushed cheap nameless special assortments. Lever Brothers' advertising now sent plow hands and cotton pickers to their daily tasks smelling of carbolic acid and proclaimed that they had no body odors. Advertising in the rural South had achieved a major victory. At last it was to dignify the smell of soap on a plow hand.

In time soap became a big source of profit for the stores. Even the most illiterate sharecroppers were conscious of its distinct social advantages, and their notes became mixed orders for soap and tobacco. Such was that of a South Carolinian whose blithe disregard for the civilized art of Noah Webster was complete. He asked, "Please give to barrow for me Dick Kennedy one plug of to Baco and a Bar of Soapie i am Busy my Sef trying to get a Bale cooton to you or i would acome."

Throughout the post–Civil War years agitators and reformers vigorously sought to secure the freedom of women. But the emancipationists were men and city women who had never been enslaved to the acrid fumes of potash and lye of steaming soap kettles, or they would not have had time for campaigning. To farm women the greatest reform was the appearance in the eighties of cheap factory-made laundry soap. Charles Fels, a country merchant from Yanceyville, North Carolina, saw an opportunity to compete with the household soapmakers, and by way of Baltimore and Philadelphia he placed his famous Fels-Naptha on the market. In constant competition there were other thrifty names such as Big Deal, Easy Clean, Yellow Tag, Procter and Gamble, and a host of others.

School children read the story of the early settlement of America and were impressed with the amazement of the English at Sir Walter Raleigh's dramatic display of tobacco. For them it was impossible to imagine a world in which tobacco was unknown. The tobacco habit was a pastime of universal enjoyment as many a merchant could prove. Desperate tobacco chewers flooded the merchants with notes like that of George W. Bell. With a hint of anxiety, he wrote, "Please send me one caddie of Snaps [Scnapp's] tobacco 10# or 15# or something Similar Monarch will do be sure and send me something about same grade. *I am out.*" Even General John Bratton spent hours scribbling out notes such as the following: "See that Gander Gaines be sent 1 lb. of tobacco. Pat; 1 lb. tobacco." The General himself sent regular orders for bags of pipe tobacco.

New South chewers consumed more than their proportionate share of compressed light and dark leaves. In Piedmont, North Carolina, and southern Virginia the plug houses sprang up like mushrooms. It would seem that every farmer with a stock of raw tobacco, a mortgage, a case of licorice, a pillowcase full of dried apples, and a homemade plug press introduced some romantically named product to the nation's chewers. Merchants supplied licorice, dried fruit, tobacco sacks, and sack strings by the case to these small manufacturers and then realized a second profit from the processed goods.

By 1870 naming plug tobacco became almost as exciting a pastime as naming steamboats, fighting cocks, and race horses. Keeping up with trends, the manufacturers were ever on the alert for eye-catching names. With both deep sentiment and business acumen William Lindsey of Riedsville, North Carolina, named a plug Johnny Reb. His competitors, G. Penn, Sons and Company sold the Rebel Girl. R. L. Candler of Winston produced the Rebel Boy and Confederate.

Gentle aspects of the Old South were represented by Southern Rose, Bonny Jean, Little Rosebud, Little Ethell, Little Ruth, Little Alice, Annie V., Kitty May, Lucy Ashton, Edna Lindsey, Maggie Mitchell, and Sunny Hours. Likewise, there was the robust South with its lusty names such as Georgia Buck, Bull Tongue, Stud Horse, Captain Cash, Panther, Albion, Iron Clad, Bull Head, Blood Hound, and Good and Tough.

In 1892, when the Populists went wild in their Cincinnati convention and the Bland-Allison and Sherman Silver Purchase Acts were in the news, free silver was a popular topic of conversation. William Lindsey introduced a new strong plug named Free Silver and another called Legal Tender, designed specifically to catch the lush nervous Populist market.

That same year Budd Doble drove the famous Bluegrass Kentucky mare, Nancy Hanks, to a new world's trotting record. She broke the long-time record of Maud S and went on to establish the sensational time of 2:04 for the mile. Quickly the Penns made a Nancy Hanks plug to honor, not Kentucky's mother of Lincoln, but her proud little trotting mare.

There were appetizing brands such as Peach Pie, Apple, Pound Cake, Peaches and Cream, Cornbread, Sponge Cake, and Pure Honey, whose names were pleasant subterfuges for plain chews with only imaginary differences in taste.

One by one the fancy names fell by the way as more highly centralized systems of manufacturing and distribution were created. At an early date R. J. Reynolds entered the country-store field with his great rural favorite, Brown Mule, packed in caddies. Full plugs were creased in nickel squares and each square bore the famous red tin mule. There were Apple, Day's Work, Blood Hound, Penn's, RJR, Star Navy, Seal of North Carolina, and Picnic Twist. With the disappearance of the period when manufacturers gave plugs their daughter's names, only the romance of the brands was lost; certainly the South lost none of its fondness for the tightly compressed, sweetened, licorice-and-apple-flavored product.

Dipping was a handmaiden of chewing, and ledgers contain one entry after another for snuff. There were Railroad Mills, Garrett's, Ralph's, Lorillard's, Railroad, Tube Rose, Dental, Rooster, Lady Belle, and DeVoe's. Unlike chewing tobacco, snuff brands were highly sensitive to regional demands. Railroad Mills, Railroad, and some of the other brands were never sold in the lower Appalachian and Valley South and West, nor were Garrett's, Ralph's, DeVoe's, Rooster, Bruton's, and Tube Rose sold extensively along the Atlantic seaboard.

Use of snuff involved a peculiar southern folkway. It was indecent for a woman to chew tobacco and downright sinful for her, while under the age of sixty-five, to smoke a pipe. Filling her lower lips, or rolling frazzled ends of black-gum toothbrushes in ounce tin pocket boxes, females consumed huge quantities of tobacco in its vilest form. In the age of careful observations of social customs, it is doubtful that a woman could have kept her self-respect in the years 1865 to 1915 if she had smoked either a cigarette or a cigar. Even one tiny Virginia cheroot smoked in public would have laid permanently to rest her reputation as a "fine woman." But snuff was quite all right, and many a dozen eggs were exchanged for it.

Among the hosts of "dippers" there was a curious folk legend about judging the quality of snuff from the outside of the bottle. The signs were in the pontil marks on the bottom of the bottles, and those which had three slight protrusions were superior. This was especially true of Garrett's, which came in six-ounce brownglass bottles. Clerks were hounded to death by insistent customers who wanted "good" snuff, and only good snuff had "three tits on the bottom of the bottle."

Oldest of all forms of prepared tobacco was that used for pipe smoking. From the very beginning some type of pipe tobacco was offered for sale. In country stores quantities of it were shoved into cases or piled on shelves, and along with pipes of dozens of different shapes and materials, it was very much in demand. From the fields of North Carolina following the Civil War came light leaves which quickly gave rise to a profitable business of tobacco manufacturing.

Most interesting of the many stories back of the introduction of new types of pipe tobacco was that of John R. Green's famous bull. The manufacture of Best Flavored Spanish tobacco, and later Bull Durham, was the beginning of the extensive enterprise of manufacturing, advertising, and selling specific brands of tobacco. The Bull of Durham eventually made his way to every southern store shelf from North Caroline to Texas, and its users soon became as ardent in proclaiming its merits as they were in supporting their respective sides in community election rows.

Imaginative advertising men, following the custom of their times, gave razors, clocks, hammocks, soap, loud-striped couches, and dozens of other bargain-house premiums with the purchase of Bull Durham. As a result of wide-sweeping advertising campaigns, store walls, fence posts, barns, and trees were plastered with likenesses of the rugged tobacco bull. An army of sign painters visited the South, and people quickly became tobacco conscious. Farmers looked at Green's artistic portrayal of his famous bull and dreamed of the profits they could make if he were only in their pastures in the flesh.

The market was too good, however, to be enjoyed by one manufacturer with a single brand of pipe tobacco. Over at Winston-Salem, R. J. Reynolds began to compete for trade with huge, fluffy bargain packages of Our Advertiser or RJR. Later Richardson and Company placed great emphasis upon a fine-cut tobacco labeled Old North State, which was tightly packed in little bags for combination use in cigarettes and pipes.

There were scores of other brands of smoking tobacco which competed for the rich store trade. Some of them appeared one year and were gone the next, some caught on in one section and rotted on shelves elsewhere. Out of these many brands came one which ran a tight race with the Reynolds' products. This was Stud. Each package had the picture of a rearing white stallion on it, and a round tag with the same picture as the label fastened in the end of one of the draw strings. For years it was a neck-and-neck race between the stallion, the bull, and RJR for the country's business. Young bloods just getting their first taste of being "bad" strutted around with the stud-horse tag flying from a breast pocket. Along with the ownership of a cheap pistol, the use of Stud tobacco was indicative of robust manhood.

After 1867 cigarettes were manufactured in the United States. At Durham, North Carolina, in 1881, Washington Duke and Sons were producing the immoral "coffin tacks," and the South was off on a new trail of vice. Almost from the beginning cigarettes appeared on store invoices. At first there were conservative orders for five hundred and one thousand, and then they climbed up to ten and twenty thousand at a time. Among the first North Carolina cigarettes were Cablegrams, which came packed in tight little cylindrical packages from which it was extremely difficult to extract the "tacks."

Later Duke of Durham, Sweet Caporal, Cycle, Richmond Straight Cut, Center Rush, Ten Strike, and American Beauty brands appeared in flat boxes with sliding covers containing ten cigarettes each. Capitalizing on the currently popular fads, the companies used the same advertising devices as did the soap, thread, and soda companies. They published series of bright-colored pictures of birds, American scenes, "daring girls," and baseball players of the southern leagues. For a smoker to get all the birds, ball players, and an exciting collection of girls, it was necessary to buy a considerable number of cigarettes. Thus, with another of Satan's subtle devices, the tobacco companies were sending southern youth to sinners' graves with "coffin tacks," baseball, and bad girls.

For some reason, tobacco rolled in paper became a hand-picked tool of the devil. Cigarettes were especially evil things in the eyes of the ardent reformers of the late nineties and early nineteen hundreds. Preachers with snuff- and tobacco-stained lips condemned cigarette smokers to a scorching hell for eternal punishment without ever appreciating their own inconsistency.

Tack by tack eloquent defamers of the Bull of Durham and the Stud Horse hammered down coffin lids over the bloated faces of ruined cigarette users. It soon got to the place where a man with a cigarette in his mouth was almost as much a symbol of death as were a skull and crossbones. But paradoxically the louder the dirge of reformers, the more cigarettes they helped to sell. It became a matter of curiosity on the part of customers to see what a "coffin tack" really tasted like. Before many years had passed, customers were joking about their sin, and this was excellent free advertising. Soon the bars were down, and the tobacco sections of the stores had to be enlarged and invoice books bulged with orders.

With the growing cigarette craze, the Stud, the Bull of Durham, paunchy bags of RJR, Our Advertiser, Old North State, and numerous other brands were sold with packages of cigarette papers attached. The fancy packages of "ready rolled" with their stiff board sliding covers and their colorful pictures in time disappeared from the market, and a larger and more practical package was in its place. By the end of World War I, cigarette and smoking-tobacco ads monopolized the store walls. Dignified, bald, and bearded Prince Albert stared icily at the passing throng and symbolized the aristocracy of the pipe and hand-rolled cigarette tobacco. The newer brands of ready-made cigarettes which came out of the war carried on a battle of slogans and catch phrases of long-distance hikes, coughing, and general satisfaction.

Cigarettes ceased to be special sinful wretches hidden away in the glass cases along with contraceptives, dice, and playing cards. At last the great social barrier which kept women from smoking was lowered, but in its lowering there was a comical step-by-step advance toward the use of woman in advertising the various brands. Even John R. Green's heavy-necked bull was portrayed against a bucolic signboard background with a dreamy-eyed matronly jersey warbling, "My hero!"

While reformers and manufacturers were ironing out the kinks of the cigarette business, chewing gum laid a firm claim upon a place of favoritism on the store counters. A dozen compounders of cornstarch, sugar, flavoring, and chicle offered to keep lean jaws working.

Chewing tobacco was so common that it hardly seemed natural for an individual not to be gnawing on something. For women and children and a few abstemious males, chewing gum was a compromise and, as a gaudy merchandising product, it came on the market during an age which made a loud display of itself.

The Baltimore Chewing Gum Company, quoting A. T. Stewart, the wealthy New York merchant, approached dealers with, "I seek the lowest market on the most trivial article and always place my order with a house that gives the lowest figure and never divulge prices to get another to meet them. It is the small items that count in business." Gum was a small item and it counted for much in the country store. From Baltimore came Seltzer's Pepsin, Crown Pepsin, Lily Pepsin, and Daisy. These were sold at a penny a package for what now amounts to five sticks. At Louisville the American Chicle Company sold Kis-me gum, which was famous throughout the South. Right after the Civil War this house was selling Tolu Taffy, which was perhaps the first brand of chewing gum put on the country-store shelves.

Masters of the chewing-gum business, however, were William Wrigley, Jr., and Company. Immediately after 1865 these Chicago manufacturers were selling the country their famous brands. With each purchase of sixteen boxes of Juicy Fruit, Sweet Sixteen, Vassar, and Pepsin gum they gave six pot-bellied, hand-colored parlor lamps. Then there were more modest prizes given with smaller orders. Among these were brass hand lamps, electrical seal collarettes and muffs, spindle-legged brass tables with ornamental onyx tops, knives and forks, mackintoshes, skirts, shirtwaists, and couches.

This company offered a six-foot couch with thirty-three tempered steel springs, fully tufted and fringed, with the purchase of eleven dollars' worth of gum. Its gaudy back was one of the most reckless eye-catchers of its age. The long orange and blue stripes which ran from head to foot gave it the appearance of the bed of a temptress. Customers and storekeepers who took the Wrigley offer seriously no doubt had in mind the picture of Samson and Delilah in the gaily colored Bible books.

The Zeno Gum Company went its competitors one better and distributed vending machines which dispensed small pieces of inferior gum for a penny. These machines had ingenious clowns that turned around jerkily on pedestals as if they were personally delivering the Zeno Company's wares. There was a sardonic expression on the little clowns' faces which seemed to say as they snapped back into place, "It is the small items that count in business."

9

BIG HOGS GREW IN IOWA

A Georgia farmer wrote, "Our Fathers which art in Troy, Wiley & Murphy be thy names, thy kingdom of provisions come, thy will be done on my farm as it is at your store. Give us this day our daily bread. Forgive us our trespasses on your barn as we forgive those who tresspass upon ours, lead us not into temptation but deliver us from hungriness, for thine shall be the crop, the mules and the land forever and ever if we don't pay—Amen. P.S. If this is good for ten bushels of corn and three hundred pounds of bacon, fling it in the wagon."

George Bevlry, an Alabama farmer, and his neighbors were most numerous in the South's rural population. In March, 1893, he requested a merchant to "sen me six pounds of meat & one galon of lassies, [give] Jack Hern five pounds of meat fer Wilson Hern & [one gallon] lassies fer John Hern & sen me the Bil of it." It was March of the hard year of 1893, and these cotton-belt farmers were already out of home-grown meat, meal, and molasses.

Back of George Bevlry's illiterate note was a significant story in domestic economy. Perhaps this was the major chapter in the history of southern storekeeping, and here the merchants exerted an influence which was to affect the very sinew and bone of the region. The whole big question of regional diet stemmed from the meat boxes and bread barrels of the storehouses and their shed rooms. Merchants converted their neighbors to an economy of getting food supplies from elsewhere.

Thus the basic fare of the store became as monotonous as the prevailing system of agriculture and politics, and was a subject which provoked the wrath of editors, agrarian reformers, and apostles of the New South. When a country editor found himself without a subject for an editorial, he could always turn to the failure of most of his subscribers to supply their foodstuff.

Perhaps it would do the dignity of the good people of Alabama no great injustice to compare the human population with the number of hogs they owned in 1870, 1880, and 1890. In the first tabulation following the war the census takers accounted for 996,884 persons and 719,757 hogs. Ten years later, when figures were more accurate, the ratio between people and hogs was still out of balance; there were 1,262,505 people and 1,252,462 hogs. In 1890, when the New South was developing and farmers were again on their feet, emphasis in this pork-loving state was still on cotton and people. The human population climbed to 1,513,017, and hogs were behind at 1,421,884. In most of the Confederate states during these three decades the picture was not materially different from that in Alabama. Occasionally the increase in hogs ran slightly ahead of that of human beings, but in most it dropped behind.

It was a great contradiction in economics that southern farmers liked pork and disliked hogs. There was a sentiment that "a dad-blamed hog and a dad-gummed cow were the most aggravating things that ever made tracks on a piece of cotton land." Farmers generally regarded the hog in the same unfavorable light as a Fayetteville, Alabama, merchant who declared vigorously that it was a destructive thing to have about. In a brief paragraph he wrote the hog's obituary. "A two dollar hog," he declared, "can hoist the front gate off its hinges at night, when you are asleep; root up the herbs in the garden that cost us years of trouble to get; eat all the chickens and ducks in the fowl yard; root the yard into holes; root down the side walks; fill up the ditches, enter your store, while you are engaged in waiting on a customer, turn over a barrel of molasses and let it run all over the house, damaging other goods to the amount of hundreds of dollars in less time than you can say sooey! rip up everything in their reach; and do any other thing which is too bad to be endured."

This was an attitude which prevailed in much of the South. The hog was too difficult for cotton farmers to handle. They refused to fence in productive land for pasturage or to build good fences. Usually they penned two or three half-starved hogs in a hillside pen as bare of vegetation as a marble floor, gave them a pot of kitchen slop once a day, and then wondered why the devil the brutes were always shoving the fence down and rooting up the place.

Disgruntled croppers sat for hours about the stores conversing on the general cussedness of a hungry brood sow, yet the busiest place in the stores were the lard barrels and the meat boxes. Literally millions of pounds of meat were shipped south every month. Broad thick sides of Iowa, Illinois, Ohio, and Indiana salt pork were sliced into five- and ten-pound orders on Saturdays for hungry families of cotton farmers.

A local observer, in 1872, wrote that the towns of Selma, Rome, and Dalton were packed with freight. Hundreds of carloads of meat and grain products rolled in from the Northwest. Cincinnati, Louisville, Des Moines, Chicago, and Indianapolis sent shipments of foodstuffs to feed the cotton growers.

Every Saturday in the stores was a day of sending out rations for the forthcoming week. Clerks kept busy about the meat boxes supplying requests for what was euphemistically called "bacon." It was an every-week occurrence for malnourished customers, sated with salt meat, to plead with meat cutters to find them pieces with streaks of lean. They knew too well the lack of variety in fat slices of Iowa meat which had only a dividing line of tissue to break its angelical whiteness.

Actually the bacon trade was the point of departure for the southern supply business. It brought the high and the low among the reformers to the salt boxes in the back rooms of the stores to read the unpleasant fate of the agrarian South. That high priest of progress in Atlanta, Henry W. Grady, took time out from his vigorous sermonizing on industrial hopefulness to lecture his people on the evils of the meat box in the country stores. Like that other famous legendary Georgian, Uncle Remus, Grady couched his sermon in a simple folk allegorical style so that all might understand. Using a sunburned and tattered cotton farmer as interlocutor, he opened his drama with the monotonous question, "How do you sell bacon?"

"Fourteen cents," was the laconic answer.

"He looked long and anxiously into space, as if ruminating upon the hungry children at home and the wan work-worn wife—again he ventured, 'how's corn?'

" 'A dollar ten!'

"And again the look of anxious thought overspread his face. A farmer without meat, without corn, with his patch of cotton mortgaged to the guano man, five mangy fice dogs at home, five children almost nude, a wife wearing a three year old four cent calico, he was indeed a picture to behold. Throwing out an ancient looking sock he mumbled,

" 'Half a bushel!'

"The half bushel was filled. Payment was made in dirty, greasy nickels, and the man with his smokehouse in the West drove off.

"He wore a suit of clothes, the material of which was furnished by an Ohio ram, his half starved mules were imported from Kentucky, his flimsy wagon was from Indiana, his hat was from Massachusetts, his brogans were from Lynn, his harness was from Cincinnati, his corn from St. Louis, his meat—was from nowhere, because he did not have the money to buy it.

"What was there of Georgia? Nothing! For he had fed so long on western corn that his very flesh and bones were the growth of western sustenance. All that there ever had been of Georgia in him was starved out, and all there was of him was Missourian!

"Poor Georgia farmer! and how little it would take to convert this pitiable object into a high spirited, self sustained citizen. Appeal to Georgia soil for your opportunities, avoid cotton, and you will master the situation."

Eloquently the editor of the Atlanta *Constitution* personified his sermon. Four-fifths of the southern farmers could understand his point that their bodies were more Missouri, Ohio, Iowa, or Illinois than they were Alabama, Mississippi, Georgia, or South Carolina. They could have told the prophetic editor more of the actual details of his story than he knew. For instance, E. P. Mobley, Sr., of South Carolina, knew more intimately the details of the southern cotton system. Weekly this landlord prepared notes such as the one which he gave his tenant Coburn on July 13, 1889. He ordered a gallon of molasses, twelve pounds of bacon, and a bushel of meal "on his liean." Every Saturday morning an army of cotton farmers sat down to order those same items for their families and those of their tenants.

Merchants were called upon to "let Jim Wylie have a side of bacon & 2 gallons of molasses, and Steven Coleman a side of Bacon & a gal of molasses. Charge to their acts. They will be down next week to fix up their lien. Ples send me a good pair of baby shoes." As spring advanced other orders came along asking for meat, meal and plow tools. A farmer in Alabama wanted "50 # of side meat 6½ bu of meal 3 Avury scooter stocks, 10 weeding hoes no 3, 3 sixteen inch sweeps."

Saturday night at the stores, greasy and exhausted clerks stood between meat boxes and scales slicing off pieces of fat backs. All day they had wielded heavy butcher knives on flabby slabs of sowbelly and fat back. A timid Negro ambled up to the box and asked for eight pounds of meat, five pounds of lard or a gallon of cooking oil. A white farmer bought a side of meat and a five-gallon can of lard which he parceled out a little at a time at home.

All afternoon and night cotton wagons rattled away from the stores with their pitiful loads of rations. Hunched over a spring seat a cotton farmer jolted homeward behind a jaded pair of mules with a can of kerosene, a hunk of meat, a pail of compound lard, and dust-covered bags of flour and meal.

This was the store diet in transport. At home wives sliced off thick pieces of the Iowa meat and fried it for breakfast, boiled hunks of it for dinner, and fried more of it for supper. They thickened the gravy with flour and served it and molasses as sop for corn bread and biscuit. Three times a day and fifty-two weeks a year, for many, was a long monotonous year of meat, corn bread, biscuit, gravy, and molasses. Farmers complained of "burning out" on them, and some ingenious wives hit upon the idea of rolling slices of meat in cornbread and momentarily camouflaging them as fish. This was food for what the rampant editors often called "cotton tots and tobacco worms."

Life for most of the customers was of a marked degree of whiteness. There was white meat, white gravy, white bread, and white shortening for the table, white supremacy at the polls and white gloves for the pall bearers at the graveside. Next to meat in demand at the stores was corn meal. Since the days of John Smith and Jamestown corn bread has been a mainstay of southern diet. There may be much room for debating the question of how near southern farmers, since early ante bellum days to 1920, came to supplying their demand for corn from the home fields, but there is no room for argument about their taste for corn bread. Stores sold meal by the hundreds of thousands of dollars' worth. During 1881 it was estimated that corn from the Northwest to the South sold for $50,000,000, with perhaps an additional $25,000,000 worth over the counters as meal.

This was a sectional issue which at times was almost as important as the Civil War itself. Milling companies at almost every railway siding in the intensive grain areas were grinding meal and flour for the southern trade. Bigger manufacturers like C. C. Washburne and Charles Pillsbury were busy putting Minneapolis on the economic map. At Louisville, Ballard and Ballard were developing their southern trade. In all of these, improved mills were grinding flour and sifting out all of the coloring properties. Out in the new state of Iowa, and in the older settled ones of Indiana, Ohio, and Illinois, grist and flour mills hummed with activity. The South was a rich market for their products, and the steamboat and railway lines were burdened with bolted meal and bleached flour on the way to the racks in the stores to supply a workaday appetite.

In colorful rows, twenty-four-pound bags were piled high each week to be sold by the next Saturday night. Gaudily printed labels showing an Easter lily in full bloom, a banjo, an opossum, a smiling Negro, or a beautiful girl all lent an air of "good old southern" atmosphere to a commonplace business. There was one major objection to the printed bags. Lithographed labels washed away quickly enough, but the weight and manufacturers' names were indelibly printed and sometimes rural clotheslines sagged under the weight of homemade underwear bearing weight labels in most inappropriate places.

Southern merchants in buying corn from the Northwest were indeed the sons of Jacob seeking bread for their people. But neither the Josephs in Iowa, Indiana, and Illinois nor the hungry scions of Jacob of Alabama, Mississippi, and Georgia were always just in their dealings. It was said that the "Egyptians" above the Ohio were forever stuffing their bags with faulty corn. At least many of the scribes of the southern Israel cried out loudly in their rebuke of the Northwest for shipping a poor grade of immature shocked corn to the South. While the wrathful sons of Jacob railed out at their bread suppliers because of their inferior product, a more astute "Israelite" purchased ten thousand bushels of corn in Iowa for fifteen cents and sold it in Montgomery for a dollar and a quarter.

Corn was ever a scarce commodity in the cotton, sugar, and tobacco South. It was rarely true that the average small farmer had enough to supply his needs from the time the rats and weevils left off with their destruction of the old until the new corn was hard enough to grind. The invoice books and ledgers supply a flood of evidence of this fact. One of the major items in the books is grain for human food and feed for livestock. Many merchants maintained gristmills in connection with their stores so that they not only reaped a profit from the sale of meal and took toll of the grinding, but gristmills were good trade getters because of the crowds they attracted. Often home-ground meal was sold through the stores, because corn in the form of meal always brought a much higher price.

Merchants, unlike the editors, worried little that there was insufficient corn grown in the South to supply the food demand. Some critics even accused the merchants of blocking the planting of grains in order to secure larger amounts of cotton. Thus caught between the upper and nether millstones of the editors and the merchants, the customers usually saw themselves badly scolded and abused. A Georgia country editor in scolding his subscribers said that "we can tell a man who has corn enough a mile off. The corn man cocks his hat on one side and swings along at an easy stride. The 'no corn' man has his hat pulled over his eyes and shambles along with a slouching gait and a side long look as if he expected every minute for someone to sing out 'I know what ails you. You haven't corn enough to last until March.' He takes the bray of any casual hungry or lonesome mule as a personal reflection and can't look the critter in the face, thinking he is saying to himself 'there goes a cotton lunatic—may the devil fly away with him.'

"We don't know a man who has gone to pot since the war for planting too much corn."

Thus it was that both merchant and customer were harassed. The merchant was accused of making the farmer plant cotton so he could make money to pay his bill at the store. At the same time there was a profit in selling corn and meal.

Sentimentalists have waxed eloquent in their writings of corn pone and potlikker. Even United States senators have been known to make public spectacles of themselves, and sometimes southern governors have made folksy appeals to red-necked constituencies with the subject. Next to "corn bread and potlikker" has been corn bread and buttermilk—when there was buttermilk. Corn bread went with everything. It is a wonder that the picturesque colonels of southern romance were not made to appear sitting on their high-columned porches with slices of hot buttered egg bread in one hand

and frosty juleps in the other. Always it was the *pièce de résistance* of the meal, yet this innocent food was charged with the heinous crime of causing pellagra. By 1910 the twenty-four-pound bags of bolted meal on the counters of stores were suggestive of the southern scourge. Actually bolted meal was only one of the sources of regional malnourishment. There were many other factors in the cause of this disease, and most of them stemmed from the types of food carried on the pages of store ledgers.

A slight degree higher in the culinary-social scale was the inferior chalky-white flour from the mills over the Ohio. Flour bread was a sort of mark of food gentility. It was all right to serve corn bread with vegetables, and occasionally to offer hot corn bread to guests on other occasions if the hostess "smiled" in doing so, but biscuits were definitely company bread. Hot biscuits with the hospitable admonition to "take two and butter them while they're hot" was a great rural favorite. Southerners generally loved hot biscuits. Three times a day they wanted them, and they ranged in size from the dainty little mouthfuls cut by the fastidious tin cutters from the stores to the sprawling islands of dough cooked three and four to the pan. One southern geologist observed that biscuits spread out conversely to the nature of the topography of the country. Certainly the quality of biscuit served on southern tables varied with the social backgrounds of their makers.

Both high and low among the social groups found flour an indispensable commodity. A human note from General John Bratton adequately describes the necessity of flour. "Please send me a small sack of flour," he wrote, "we ran out entirely Sir before I was informed of it and there are more people in my house than at any time for a year past. So be sure to send me a little Flour, whether you have it in small sacks that boy can bring on horse or not."

Flour by the barrel became the gauge by which the prices were adjudged. In times of fair economic balance a barrel of flour sold for $3.50 to $7.00. When these prices crept upward, either the economic balance was being disturbed or merchants were guilty of charging exorbitant prices. That the sale of flour was heavy is attested by the fact that counters and warerooms were always filled with sacks and barrels. Invoices give the picture of this trade with almost statistical accuracy. A whole barrel weighed 196 pounds and a half-barrel 98 pounds; a quarter-barrel sack was 48 pounds, and the small sacks weighed 24 pounds.

Barrelheads were places where commercial artists let their imagination run away with them. Fierce American eagles with widespread wings and claws full of arrows skimming over the national shield was the mark of Spread Eagle brand. A large circular label portraying an Egyptian obelisk was the mark of a famous Louisville product. Among the hundreds of others were Grand Republic, Homeland, Elite, Blue Ribbon, White Rose, Mama's Pride, Sunny Side, Ever Thine, White Lily, and Omega. These brands represented the output of as many factories, and nearly every one of them was indicative of a certain quality. Generally the stores handled a poor grade of flour which was purchased at wholesale prices from $2.50 to $5.00 per barrel and was retailed at prices ranging from $5.00 to $9.00. That some customers were conscious of the fact that there was a difference in quality was sometimes noticeable in order notes which asked for a "good grade of family flour."

When the acute economic pinch came in the seventies and again in the nineties, a veritable storm of wrath broke out against the merchants and the millers. The price of flour was pounced upon nearly every time a critic of the southern way of life raised his voice. It was regarded as a fairly accurate index factor in the discriminatory cost of living. The whole margin of mercantile profits, it seemed, could be established by checking the buying and selling prices of flour. Thus it was that this important source of bread was often caught up in the arguments shouted from the platforms by ranting demagogues and agrarian reformers. But more fundamental, however, was the fact that it was one of the strong links which bound the staple farmers of the South to the grain farmers of the Northwest.

Paradoxically the grain and meat trade was a factor in making common cause between the farmers of the South and the Northwest, yet it set them against each other. Like the southern farmers, the meat and bread producers wished to get as much as they could for what they sold and pay as little as possible for what they bought.

From Virginia to Texas food purchases were pretty much alike. Every personal account of any consequence included frequent purchases of the staples, meat, meal, molasses, flour, sugar, salt, and coffee. Molasses was made in all of the southern states, and was of three grades. There was the lowly sorghum which grew throughout the region from Kentucky to the Gulf, and which was converted into thick syrup in the early fall. All during the year it was sold through the stores for thirty to fifty cents a gallon, and made a decided appeal to Negro customers. After it had been in a barrel for six months, it reached a stage of mild fermentation in which a heavy white collar stood on jugs and cans, and it gave off a loud odor of cane.

That much of the molasses sold in the stores was of an inferior quality was illustrated by the frequent notes of complaint. A lower South customer wrote in 1893 that "there must have been some mistake about the molasses. My family cant use what you sent so I return it. I have plenty of the same kind you need not send the Bar. back. Will not trouble you to Draw It. Please send bar of flour." A South Carolinian, however, was less hard to please about his "morlassies." In February, 1886, he wrote T. G. Patrick, "Please send me and Bob one ballriel of them morlassies that you sold Bill and Jorden Charge one half of the Balriel to me and the other to Bob—the very same morlasis that you sold Bob and Jorden."

Louisiana and Georgia ribbon cane syrup from which the sucrose had not been removed was the choicest product. It was far superior to either sorghum or cheap blackstrap which was a by-product of the Louisiana sugar houses. Distributors such as John M. Parker and Company and the Louisiana Molasses Company of New Orleans supplied a large portion of the molasses which found its way into the throng of jugs which passed through the stores. Frequently order notes asked for molasses, and with a large number of customers the molasses jug was more a necessity than was the coal-oil can. Most southerners were extremely fond of sopping their bread in either gravy or molasses. The latter was more relished because its sweetness offset the monotony of the corn-bread–salt-meat combination. In fact molasses went a long way toward making salt meat palatable, and this is one of the reasons that it has often been charged with being one of the sinful dietary trio.

Characteristic purchases of food were the two entries taken from the daybook of R. W. Brice and Company of South Carolina. In June, 1878, George Caldwell bought eight bushels of meal, two gallons of molasses, thirty-six pounds of "bacon," and one hundred pounds of flour, while his neighbor A. J. Mobley purchased twenty-five pounds of sugar, twelve pounds of coffee, a gallon of "lamp oil," fifty pounds of bacon, two gallons of molasses, six bushels of meal, two fans, and three and one-third yards of calico. These early ledger pictures hold true for most of the southern supply trade during the five decades following the Civil War.

Aside from the staples which have been mentioned there was the steady demand for coffee. Every customer was a potential purchaser of this commodity. In most instances merchants bought coffee in the green-bean stage and dipped it out pound at a time from the large jute bags in which it was packed in Brazil. Nearly every household parched and ground its own coffee, and it was more from this custom than from the much famed magnolias that the countryside took on one of its most fragrant odors. Customarily green coffee sold all the way from a bit a pound to three pounds for a dollar, and it was as much a necessity as were tobacco, molasses and bacon.

Sugar and salt ranked with coffee in importance. Both of these commodities originated in the region. Sugar came from the Louisiana, Carolina, and Georgia cane fields. Stores in the upper part of the region secured salt from the Kanawha River source, while those in the lower South secured their supply from the Jefferson Island mines in Louisiana. It came in barrels and coarse sacks, and if less than a hundred pounds was sold, a clerk had to break the bag and weigh out the required amount. It was not until the later years of highly imaginative packaging and increased urban living that salt was sold in small quantities. Although the money involved in the purchase of salt was trivial in comparison with other aspects of the store business, it was a major factor in trade.

Open barrels of white and brown sugar were kept on hand to meet the constant demand for it. Southerners working at the arduous task of farming needed large quantities of food, and sweetening was a favorite. Like molasses, sugar helped to enliven the traditional fare which was served in most families. Cane fields of the subtropical Gulf coastal area, like the grain fields and hog pastures of Iowa, found an outlet through the stores. Cane farmers exploited tobacco and cotton growers by continually presenting their case to Congress and begging for a higher sugar tariff so they could get more for what they grew and, perhaps, pay less for what they bought. For several decades no bright-colored signs were nailed to store fronts proclaiming the virtues of one brand of sugar over another, nor of one particular brand of salt—yet these commodities were high up in the list of the standards.

Not all of the store trade in food had to do with the sale of goods which were outgoing. There was a fairly rich produce trade which yielded a steady year-round profit to merchants. Housewives longing for special clothes and knick-knacks saved their chickens, butter, eggs, nuts, and other marketable produce and traded them off to merchants. Although much the same attitude which prevailed against the hog and the cow was applied to the chicken, there was a rather steady flow of eggs into the stores. Boxes, cans, and baskets filled with eggs packed down in cottonseed came in on Saturdays to be emptied and their contents counted. Patient clerks spent hours digging eggs out of cottonseed, shaking them in the precandling days to see that they were reasonably sound and then counting them. It was a tedious job to count a large quantity of eggs, especially when heartless pranksters stood around waiting to start a commotion at the moment when a tub was filled to the brim with a day's purchase. Likewise, it was maddening to have to concentrate on counting eggs with a hot political argument going on about the stove, but business was business. If a clerk miscounted a basket of eggs sent in by a woman customer, there would be a serious repercussion, and most often the customer's claim prevailed.

As typical of the country-store trade as the rows of patent-medicine bottles and drums of kerosene were the bags, barrels, and papers of seed which were put on seasonal display. This was almost as much a reflective factor of the southern diet as was the sale of the "staples." Each February when plows, plow-lines, horse collars, axes, and hoes were put on display, bags of onion sets were unlaced and bag tops rolled down so as to show off their red and white wares. When this happened, there was an aroma of hopefulness to the stores. Nothing ever came quite so near to expressing the approach of spring as did the pungent smell of onion sets. They bespoke early gardens, turnip greens, green onions, fresh cabbage, and radishes, but, most of all, relief from the everyday winter victuals. Rural southerners were little better off than medieval Englishmen in this respect. They sated their hunger during the drab winter months with salt-cured or dried foods and looked hopefully to spring for a change. Green onions added zest to meat and gravy, turnip greens and peas, or just to hot biscuit. The frequent and almost universal entries in the store seem to indicate that southerners liked onions best of all vegetables.

At the same time onion sets were placed on sale, bags and barrels of Irish potatoes were put in stock. They cluttered the aisles and were within themselves harbingers of spring. Rice and grits filled the place of potatoes in the regional list of foods except for the spring and summer months when "new" potatoes were available. Customers ordered seed "Ish taters" by the peck and then cut them with an eye to saving enough of the meat for one meal without robbing the sprouts of too much sustenance. Actually potatoes were a rare delicacy for a large portion of the southern population except for about four months of the year.

When onion sets and potatoes appeared in the stores, the fancy seed boxes were put in a prominent place atop counters. With their lids propped upright they showed off to excellent advantage the extravagantly lithographed cabbage heads, beets, radishes, and turnip greens. Each seed packet was within itself a masterpiece in the art of commercial advertising. With few or no seed inspection laws to block their labors, artists and composers of package legends soared high in their calling. A drowsy farmer sat by the stove and gazed dreamily at the fancy vegetables on the seed packets and planned for a garden that would waft him away forever from the uninteresting food which he ate three times a day. He almost forgot the presence of the meat box, the molasses barrel, and the stack of meal sacks in the back of the store.

Yet in the idylls of the seed displays there was a strong current of conservatism. Southern taste was for the more commonplace vegetables. Orders came in like the one written by William Mabby in 1892: "please send me ½ gal onion sets 1 pack Drum head cabbage seed 1 pack collard seed 1 pack beet seed if you haven't got them on hand please get them for me and take pay out of money I left with you please send seed and amt of cost by Dick." Another wanted "2 papers cabbage seed 1 of collards & 2 of tomatoes," and a female gardener asked for "2 papers each of flat Dutch Drum Head & Winningstadt cabbage seed."

Prominent among the seed orders was a demand for collards. This vegetable was peculiar to the South, and it offered some degree of salvation to the malnourished parts of the population. But because of the taste for it by white and black alike and the ease with which it was grown, it fell low in the social scale. Nevertheless, as a matter of everyday eating and of sale of seed in the stores, the lowly collard occupied a top place in popularity.

Generally missing from the rather limited choice of seeds

were string beans, peas, and okra, which, like watermelon, cantaloupe, and turnips, were propagated by growers saving their own seeds from year to year and planting them with little thought of selection and breeding. Some of these seeds actually became a part of family traditions. For two or three generations certain bean and watermelon seeds were held in high esteem, and in the case of the watermelon, efforts were made to control the distribution of the variety. Nevertheless, several favorite varieties of melons were distributed over the South through the stores. Of these there were the favorites, such as Augusta and Georgia rattlesnake, Kolb's Gem, Tom Watson, Kleckley Sweet, and Stone Mountain.

Despite the conservatism of taste for vegetables and the large amount of home production of seeds, the seductive display cases in the stores were vital parts of the institution. Immediately after the war D. M. Ferry, of Philadelphia, entered the southern market with his famous combination shipping and exhibit boxes. Keenly aware of the regional demand, he packed his cases each fall with abundant supplies of the more popular numbers and sent them away to country merchants to be handled on consignment. At the end of the season he split his profits with the dealer, reclaimed his cases and the unsold stock and began all over the cycle of "catching the trade."

The imaginative Ferry was not without competitors. The Shakers from Pleasant Hill, Kentucky, sold seed all over the South. At Richmond, Virginia, T. W. Woods and Sons had a claim on much of the southern trade, and where they left off, the Alexander Drug and Seed Company of Augusta took up and competed with the outsiders. Later all of the seed houses found strong competition from the H. G. Hastings Company, which developed a large mail-order business from the red acres south of Atlanta. Selling seed was closely akin to the medicine business: there were many distributors who competed for the country-store market with far more knowledge of the drawing powers of lithography than of garden seeds. For the stores themselves the rather generous profit returned by the sale of seed was not large, but few stores wanted to be without their colorful displays. They comprised a flashy part of the over-all picture of the store itself and marked a major departure from the sale of "imported" foods over the counter.

Thus the stores became active centers of southern human welfare. There was in both their stocks and records eloquent testimony describing as accurately perhaps as a statistical table the basis of life in the region. The story of the store's food sales was often sinful and was always dramatically symbolized by a weary man shambling away from its porch weighted down with a sack of meal, a slab of meat, and a bucket of molasses.

A little bit of everything: Tools and harness hang from the ceiling, while counters are stacked with clothing, tobacco, and sundries. (Photograph courtesy J. Winston Coleman, Jr.)

Here Uncle Sam's humble servant, the postmaster, carried on the business of the Post Office. (Photograph courtesy J. Winston Coleman, Jr.)

Whatever you need . . .

Everything from fresh meat and vegetables to snuff and chewing tobacco to lamp globes and coal oil (out front.)

10

MR. McGUFFEY AT THE CROSSROADS

THE COUNTRY STORE and the one-room schoolhouse developed simultaneously, and they were closely associated. Sometimes they were near neighbors, and always the stores were sources of supplies for the schoolrooms. In March, July, and October, account books tell the stories of school openings. Within three or four days after each term began, ragged orders for textbooks, writing materials, clothing, and extra food supplies appeared in the stores.

A schoolmaster wrote J. L. Williams of Eagleville, Tennessee, in a semimilitary manner: "Sir, by order from the Director and Clerk Mr. Lowe I ask you to please send me Two buckets two dippers, a broom and a box of crayon and charge the same to the board? Do this and oblige yours as ever, customer? Fred M. Jordan."

Fred Jordan's pupils and those like them all over the South bought books, tobacco, slates and slate pencils. An Alabama mother wanted a merchant "To please let the bearer have sixty cents in trade. Send me McGuffey's 1st reader, McGuffey's third Reader, 2 Webster's spellers. If you have not got them, please get them and send me bill by bearer." A South Carolinian sought "1 book Appleton's Second Reader. 1 Ten cent Slate—and fifty Cts worth of Good Ten cent Tobacco and Charge to me."

Consistently there were orders for McGuffey's, Goodrich's, Appleton's, Butler's, and Harper's readers, Ray's arithmetic, Webster's *Elementary Spelling Book,* Barnes' and Stephens' histories, Guyot's and the New Eclectic geographies, and Harvey's grammar.

The famous McGuffey series of *Eclectic Readers* was the keystone of rural southern education. Before the Civil War, William Holmes McGuffey's publishers, Truman and Smith Company, sold thousands of their texts to the region's schools. In 1860, Winthrop B. Smith, president of Truman and Smith, conducted a sales campaign south of the Potomac, and when the war began, he had many uncollected accounts. This largely explains why Confederate school children were supplied McGuffer's readers. These books were printed by the Methodist Book Concern of Nashville until that region was occupied by Federal forces, and then the trade moved back to Cinncinati.

When the war was over, the *Eclectic Readers* were again sold by the Cincinnati publishers. Wilson, Hinkle and Company (after 1877, Van Antwerp, Bragg and Company) again secured the southern book trade. Working through new state superintendents of education, with poorly organized school boards, and through country merchants, their company secured a growing patronage. This company was able to win in the bitter rivalry with Morton and Griswold Company of Louisville, who published the famous Goodrich readers and spellers.

McGuffey's readers were well suited for the vagaries of the crossroads textbook trade. The original texts were prepared at a time when America was in a most exciting period of fermentation but the author believed there were certain fundamental human impulses and reactions which were unchanging, and he stuck to these. Like his famous contemporary, Stephen Collins Foster, McGuffey was able to divest his work of sectional bias.

The stories in his readers were simple and forceful accounts of everyday life. Sentimental admonitory pieces like "Meddlesome Matty" found a ready audience. Mrs. E. L. Beers' "Which" was a glorification of poverty and large families. These were selections which at once appealed to sentimental and highly moral ante bellum southerners, and later to simple rural folk who were getting their first real taste of popular education.

Within the first decade of the existence of the new schools one-third of the rural southern people were unable to tell whether Robinson Crusoe was a marooned character from Defoe's writings, the Old Testament, or the Fourth Reader, or whether "Dare to Do Right" was a chapter from Proverbs or an English schoolboy story written by Thomas Hughes. Many McGuffey illustrations even validated the scriptures. In the scene where a boat of a whaling crew was upset, one hapless victim was represented as falling headlong past the whale's mouth to convince the most skeptical that Jonah could have suffered his famous catastrophe.

In the midst of the Civil War, E. J. Whitney was employed to make new plates for the readers, and the famous textbooks took on a modernized graphic tone. Progress in engraving improved the appearance of the textbooks. Hand-drawn pictures were cut on wood blocks, then transferred by electrotyping onto metal plates. For the rural South the pictures in McGuffey's readers were a sort of artistic *hors d'oeuvre.* Engravers were able to put in each of their scenes the same aphoristic lessons that were written into the text, and for those who were unable to grasp the full meaning of the stories the pictures gave wonderful aid.

Pupils generally kept account of their progress through school by passage from primer to first, second, third, and fourth readers and life in earnest. A fourth-grade education enabled the average pupil to read with some certainty, to spell most of the words in the first half of Noah Webster's *Elementary Spelling Book,* and to cipher a reasonable portion of the problems in Joseph Ray's *New Primary* and *Practical Arithmetics.*

Arithmetic was an important subject in the South. Van Antwerp, Bragg and Company sold thousands of their famous book prepared by Joseph Ray of Woodward College through the country stores. These were copyrighted first in 1877 and quickly became everyday stock in the stores.

At Booneville, Mississippi, Dr. Ray had a competitor in S. H. Morrow, a roving mathematician, who sought the southern trade with his little book, *The Practical Arithmetic; Containing the Shortest Process Extant of Solving Practical Questions*. In the face of such a giant as Ray's arithmetic there must have been some misgivings in Professor Morrow's mind about the possibilities of his sixty-four-page book. He printed the legend, "What Man Has Done, Others May Do. I'll Try." The printing was done in Louisville, Kentucky, and it was sold first for one dollar a copy; later the price was marked down to fifty cents. The author's market was the New South, and figures of a practical sort were beginning to have meaning as never before. Long division and computing interest became a vital part of life. Lien notes and sharecropping demanded an elementary knowledge of these mathematical disciplines by even the most illiterate. "The age in which we live," says the preface, "demands that every man should at least have such a practical knowledge of the principles in the solution of examples that occur in daily business transactions."

Dr. Ray showed a like practical turn of mind in planning his problems. His *Practical Arithmetic* set forth both maximum and minimum interest rates and explained that "usury is now practically abolished in nearly half of the states and territories," which was a wary general statement by an alert textbook writer. Just in case his book was used in states where lien notes and stiff interest rates and credit prices were charged on annual accounts, he supplied examples of 12.5 per cent which could easily be doubled by simple multiplication.

Geography for the average southerner was purely a science of aesthetic education. The Home Geography, Carpenter's, the "Eclectic Series," and Frye's "Little and Big" geographies tried in vain to give it an element of usefulness. The "Eclectic Series" was divided into two parts, first the *Primary* and then the *Complete Geography*. After dismissing the constellations in summary fashion, the author went around the globe in a systematic order, giving quick glances at the world's sensational spots. The story of North America began with a crushing assault of a herd of buffalo upon a grizzly bear in the presence of two entranced rattlesnakes sporting rattles as large as saucers. Niagara Falls poured over a mighty rock precipice in mad fury, and in keeping with these robust introductions, much of the rest of North America was illustrated with lusty scenes from various sections. Too, there were idyllic views of woods hunting, of steamboats idling on low country rivers between rows of moss-festooned trees. As late as 1898 slaves were still feeding horse gins and rolling bales of cotton around the wharf at New Orleans.

It was thrilling to travel with Chinese junks down Oriental rivers, to catch wild horses around Turkoman wrangler camps, to stalk the wild animals of Africa, and to view the strange varmints of Australian jungles. The "Big Geography" was a more exciting volume because of its illustrations. For the South, it showed cotton, tobacco, and cane culture from a romantic mammy-song point of view. Its artist conceived of a southern cotton field as something taken from a sentimental novel, and he portrayed bolls as wide as dinner plates. The world of the eclectic geographies, like Sister Noah, was fearfully and wondrously made with more than a suggestive touch of Phineas Taylor Barnum.

It cost southerners more money to learn that the St. Johns River in Florida flowed north, that cove oysters came from Biloxi and Baltimore, that an island was a body of land, and that "the goods that are not used in our country are bought by merchants and shipped to foreign countries," than it did to apprise them of the practical influences of climate, soil, and drainage of their own environment. For instance, a Mississippi pupil in a one-room school got a fantastic notion of Asia, but no conception of his own state.

The "Little Geography" was a combination of moral lessons, socratic questions and definitions, and tourist information. "Jews," said the brief little book, "were people who do not believe that Christ is the Son of God, but that the Savior is yet to appear." With equal brevity, "Mohammedans believe that Mohammed, the founder of their religion, was a true prophet." The student, however, is left in total ignorance as to the global whereabouts of these pagan races whose religious beliefs were contrary to those of the South. The "Big Geography" sold on the credit across the counter for two dollars, and it was purchased from the American Book Company for less than one dollar. It was the epitome of world knowledge.

Fortunately for the publishers they were able accurately to gauge the sentiments of the age. They knew only too well that Darwin's *Origin of Species,* the Hegelian philosophies of William T. Harris and the St. Louis Group, and the pragmatic teachings of William James, Charles Pierce, and John Dewey were still confined to the ivory towers of the universities. Although the wonders of nature were given much attention, they were purely surface manifestations. All of the elementary books ignored the science of geology which had had such fascination for Thomas Jefferson.

While Milton H. Smith, president, and Albert Fink, chief engineer, of the Louisville and Nashville Railroad, Henry F. DeBardeleben, Truman H. Aldrick, W. S. Gurnee, Enoch Ensley, and Tannehill T. Hillman were developing the Birmingham coal and iron area, the geographies were concerned with eclectic morality. Southern cotton fields were being gutted with erosion, but geographies still presented pictures of ante bellum horse gins and made known the laconic fact that "an iceberg is a large mass of ice floating in the sea." Perhaps the most impressionable lesson carried away from the one-room schoolhouse was that *g-e-o-g-r-a-p-h-y* really meant "grandpap et old gray rats at Paul's house yesterday."

History was a subject of great practical moment in a South which had passed through the Civil War. There was an assortment of texts on the subject. Occurring frequently among the book accounts was Barnes' *Universal History,* which took a broad chronological and cosmic view of the subject. For $1.65 a southern cotton farmer's child could gallop the armies of Greece, Rome, France, and America right up to his weather-beaten schoolhouse door. Barnes' conception of history was "universal" only in the sense that he conceived it to be a succession of wars, overturned thrones, and the lives of the great.

Samuel G. Goodrich (Peter Parley), a textbook writer who recognized few subject limitations, supplied many southern schools with some of his assortment of ten books. In copiously illustrated volumes he portrayed the whole scope of world history. Most popular were his *Pictorial History of the United States, A History of Europe, A History of Asia and Oceania,* and his *Common School History of the World.* His historical figures were creatures in caricature. Henry VIII, for instance, stared at the shivering ewe, Anne Boleyn, as if she were a butcher following his daily routine of slaughter. Locke, Addison, Pope, Swift, and Newton were portrayed as a sort of steel-engraved gallery of cutthroats. Goodrich's text was little more than narrated chronology which covered wide sweeps of history in a skimpy fast-moving narrative with scarcely a hint of either timeliness or interpretation.

Competing with versatile professors who wrote from austere professional points of view, Alexander H. Stephens managed to take time out of a busy political career for the task of writing a history text. He presented to the South what has often been jokingly described as an "unbiased history of the United States written from the southern viewpoint." "Little Aleck" attempted to achieve results which have frustrated many ambitious textbook writers. Publishing special editions from the capital cities of the southern states, he announced on his title page that the book was "A compendium of the History of the United States from the Earliest Settlements to 1872. Designed to Answer the Purpose of a Textbook in the Schools and Colleges as well as to Meet the Wants of General Readers."

In some parts of the South, Stephens' book was regarded as a standard treatise on the history of the Republic. He was, however, surely a chronologist with a certain amount of prejudice and personal bias. His account of Lincoln's first inauguration is a fascinating bit of indefinite historical writing. "Abraham Lincoln, of Illinois, 16th President of the United States," said this author, "was duly inaugurated at the usual place on the 4th of March, 1861, aged 52 years and 20 days. Borne in an open carriage, he was escorted and guarded from Willard's Hotel to the Capital by an armed military force under the direction of Gen. Scott, the General-in-Chief of the Army of the United States. . . . His Inaugural Address was read from a manuscript. It indicated no decisive policy, except the maintenance of the 'Union' which he claimed to 'be older than the States.' . . . "Little Aleck's" treatment of the founding of the Confederacy was more explicit, and his accounts of the campaigns of the war were planned to hold the reader's interest.

Dr. Noah Webster's famous "blue-back" *Elementary Spelling Book* was sold over the counter for fifteen cents a copy. In 1885, D. Appleton Century Company advertised that they were selling a million copies of this text annually. It was around this book as much as McGuffey's readers that southern school traditions centered.

Beginning with the simple words like "b-a *ba,* k-e-r *ker, baker*" it took the young learner step by step, syllable by syllable, over the high hurdles of "perspicacious," "pertinacious," "legerdemain," "rubific," and "schismatic" and tapered off with "bacon," "beechen," "bidden," "chosen,"and "cloven."

Many a snaggle-toothed youngster resolved in his own mind that the name Webster should forever be stricken from the annals of southern education. When an unyielding schoolmaster called upon him to stammer through the great spelling-book shibboleth: "i-n *in,* c-o-m *com,* p-r-e *pre,* h-e-n *hen,* s-i *si,* b-i-l *bil,* i *i,* t-y *ty; in com pre hen si bil i ty,* and when he had spelled the word giving the sound of every syllable, he was then called upon to give its meaning; here was realism in its starkest form. This, along with many other words in the spelling book, came to be a symbol of juvenile humiliation.

Noah Webster, too, kept uppermost in mind the obligations of moral teaching. "Keep your mouth clean, and save your teeth," admonished the little blue book before the days of patented tooth pastes, smiling movie actresses, and pampered socialites. Supporting temperance sentiments of the times,

Webster wrote that "drunkards are worthless fellows, and despised." In true New England fashion the author declared that "a love for trifling amusement is derogatory to the Christian character." At the end of the book there was a series of stories and illustrations which left with several generations a sense of the virtues of right and industrious living. There were stories of the dogs and lion, the stag, the boy who stole apples, the country milkmaid, and the crafty story of the cat and the rat.

Looking back historically upon the age when "b-a was *ba* and k-e-r was *ker,* and b-a-k-e-r *was baker,*" it is hard to determine whether Webster's "Blue-Back Speller" was in reality an educational textbook or an amusement device. Innumerable spelling bees were held in schoolhouses or in lodge rooms over the stores. There were perennial scholars who never forgot that in school they had stood at the head of the line in spelling. Just as playing baseball or pitching horseshoes was a sport with them, so was spelling. Ignoring the book's puritanical pronouncement that "a love of trifling amusement is derogatory to Christian character," promoters of spelling matches lined up teams and spent Saturday nights spelling down their neighbors.

Spelling classes in schools, however, were anything but frolics. Impatient schoolmasters waited for stammering pupils to get through their stints of spelling, syllabication, and accentuation. Luckless scholars went to the foot of the line for missing words. Sometimes humiliation at "going foot" was insufficient punishment, and the master's flail fell heavily as a reminder that spelling was one of man's major achievements. But with all the emphasis upon spelling in the schoolroom, abundant evidence of which is in merchants' ledgers, there was marked lack of spelling ability in the South.

Notes which poured into the stores followed consistently two principles: Words were spelled the way the writer understood them, or they were spelled the way he thought they should sound. Clerks had to master not so much the art of deciphering illegible notes, as of interpreting words which observed none of the rules set forth in the Blue-Back Speller. Alick Woods' note to T. G. Patrick's store was a shining example of phonetic spelling. "i Wish you Would let uncol Same formme have 225 D and twent sent Worth At Capt Price i did Make a little miss take But i hope you will undorstand it." There were literally thousands of Alick Woodses who knew just enough about writing the English language to scrawl their ragged little order notes requesting goods "on the credit." But even more indicative of the lack of education in the South were the bales of legal papers signed by cross marks, because the signers could not write their names.

One of the commonest arguments used against public education was its high cost. From 1865 to date, southerners have raised the cost-of-books issue to explain away failure to progress educationally. Actually the book cost involved in the acquisition of a sixth-grade education was less than a year's supply of snuff and chewing tobacco. At most, it required no more than ten dollars to buy the books for the average rural education, and it required only fifteen cents to secure a book which would teach one to spell every word in the English language. Harvey's and Noble Butler's grammars came a little higher, but for a dollar a southern pupil attending an "old field" school could acquire the fundamental rules of the language.

Publishers of textbooks in the four decades following the war were the same shrewd businessmen as were other trust-forming capitalists. They focused their attention upon the moral lessons of their wares rather than upon the production of new books. They were so busy reprinting old standards and heading off competition that they had little time either for new authors or for the production of new and imaginative texts. Thus it was that used textbooks, like outgrown jeans breeches, were passed on from one member of a family to another until they were worn and scuffed beyond recognition. This was the main reason why the McGuffey books descended from father to son, and sometimes from grandfather, without fundamental change in ideas.

A progressive county superintendent in Kentucky wrote in the nineties that "it looked at one time like nothing short of the state militia would put down the 'blue back' speller." He was saying, of course, that the time had come to introduce new and timely ideas into the process of southern education.

Before a child could begin school during the early years after the war, he needed the maximum equipment of a slate, a pack of slate pencils, half a quire of foolscap paper, a bottle of ink, a pencil, half a dozen steel pens, and a dictionary.

Perhaps not all of these things were necessary, but at least the slate and pencils were. There seems to have been an affinity between the red-felt-bound, wood-frame slates and their juvenile owners. Large slates (8 x 12) cost a quarter and the smaller ones (5 x 7) fifteen cents. In a South which was destitute for writing paper, they were the only satisfactory writing surfaces which many of the people had. Where school children managed to stay on their feet or resisted savage impulses to break somebody's head with their slates, they lasted for two or three generations. For a nickel, merchants supplied five slender pencils draped in the United States flag, and from these could have come enough words to fill the dictionary and enough pictures to decorate Belknap's giant hardware catalogue.

The slates and pencils of the one-room school gave students their one opportunity to be original. The paper-starved child could write and draw to his heart's content without fear of wasting precious materials. Teachers set examples of letters, and pupils copied them over and over. Enterprising publishers, however, were quick to see the importance of teaching by example, and they began issuing copybooks, which were sold through the stores.

An overworked or poorly trained teacher could, with copybooks, conduct a writing course without giving it too much attention. These guides were always the work of some Victorian writing master who struck off round-bodied letters to be copied on a series of blank lines. Occasionally a dexterous Spencerian copybook artist became so infatuated with his writing that he drew flitting birds and ornate curlicues with his pen. Flowery handwriting, like flowery oratory, was one characteristic of the age, and the artistry of the masters showed up in the notes of customers and on the pages of ledgers and journals. In most cases store books were posted by men who had learned to write in one-room schools and many of their entries were of the same laborious copybook style. Nearly always the writing is legible even where the spelling and sentence structures are illiterate. One waggish observer said that many people could write fine Spencerian hands, and many of them could make birds, trees, and other fancy ornamental objects with their pens, but they could not spell. In such cases he likened their art, in apt rural phraseology, to "a new saddle on a cow."

Schoolkeeping's first consideration was drinking water. Large tin buckets, common dippers, ropes, and chains were necessary equipment purchased at the beginning of each term. Schoolhouse wells were scenes of many an act of devilment. Someone was always jabbing a hole in the side of the well bucket and then leaving it to spray everybody else. Periodically brigands threw buckets, chairs, and pulleys—as well as other objects fair and foul—into the well. When this happened, it took most of a school day for two of the larger boys to go to distant wells or springs.

Flimsy school buildings were heated with cast-iron stoves which teetered uncertainly on brickbats in the middle of the floor. They too were objects of temptation. Coltish boys could not refrain from giving them sly kicks to see the joints of pipe come sprawling onto the floor and break up school for an hour or two while the stove and pipe were put back into place and the soot swept out. Schoolhouse flues were always held together by an intricate system of twisted wire and bent nails. Schoolmasters became so clever in this art of tying that when a stove was shoved over, its pipe usually remained suspended and intact.

Blackboards and erasers were crude. Most of the times blackboards were coated with paint which came from the stores and erasers were bits of sheepskin. Teachers were expected to purchase crayons out of their slender incomes, and they kept a miser's eye on its use.

Not until the second decade of the present century did a revolutionary change take place in the rural schools. Publishers began to use more imagination in the contents of their textbooks and they brought them up to date. The curriculum was expanded, and the level of education generally was lifted. Populists crusading for advantages for southern farm people helped to plant an educational germ which was to grow. Agricultural and mechanical colleges, born of the Morrill Act, introduced new conceptions of learning. With the exception of having to read city-inspired and written textbooks, the southern child of the 1920's was at last freed from the restrictions of the ancient textbook combine. The progressive arguments for greater educational advantages finally removed the book trade from the stores and transferred it to the hands of the specialists in state departments of education. Bacteriologists discovered that common dippers were carriers of measles, whooping cough, itch, mumps, and chicken pox, along with every other infectious disease known to mankind. And the stores tripled their dipper business in the sale of the new-style collapsible aluminum drinking cups.

There were other revolutionary changes in the schoolhouses of the postwar years. Furnaces supplanted rickety stoves with their flimsy smoke stacks, three and four rooms were added to the house, pupils came from a larger area and were herded into separate grades. Storekeepers ceased to be controlling factors and lost the privilege of determining who should and should not teach. But it was these merchants who actually nurtured the schools through their formative years.

The revolution in public education was to go farther than the physical appurtenances of the schoolroom. Before it ran its course, it was to strike a mortal blow to the traditional one-room school itself. Even school financing was eventually to be placed on a more satisfactory basis. No longer were teachers paid with county warrants and then forced to discount them with local storekeepers for 40 to 60 per cent of their face value in order to get their money within six months or a year after they had performed their services.

Changing attitudes toward community responsibility for education were seen everywhere in the South. A manifestation of this was that ring of farmers who on a spring night in 1919 squatted before the Calvary Baptist Church in Winston County, Mississippi. Some of them dug miniature furrows with their knives while others whittled on sticks. This group of landlords and tenants were planning to consolidate the one-room schools of Providence, Gum Branch, and Scott's Spring. They wanted a school with several teachers in it who could offer better instruction. The grades were to be separated, and their children were to have more attention than was possible under the old system. There were other advantages which would come with the pooling of finances and teaching facilities. The larger school would give more meaning to the whole learning process.

Without knowing it, these southerners were shaping the end of an educational era. People in their backward state had been slow to appreciate the advantages of consolidation. One discordant note, however, was sounded in this informal forum: Constable Jefferson Banes, a tenant farmer, raised loud objections. The new school would bring higher taxes, needless extravagance in salaries, and force his children to attend when they ought to be picking cotton and peas and making molasses. In a futile gesture the defeated constable threatened to hire a tutor and leave the new school in need of students by the absence of his brood.

Fifty years before, Jefferson Banes's frantic opposition would have found much support. Southerners were baffled by educational ideas and philosophies which came out of the war. On the face of things, this new educational movement seemed to be a part of radical reconstruction. It was associated with the freedom of the slaves, with political activities of the

Freedman's Bureau, and even with the military governments. Some southerners regarded public education and civil rights as insidious devices for putting the bottom rail on top. Little did they understand, however, that meager one-room schools with their hopelessly unprepared teachers were the first fruits of vines which had long remained dormant. The process of reconstruction only fanned anew a smoldering spark of general public education which was kindled in the ante bellum South.

Die-hards like Dr. R. L. Dabney, a preacher and professor in Hampden-Sidney College, even went beyond associating public education with reconstruction to expose its fundamental weaknesses. Dr. Dabney, in his arguments, spoke for the ancient classicism of tight-minded ante bellum Virginia, and he saw in public education a symbol of social and economic degradation.

In a newspaper argument with the superintendent of public instruction in Virginia in the seventies, Dr. Dabney said, "Your free schools like not a few other pretensions of radicalism, are in fact exactly opposite to the name falsely assumed. The great bulk of those who pay money for them, do it, not 'freely,' but by compulsion. It has become mischievous and tyrannical, in that it forces on us the useless, impractical, mischievous, and dishonest attempt to teach literary arts to all Negroes, when the state is unable to pay its debts and provide for its welfare. . . ." Then he argued that "the state intrudes into parental obligation and function of educating all children is dangerous and agrarian." Fortunately for southern youth this opposition was ignored and the new state constitutions framed during the years 1865–72 contained provisions for free public schools.

There was much truth in Dr. Dabney's contentions, but likely he never understood it. Somewhere during the years of reconstruction the South lost much of its productive facilities for nurturing intellectual and political leadership, and before the new school system was organized, there was a change in modes of instruction. However, during this unproductive period of 1865–1912, when a fourth-grade education epitomized much of southern schooling, the country merchants with the one-room-school teachers helped to keep alive the spark of learning which was to blaze anew in the modern South.

11

ADMIRAL DEWEY CORSETS AND BONTON PETTICOATS

On Sunday afternoon, May 1, 1898, the populace of Washington was stirred with great excitement. The secretaries of war and state remained in their offices anxiously awaiting news from Admiral Dewey and his exploits inside Boca Grande. Messengers scurried to and from the War, Navy, and State building. Then there came a fragmentary message dispatched from Madrid that there was a naval battle in Philippine waters, though it was silent as regarding the outcome.

For three or four days the nation waited to hear what had happened to Admiral Dewey and his fleet. Then people began to speculate: "If there has been a battle, we, of course, won; but what are the details?"

Going on the strong assumption that Admiral Dewey had put Admiral Montojo and his fleet permanently at rest, enterprising New York dressmakers were busy capitalizing on his victory. By the time the celebrations were under way in the East, ladies were parading the streets in Dewey Victory dresses. They had a wide flaring blue skirt with brown stripes down each side; waists were white and blue striped, topped off with Zouave jackets caught at the throat with gold frogs. For variation, and as an impartial tribute to that other American hero, Teddy Roosevelt, who was in Tampa preparing to rush headlong into victory, the naval victory costumes were topped off with Rough Rider hats adorned with crossed sabers. Everywhere there were Dewey lapel buttons, and in the restaurants there were special Dewey dishes. Along the streets throngs of jubilant smart alecks were repeating the idiotic catch phrase, "We didn't Dew-ey t'ing to 'em!"

Admiral Dewey's popularity was far reaching and it was to go beneath the gaudy white-and-blue-striped waists. Soon ingenious manufacturers offered the Admiral Dewey Health Corsets to female idolaters. Its shape was a swirling twist which gave it the grace of Lillie Langtry and the ruggedness of Calamity Jane. Its expansive top seemed ample enough to accommodate the foredeck of Dewey's flagship *Olympia,* and below its sinuous waist there was an embouchure sufficient to cover the most ample hips. "The Admiral Dewey," said its manufacturer, "has a perfect made bust, silk stitched, six hooks, carded hip gore, heavy trim wire back. The most perfect fitting health corset on earth."

There were scores of other corsets which served effectively to give form to the shapeless and charm to the graceless as did the Dewey. For young maidens just entering their period of waist consciousness there were such tender little binders as Darling, Little Pet, and Young Ladies' Beauty, which compressed adolescent middles with the gentleness of heavy woolen undershirts. As girls grew into womanhood they girded themselves with the more robust Victoria, a matronly compressor pulled together by two strong laces fore and aft, which held its shape with the aid of steel and whalebone stays. For torsos which had not reached too serious a stage of distortion there was the seductive Primrose Path. It was "blue and white, the latest French white sateen strips, six narrow zones on each side, point lace embroidered top, satin ribbon drawn, five-hook clasp, a most comfortable and easy fitting corset." Equally fetching was *A La Spirite* made of "heavy English coutille, long waist, silk flouncing on bust, embroidered on top, known all over the country as the best wearing goods made." *A La Spirite* was awarded a gold medal at the Paris Exposition in 1889, and with a hint of the new freedom which was to come it was proud of its saucy "flexible hip."

The corset business in the country store was good. Female members of customers' families can be accounted for by the number of corsets ordered in the spring together with spools of thread, molasses, onion sets, tobacco, batter spoons, roach combs, shuck collars, clevises, and hame strings.

For sixty cents to a dollar and a half, southern belles could buy a Talk of the Town, Annie, a Cousin Jane, Daisy, or a Beauty corset which would give their figures the coveted hourglass appearance. Even the prize winner, *A La Spirite,* could be had for a dollar, and the rugged Admiral Dewey clung snugly to its victims for the nominal price of sixty cents.

Every dry-goods invoice had its corset orders, and distributors like the Worcester (Massachusetts) Corset Company enjoyed a brisk trade in the South. For women above the age of fifteen to show their contours out in public was vulgar. She was a coarse character who appeared without a retaining wall of jeans, steel, whalebone, and bamboo stays. Even mothers with babes at breast were forced to bind their torsos with rigid steel. There were nursing corsets with ingenious flaps which made it possible for a mother to keep her shape and nurse the baby at the same time. The W.P.C. Improved Corset was characteristic. It had a "long waist, French model, reinforced sides, patent slip button on nursing flaps, of white jeans, with sateen stripe, silk galloon lace top."

Pictures of females for the decades prior to 1910 show such a remarkable bust development as to cause one to believe the modern woman is in an advanced state of physical decline.

It was difficult even upon close examination to distinguish the genuine from the spurious. Imaginative Yankee dry-goods brokers sold a heavy ten-gauge wire coil in the shape of a double cone which was held in place by a web band through its middle. This stout expander was covered with soft quilted material, and when it was strapped into place in the top of a corset, even the flattest-chested Mary became a pleasing advertisement for the constructive powers of Lydia E. Pinkham's Compound.

Balancing off the plump touch about the breasts was the crescent-shaped bustle which made an abject apology for nature's shortcomings about the hips. Ever conscious of the dire potentialities of bustles being sat upon, manufacturers created them out of stout bias woven wire, and they were molded in the shape of halfmoon pillows. Like the forward bustle they, too, were held in place by a series of web straps and short buckle hitches. The tiny *carte de visite* photographs of the seventies, eighties, and nineties portray females looking pridefully over their shoulders at their trains.

One other bit of webbing in the foundation bulwark was necessary. A lady's stockings could never sag, even if they never showed. There was always danger of the unexpected. For instance, a horse might run away and theoretically stockings had to be in place. Corset makers supplied hose supporters, or side corsets, called "Langtry lengtheners," with long, coupled straps which could be fastened to the corset at one end and stockings at the other.

Thus rigged, the "stylishly" dressed woman was ready for flowered corset covers and molded petticoats. Dressmakers before 1900 conceived of the ideal female figure as being that of a newly blown crystal hourglass which had been set out to cool. Petticoats were shaped so as to cover a bustle, and hang in such a manner as to give the general impression of forward movement. Such a skirt was the "Bonton," a brand-new number for the spring season of 1899, of "fine quality sateen moire effect, very latest stripe patterns, lined with plain flannelette, deep flounce cut on the bias, with five inch accordion pleat ruffle and one inch fancy tape strap, flounce lined with heavy leno." Here was a limb concealer and shadow breaker of major proportions. It hung to the floor, weighed as much as a light-overcoat and sold for $2.50.

Over the heavy subsurface garments went skirts and shirtwaists. Styles for these garments went through a process of annual metamorphosis, but seldom, if ever, were the fundamental principles of length, flair, and waistline involved. In the nineties the average shirtwaist sold in the country stores was "lined throughout with good quality percaline lining, sleeves lined, double-stitched yoke, felled seams, pleated backs, full front, trimmed on each side with six rows of black Hercules braid half an inch wide and seven rows narrow braid, giving waist a rich appearance, standing detached soft collar, soft cuffs to match waist, fly front, and cardinal and blue color."

Skirts were equally as formidable as petticoats. Carrying out the cardinal idea of absolute concealment and weight, a $4.00 best-seller of the latest pattern was made of "extra fine quality figured mohair brilliantine, silky effect, very full skirt, double lined throughout, seven gores, fan back, rubber band attached on inside of skirt, giving same a beautiful hang, bottom of skirt bound with waterproof binding, which is a great advantage to the wearer."

Underwear was a highly seasonal matter, but seldom was merchandise commensurate to southern weather. It was purely of Yankee conception, and since the factories were located north of the Potomac, there was considerable miscomprehension of the demand for light-weight materials in the South. Two favorites were "medicated scarlet" and "medicated Australian." "Medicated scarlet," the greatest favorite, was warranted to be knitted from select washed sheep's wool, "finished in most durable manner, silk embroidered inside yoke, silk tape bound neck, front and bosom pockets, cat-stitched neck, full regular made shoulders, elastic ribbed cuffs, pearl buttons, hemmed tail." Pants to match were "style U," banjo seat with tight-fitting legs and long elastic cuffs. Usually the idea of medication was just another instance of humbuggery of the postwar decades, but the scarlet tradition was of Biblical origin. In praise of woman, the appreciative scribes of Proverbs had written, "She perceiveth that her merchandise *is* good; her candle goeth not out by night. . . . She stretcheth out her hand to the poor. . . . She is not afraid of the snow for her household: for all her household are clothed with scarlet."

For fifty years the general meaningless term "Dongola" was applied to women's shoes. It was not until the age of annual stylistic variations that shoes underwent significant changes of designs. Shoes had high tops, long, slender, oval toes, and low heels, and they were securely fastened with either laces or buttons. Heels and toes were "common sense," and the tops gave wearers' legs and ankles an unusually plump appearance. Uppers were made of combinations of cloth and leather, and, laced up, they covered the leg halfway to the knee. Some of the earlier types, like one style called "peaches and cream," had gaily figured uppers, but these were never displayed to the public gaze. Some of the tops were scalloped, and others were figured with fancy cross-stitching.

When the Hawaiian Queen Liliuokalani called on President Cleveland to protest the highhanded act of the Harrisonian missionaries of imperialism, Sanford B. Dole and John L. Stevens, she at least captured the imagination of the country with her impressive appeal for the withdrawal of the Americans from Hawaii. The press carried accounts of her visit, and soon there were Queen Lil shoes for the ladies. They were advertised by one broker as "royal in name, royal in make, royal in stock, but beggarly in price." For $1.75 a customer could sport a pair of medium-high-heeled coin patent-leather-top shoes of distinctive style and taste.

There were numerous other trade names such as Prosperity, Anchor, Fly, and Rachael, long lists of which appeared each spring among the invoices. Every variation in style and material bore a special classification and description. It was not until dresses crept upward that manufacturers attempted radical transformation. Sweethearts of World War I perched perilously atop tiny spike heels, but the tops remained high enough to reach the hem of their dresses. At the same time, toes were as sharp as toothpicks and as uncomfortable as a vise.

Stockings to go with the high-topped shoes were purely utilitarian and were worn for sake of warmth and modesty. Most popular for sixty years, outside the rugged home-knit types, were the so-called full-length or kilt hose with "shaped" ankles. Black was the prevailing color, although there was the Gallic touch, called in some lines "real French lisle." One type of "French" hose was "positive black Hermsdorf dye, extra superfine Richelieu ribbed hose running all around and down to the French toe. English heel and full-fashioned." There was another with "wide belt, extra elastic spliced heel and toe, boot pattern with lace stripes." But most common of all were the heavy-ribbed balbriggans.

After 1915, the heavy Richelieu ribbed and formless French lisles gave way to the finer spun-silk garments, and the southern crossroads strove manfully to keep abreast of the changes in styles.

Actually corsets, bustles, moire petticoats, dongola shoes, and French stockings represented the fancy counter trade. The piece-poods counter was still the stand-by and sold much larger quantities of merchandise.

Every spring and fall accounts were laden with such entries as "ten and a fourth yards stripes, three and three-fourths yards hickory, six spools of thread, twelve yards calico, thirty-one yards long cloth." A week and a half later the same family bought "six plugs of tobacco, sixty yards of calico, six yards of cottonade, a spool of thread, and a pocket knife." A Tennessee seamstress wrote, "I wante 10ct off stays fore a Dress and 5 ct off hooks and ise. Sende the things By the one that Brings this if you Pleas."

An Alabama matron was faced not only with the problem of buying cloth but another springtime necessity. She needed "a preparation of quicksilver & corrosive sublimate for bed-Bugs, 6 yds 10¼ unbleached sheeting, 12 yards blue calico for wrapper, 3 yds. good bleached domestic, 1 set glasses. Please send me about five yards of your red wrapping paper (for pattern making)."

Literally thousands of notes poured in bearing tiny samples of cloth, bits of lace, pieces of thread, buttons, and linen "stiffing" for dresses. Matching was a chore for every clerk in the house. A neighbor wanted a yard of red calico with a yellow flower in it for making "Robbie pants" (short warm-weather drawers). Another requested "25 scent of that same red cloth I got yesterday when I was thair." A notionable customer ordered "5 yards of that purple goods for a skirt & a spool of thread to match." Frantically a conservative dressmaker asked for "10 yards of cretonne like sample." Often it was impossible to match a piece of goods exactly, but it was not so much mismatching that started spring troubles in the stores as it was the incurable sample collectors. Female customers sent for samples of cloth by every passer-by, and every year scores of bolts were wasted in this manner. There was a utilitarian side to this practice. If clerks were generous, the fragments of cloth could be pieced into quilt covers. Many a rural rag bag was filled with them.

A family of six required four bolts of cloth annually in order to provide changes of clothing around. Goods came from such widely scattered wholesale houses as Daniel Miller and Company, Hurst, Purnell and Company, Joel J. Bailey and Witz, Beidler and Company of Baltimore, Thaxton and Watkins of Richmond, O'Bryan Brothers of Nashville, and J. Bacon and Sons and the Stewart Dry Goods Company of Louisville; and the New Orleans, Mobile, New York, Cincinnati, and Chicago houses catered to an extensive southern trade. Large orders were shipped directly from cotton mills in the Carolinas, Tennessee, Georgia, and Alabama. Frequently, notes on New York invoices indicated that the goods were actually originating within the southern region. A South Carolina merchant ordered cloth from New York which was made out of South Carolina cotton and shipped to him from Greenville, and Georgians bought millions of yards of Riverside plaid from northern wholesale houses only to have it shipped to their stores from Columbus.

The long list of textiles which passed annually over the counters tell a vivid story of southern clothing. The more popular fabrics were Simpson calicoes and homespuns, North Carolina, Virginia, and Kentucky jeans; Virginia Schoolboy cassimere, Virginia jersey, Mississippi, Tennessee, Alabama, Oneidas, and Riverside Plaids; California drill, red canton, red and gray flannel, hickory stripes, unbleached domestic, long cloth, lawn, linen, and osnaburgs.

These were made into garments of myriad patterns and forms, some no more than shapeless bags gathered at the necks with buttoned collars and bound in the middle by simple tie strings. Some, of course, were made into dresses after the grand styles of the moment so that a farm woman in a calico dress had the same general over-all appearance of a city woman in black silk.

The gay nineties were not colorful for patrons of the cross-road stores. On the contrary, the spirit of the South in those days approached a drab morbidity. This turn of mind kept much of southern womanhood in a dolorous state of dress. Plaids such as the famous Mississippi checks, Riverside, and Columbus checks had some dash to them, and so did some of the more daring calicoes; but stacked in among these striking colors were those bolts of spiritless textiles designed to clothe "respectfully" the married and jaded southern female.

Mrs. Nannie Clary of Alabama ordered a bill of dress goods for the spring and summer season of 1897 which was characteristic. She wanted "5 yards of dark calico, 3 yards of drab dress drilling, 1 yard of coars stiff linen, if [you do not] have that send wiggin 1 set of whalebone, 1 spool dark navy blue silk thread, 1 doz medium smoke pearl buttons." This was the kind of spring outfit which marked the end of a cheerless winter and the beginning of a wearisome summer. It was the kind of matronly dress which robed an army of perspiring females crowding their way into the left-hand corners of the protracted meeting houses. One set of whalebone included on a modest little order seemed innocent enough, but there was an unhappy sequel. Long before a garrulous preacher, intoxicated with the sound of his own voice, could blast his way through a truculent sermon, the stays of a homemade corset bit their way into a recalcitrant and badly disturbed abdomen. What had started out to be a form-creating corset became a strait-jacket, and scarcely had the wearer deposited her aching body on a spring seat in a jolting wagon headed for home than she pulled the rip cords and set the straining whalebone stays at liberty.

Nannie Clary's neighbor ordered "3 yards of plain black lawn, 1 yard of black calico, 1 spool black thread no 60, 70, 1½ yards black moire ribbon, 2½ or 3 inches wide." Another carried on the tradition of morbidity by ordering "two dress patterns 10 yards in each I want dark calico sutable for an 'Old Lady,' Wish black with some very small spray or dots. Two yds, of dark sutable for a bonnet, 3 spools of black thread, no. 50. 2 pr. black hose, 20 yds. nice sea island domestic." The term "old lady" in the lower South was at best a relative one. It did not always indicate that the lady with a black dress created from ten yards of calico, and a bonnet with enough cloth in it to make a skirt for the modern woman was a grandmother. Women in their late forties and early fifties took the country-store veil, which was a doleful splint-lined sunbonnet, and considered themselves within the shade of latter life.

In general the demand was for conservative patterns and drab colors, but there was one significant exception. All of the stores catered to a large Negro trade, and the Negro was sensitively aware of colors. He liked bright patterns with gay flowers, plaids, and brilliant solid colors, and some of the samples attached to his notes surpass in brilliance even the modern goods. Many a romantic swain made headway with an indifferent female by the purchase of four or five yards of bright dress goods.

Lace and rickrack were in constant demand. In the eighties J. Bacon and Sons, a prosperous Louisville wholesale house which had grown out of a peddler's pack, advertised throughout the South that they had on hand, "10,000 yards of cotton laces, 50,000 yards of fancy laces, 10,000 yards of Spanish laces, 25,000 yards of fancy laces in cream and white, 50,000 yards of hamburg and Swiss embroideries, and 5,000 yards of piqué." All of the other brokers carried equally as large stocks of these trimming materials. Just as carpenters and architects put gingerbread and scrollwork on houses, women put lace trimmings and bindings on their dresses at every seam and around every pocket and collar.

Most universally used of all homemade garments, except dresses, was the stave-ribbed sunbonnet. Crowns were close-fitting caps gathered from either side with draw strings, while the brims were six or eight inches wide and were held rigid by hickory splints.

The bonnet in the South became a badge both of the field and of an age of "respectability." Younger women wore bonnets purely for protection from the sun, but on women over forty-five they indicated matronhood and the end of days of youthfulness.

After the Civil War many merchants found themselves accidentally in the ready-made-hat business. Most of the hats came from Cincinnati, New York, and Chicago, and were doubtless products of sweatshops. Brokers packed cheap assortments and shipped them to merchants, often without their having been ordered. Sometimes in order to secure most of the profits from selling hats, these merchants purchased braid, feathers, patent leather and oilcloth, ribbon, pins, and ornaments, and had a neighborhood seamstress make hats for them.

At best the hat trade of the post–Civil War years was one of doubtful profit, and no merchant engaged in it with enthusiasm. If he made a mistake in fitting a neighbor's wife or daughter, he incurred her enmity. On the other hand, he frequently received hats which he could never sell. Shelves of abandoned stores tell this story. Piles of hats have accumulated over the years and remain behind in a state of tawdry confusion to feed moths and bed mice.

The fascinator, a garment which blithely belied its name, was the most practical bit of headwear available in the stores. It was a long, knitted woolen scarf which could be draped over the shoulders as a cape or tied tightly around the head. It came in drab blacks and grays, or in gay colors with a profusion of cord and ball trimmings, and with long bright-colored tassels on each end. Fichus were indoor substitutes for capes.

Over the dry-goods counter of the country store the character and taste of a people were shaped. Die-hard moralists were stirred anew with every change of style. Even the bicycle, which became popular in the late eighties, was considered an instrument of demoralization and degradation. Because roads were poor and the sand beds too deep, the bicycle never became an important vehicle in much of the South, but its influence was felt nevertheless. Its appearance marked the beginning of change from heavy, flowing skirts, wire bustles, and fantastic back bows to the unpadded slit skirts. For ages the southern woman had ridden horseback in sidesaddles in impossible dresses and with one of her legs slung in a side prong of the horn. This was nearly an impossible position for mounting a horse and expecting to control it, and it is the reason why so many women had a mortal fear of horses. But a social creed declared that all "decent women" should ride sidewise, and to woman's credit she performed some near miracles of horsemanship in sidesaddles atop rearing horses. Until the revolution in methods and attitudes toward travel, stores enjoyed a considerable sale in sidesaddles. A Harbison-Gathright saddle with modest twin horns and a single fender and stirrup strap cost as little as nine dollars.

Slit skirts came into style with the bicycle, and ladies began riding their horses like men. This was a sin. Preachers bemeaned slit skirts and improper riding, and in many eyes the new riding skirt became a badge of modernity and disgrace. Acutally it was a landmark in the freeing of southern women from another of the ridiculous customs which had restricted them for so long.

The late twenties saw the end of the big piece-goods trade. Post–world war years were marked by developing individual tastes. Children broke over and expressed positive views on their choices of patterns and designs. There was a direct relationship between the virtual disappearance of entries for bolts of goods from account books and the slackening of parental control over children. Country stores were no longer scenes of long Saturday purchasing expeditions when fathers and mothers picked out clothes for their children and made them like it.

Once a father bought cloth for his womenfolk's clothes at cotton-selling time, and they had no idea what color or pattern he had selected until he bumped home with it in a cotton wagon. Modern magazine advertising made them acutely style conscious. Cheap ready-made dresses were placed in stock, and dry-goods shelves began to go bare.

After 1915, however, the stores were caught up in the

ground swell of the new freedom. Ready-made clothes were up to date even if they were of an inferior quality. Slips, brassières, and panties were placed on prominent display. Once the technique of buying underclothes for a woman had closely resembled that of buying liquor in prohibition days. Women customers no longer had sartorial secrets. The spirit of the times was reflected on the store shelves.

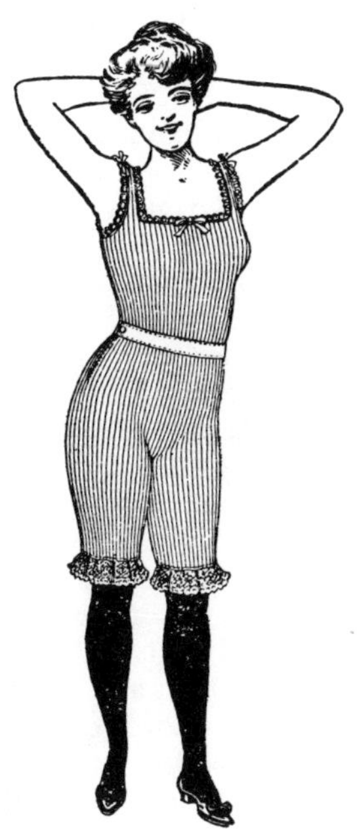

12

GENTLE JACKSON IN A DEVIL OF A FIX

THERE IS A PICTURESQUE but polite southern expression, "caught with his britches down," which is used generally to describe all uncomfortable and unexpected situations. Such seems to have been the case of an Alabamian who wrote his furnishing merchant on July 13, 1895, that he needed help at once. "Let Gentle Jackson," he ordered, "have the mount of $2.85 cts for labor and send me half of Buster's rashing and send Buster a pair of pant. So on the other half of Buster's rashons I wants some cheap panting and if you have any spair loane creator [creature] sent it to me and if you cant send me the Creator send me much as four dollars and I can high one for I am in a devil of a fix."

Need for pants was a common plea all over the South, and they were important items in the stores. A rural Tennessean stood in urgent need of "a par" of jeans pants in March, but he had no money in sight for two months. He asked the merchant to send the pants at once and "I will pay for them when my geese is picked." Another order which characterized the men's clothing trade was a note from Rufus Bratton in South Carolina who requested that "James Green have two shirt and a par of shoes and a par of pants and a hat and a par of sok. Pllease let Dubose have a pants and three yards of cloth."

Male southerners lived in an age of jeans after the Civil War, and from 1865 to 1900 this coarse type of clothing was in common demand. Most frequent of all the entries for men's clothing is that for jeans cloth with which to make trousers and coats. There was no distinctive style to these homemade trousers, and any woman who could master the rather simple mechanism of a pair of scissors, thread a needle, work a buttonhole, and comprehend so common a principle as trousers with two legs and a deep slit in the waist could make her menfolk's clothes. Legs were virtually without style, and always they were deeply wrinkled. In more modern terminology trouser legs during the first forty years after the war were filled with deep-rolled "detours."

Pictures of postwar gentlemen of all social and economic strata give the impression that their legs were those of ancient elephants. If a wearer could get his feet and shoes through the legs and if they came down reasonably close to his shoe tops and were full enough in the waist, then his pants were satisfactory.

Jeans as a fabric had a long history in yeoman America. It was intimately connected with the progress of westward expansion. In fact, frontier Kentucky jeans early made a national reputation for itself. Especially was this true in the South, where large quantities of work or slave cloth was purchased prior to the war. It was a coarse cloth of heavy weave. It had a cotton warp and a woolen woof and varied in color from red or brown to gray and green. Ordinarily trousers made from it were too rough for any but the hardiest to wear next to his skin, and it was necessary to line them with unbleached domestic. More frequently than not, entries for jeans in account books were always accompanied by purchases of the same amount of yardage of cheap cotton cloth.

Jeans sold over the postwar counters in reality took the place of the famous ante bellum butternut. This was the cloth of the working man, and quickly it became a sort of badge of southern class consciousness. In the bitter political clashes between the bourbons and the "people," coarse clothing played its spectacular part, and even candidates themselves either wore or frequently referred to the ordinary clothing of the farmer. South Carolinians of the nineties were ever conscious of the significance of everyday dress as a factor in state politics.

Many of them recall the visits of "Pitchfork" Ben Tillman, and they were impressed by his rural mode of dress. One Tillmanite remembered how an excited band of cotton farmers carried "Pitchfork" Ben through the streets on their shoulders and how his awkward legs encased in loose jeans britches flopped through the air.

Everywhere in the South politics and jeans britches were a part of the same economic and social pattern. In the piney woods and hills of Mississippi poorly dressed politicians shouted promises of reform in government to snuff and tobacco-stained constituents dressed in jeans and cottonades. Pictures of Kentucky politicians of the nineties makes the average state legislator appear to be an escaped inmate from the county jail. Even William S. Taylor, the Republican candidate for governor in the Goebel Crisis in Kentucky, attorney general, and later governor, was a perfect specimen of the "jeans-britches" state official. Kolb and Oates, the Taylor brothers in Tennessee, Tom Watson of Georgia, and a host of lesser lights depended on the jeans-britches and wool-hat boys for support. It was they who were victimized by the fluctuations of national economy and *laissez faire* exploitation. They were the properties of the southern demagogy and Populists' protests against privilege and discrimination.

Deep in the depression of the early nineties, order notes for trousers cloth grew more numerous and meeker in their requests. A farmer at Siddonville, Alabama, wanted "3¼ yds of jeans the best that you can send me if you have not got it send out and get it send drilling for pockets buttons buckle thread and lining for waist. I want the very best jeans that is made please get a gray." A less fastidious customer wanted "a pair of *common* jeans pants size 32–32 & 6 yds [shirting]—send buttons and thread."

Characteristic of the individual purchases for male members of the family in the decades after the war were "3 yds of cassimere 6.75, 1 pc. calico [for lining] .40, 1 doz pants buttons, .05, 1 spool of flax .10, 1 hat 3.00, 1 vest 2.25, 1 pr. suspenders, .50," or "1 pr. pants & coat $5.15, 1 pr. pants & coat & vest $2.50,

1 pr. shoes $1.65, 2 yds jeans .35, 2# sugar 25, 1 Bot. Cologne .35." This was the average southerner's outlay for everyday clothes, and all too frequently this was also his Sunday wear.

Next to the homely jeans, coarse cassimere, and shoddy cottonades which went into the making of pants and coats were the calicoes, prints, and hickory stripes used for shirting. As often as farmers bought commercial fertilizers, plowlines, backbands, and plow points in the spring, they purchased spring supplies of "stripes" for shirts or, occasionally, cheap ready-made shirts. For three or four decades shirting materials were bought wholesale for four to eight cents a yard and retailed to customers at credit prices of twelve to fifteen cents.

Occasionally an enterprising merchant with an unpromising female creditor on his hands supplied cloth, buttons, and thread and had her make shirts for his trade. Notes like the one from a South Carolina seamstress appear among merchants' papers. She wrote, "I send you (9) more shirts which with the (2) I made last week will make (11) I don't know as to what cloth you sent but I fear it took more than (3) yd to the shirt. I would be glad to know but I think I would prefer the wide cloth. Please send me 10 cts worth of checked pink calico & (1) or (2) of your baker loaves if they are fresh and not 'dear.' " She was making clothes for men whose wives lacked access to sewing machines or who were too busy with other affairs to cut and sew fifteen-cent cloth into shirts for their menfolk. There is the very essence of growing grass in the appeal of an anxious father who asked, "Let me and my boy have a working shirt a pace [*sic*] and will oblige me much and 10 cents worth of tobacco."

Crude work clothing was ever the uniform of the rural South. Plain wrinkled jeans and cottonade pants, heavy formless jeans coats, and calico, homespun, and hickory-striped shirts were basic garments. The hickory stripe might very well have been the flag of the New South. Since it first came on the market it was a fabric of labor. Everywhere stores displayed huge oval bolts of it with its distinguishing white transverse warp stripes and its blue woof. Where romanticists have, with foppish sentiment, described the ruffled shirts, fawn-colored vests, and broadcloth suits of the ante bellum gentry, they have been brought down to earth with the dull postwar dress. Ruffled shirts of idyllic ante bellum landlords gave way to collarless and sweat-laden garments of a most unimaginative home manufacture. There were no fawn-colored vests, and formal stocks were almost unknown.

At the same time that the rural woman was stultifying her taste for dress with osnaburgs, homespuns, simpsons, and funereal calicoes, they were buying like drab raiment for their men. Occasionally women could enliven the simpsons and osnaburgs with touches of color, but the men of the seventies and eighties were helpless. The rural South was a region of white conservatism, and there were few men so brave as to go counter to the styles of the time. This conservatism was one which was based so thoroughly upon the dignity of the white man that it remained practically an unchanging factor.

Underneath jeans britches and hickory-striped shirts for most of the year were the red flannels, white twill canton, and gray outing undershirts and drawers. Some cold-natured native son, or perhaps he was a snowbound Yankee, created the famous "string and button" drawers, which, in most instances, were gathered tightly at the waist with a stout cord. Such a garment was described by one wholesale house as "bleached canton drawers made of good, heavy quality, long front, two rows of stitching throughout, 3 patent buttons, fell seams, large banjo seat with two rows of stitching, reinforced diamond crotch, taped and faced string bottoms, eyelet back and side darts—$4.20 doz."

Undershirts were of the same general material, but they were seldom as securely bound to their victims as were the drawers. From 1865 to 1910 the average country-store customer was a wretched victim of his underwear. His undershirt bound him by its fiendish constrictions about his waist, and his legs were always hobbled by his drawers.

For the cool months of winter there were the shapeless knitted balbriggan shirts and drawers which gave a man the general appearance of an emaciated animal whose hide had drawn away from its body. The medical humbuggery of ladies' underwear was carried over to that of men. There were "special scarlet sanitary" and "medicated scarlets" on every counter. There were "pure all wool medicated underwear made from good stock of Australian wool, fine gauge, fleece brushed, silk bound neck and front, 4 pearl buttons, embroidered inside yoke, long fine elastic ribbed cuffs, regular made shaped sleeves, looped shoulders."

Most important of all the items of men's clothing, however, were shoes. Shoes have ever been the southern farmer's great concern. Walking behind plows in the sandy soils of the South, across plowed fields, or along muddy roads was always a trial even in the most favorable circumstances. But until the late nineties the common everyday shoe was the formless brogan which sold at wholesale prices for 75 and 90 cents and were retailed at the high credit prices of $1.25 to $2.25. This shoe was designed by the cobblers of Massachusetts whose itinerate salesmen followed the backroads after the Civil War looking for customers.

Until after 1880 few shoes of the common stock type were made specifically for left and right feet. Lasts were straight, and it made no difference which one of a new pair of shoes was put on first. Southern stores sold the crudest type of work shoes. Although there were several kinds of shoes on the market, the most popular with the country trade was the brogan. This work shoe came tied in pairs according to approximate sizes, and they were tumbled into bins to be fished out and fitted as they were called for.

This shoe was made either of split or hard oak-tanned leather. Soles were fastened on with hardwood pegs, and seldom if ever did the manufacturer go to the trouble either to trim the pegs or to pad the soles. Brogan toes were broad and plain without any stitching to break the lines. The shoe was universally poorly made and highly uncomfortable. Seams were often bound with heavy harness brads, and buckles were used instead of strings in about half of the shoes sold. After the first day or two of wear, these shoes became hard with deep creases across the toes, and around the ankles. Thus it was that for fifty years the American shoe manufacturer perpetrated upon the southern country a foot agony which caused a good portion of the population to go barefoot as much as possible. "Breaking in" a pair of shoes was a torturous ordeal. Often some tough-footed friend would oblige by wearing a pair of shoes just long enough to give them a hint of shape.

A pair of shoes for a two-year-old was as heavy and sturdy as is the modern heavy-built adult shoe. Toes were boxed in with brass and copper strips, and heavy uppers came well above the ankles. Manufacturers had not mastered the art of making light, flexible shoes. Despite its poor quality and general unsuitability the famous old "brass toe" was an object of sentiment which older generations of southerners recall with affection. In reality, however, their sentimentality is a bit of subconscious wonderment over the fact that they were able to wear such shoes and live with any degree of happiness.

Thus it was that from the cradle onward the problem of wearing shoes was vital. Certainly the history of the propagation and spread of hookworm is partly due to the failure of shoe manufacturers to supply country merchants with decently designed shoes of good quality and at reasonable prices.

Personal accounts are sprinkled with records of shoe sales. For $1.25 to $2.00 a pair, customers purchased carloads of brogans. Landlords wrote frequently for shoes for their family and their tenants. "Please let Ed Edwards have one pair of shoes cost not to exceed 1.50. If any at 1.25 let him have them," wrote one southerner. Ed's comfort and the wearing quality of the shoes were inconsequential factors in the purchase. That feet ached there can be no doubt. Ed Fitts, a Black Belt Alabamian, asked for a pair of "broad toed shoes even if you have to send a size larger." Another customer wrote that "I send the shoes got yesterday back by Wade. They cramp my foot. Please send a size larger of the same kind if you have them & if not a pair like those I looked at when I got them Mr. Will Patrick knows the kind." A dyspeptic boss man set a limit of $1.50 as the price his boy Sime could pay for shoes, and in the same order asked that he be sent a bottle of Carter's Little Liver Pills. A conservative customer of the "old school" ordered "a pair of Red Top boots no. 9. I will pay you when I come up."

In all the long story of maladjusted styling and poor quality, there was no racial discrimination in the matter of wary feet. Both the white man and the Negro were victimized. The fact that the Negro's feet hurt him, however, became a humorous matter. Locally he was chided for the wide gashes which gave bony toe joints and sensitive bunions relief. These slit brogans became a bit of everyday stock for the blackface minstrels which traveled through the South. The white man most often endured his suffering without resort to the knife. Yet it was the brogan with its vicious double rows of heartless pegs in the soles and the unrelenting stiffened creases which eventually revolutionized the work shoe in the South. The St. Louis manufacturers and distributors were perhaps the first to start effective competition against the brogan. The welt shoe was introduced in the late nineties, and from this beginning came the light, pliable "scout" plow shoe which quickly took its place on spring orders for everyday wear.

One major chapter of the development of the St. Louis shoe industry had its beginning in a Mississippi country store. In 1868, when James Lee Johnson died from wounds received in the battle of Franklin, he left a widow and two young sons to struggle against the odds of reconstruction days in Mississippi. The older boy, Jackson Johnson, became a bookkeeper and clerk in a country store, but in a few years he and his younger brother, Oscar, bought a store of their own. They secured capital from their uncle, H. C. Rand, to finance their country store. As the South recovered from the more serious reverses of the war and reconstruction, the Johnson brothers expanded their operations. In 1886, in partnership with H. C. Rand, they opened a general furnishing store in Holly Springs. One of the big items in their furnishing trade was shoes, and there were frequent calls for the uncomfortable brogans. Farmers bought the rough shoes, and suffered from all sorts of troubles with their feet. From handling general merchandise the Rand, Johnson and Company turned to selling shoes. The store was moved to Memphis for the purpose of specializing in the wholesale shoe trade in the South. In 1897 a yellow fever epidemic swept the lower Mississippi Valley and virtually wiped out the Memphis trade for wholesale merchants in that area. A year later the transplanted Mississippi country store was moved up the river to St. Louis, where it became the Roberts, Johnson and Rand Shoe Company, with the original storekeeper, Jackson Johnson, as its president.

The development of the Roberts, Johnson and Rand Company and other St. Louis shoe manufacturers and distributors had an important bearing on the southern shoe market. The country-store experience of the partners in the newly organized business made them conscious of the needs of the southern shoe market. First as jobbers and later as manufacturers, the St. Louis Company made serious inroads into the brogan monopoly, and by the first decade of the present century country-store customers were able to secure the new-style flexible welt shoes with sewed and tacked soles. This was the end for the shoddy pegged work shoe, and even shoe pegs themselves disappeared. Before 1920 the general-issue shoes used by soldiers in the large American Army brought a complete end to the long era of the brogan.

In earlier years when the southern male exchanged the brogan for "Sunday" shoes, he actually found that he was little better off except for general appearance. Dress shoes ran the whole gamut of the footwear trade of the times. For men with ancient feet scarred in miles of travel on sandy soil behind plows there were the relatively soft "Congress" shoes, which gave some freedom and protection. Then there were the sharp-toed patent-leather types with their stiff, unyielding soles. In the late nineties the button types with cloth tops and patent-leather counters and toes were the latest in new style appeal. It was this cheap button shoe which gave much of America an added touch of rurality. "Sunday" shoes were practically as shabby as those sold for everyday. In the catalogues and invoices they are listed for the same cheap prices, and in the account books they brought the same wide margin of profit as did work shoes.

Jeans britches, hickory-striped shirts, and brogan shoes did not, however, represent all of the southern men's furnishing trade. Gentlemen customers splurged at times and bought fancy clothes to wear courting and on Sundays. In 1870 a fastidious Mississippian dressed himself from the stock of the Nunn store at Shuqulak. He bought a pair of boots, a pair of shoes, lining for a coat, two shirt fronts, a paper of hooks and eyes, a suit of clothes, a pair of hose, a hat, a pair of gloves, two boxes of paper collars, and a watch key. His bill came to thirty-two dollars, and he was able to present himself as one of the best-dressed males in the community.

Twenty years later a rural dandy across the line in Alabama bought a coat, a pair of pants, a vest, a pair of shoes, a pair of socks, a high-standing collar, a black necktie, and a pair of gloves. His total expenditure for this outfit was less than twenty-five dollars, but he was ready for a full summer of courting with a generous number of picnics and speakings thrown in on the side.

Stores supplied the demand for ready-made clothing from racks of suits which were sold wholesale at from three to fifteen dollars a suit and were retailed at ten to twenty dollars. These originated in eastern cities or in Cincinnati and Chicago.

At best the ready-made clothes were poor in quality. They were notoriously shelf-worn and moth-eaten. Many of them had seen one or two seasons in a large city store before they reached the crossroads shelves. Typical of the complaints of customers was the note of an Alabamian to his country clothier "I send the coat back it is eat up with the moths hold it up between you & the light & you can see it is full of holes."

The pants trade, however, had three significant southern sources of supply in the Abington Pants Company in Virginia, the Greenville Pants Company in South Carolina, and the Mayfield Pants Company in Kentucky. These factories specialized in supplying cheaply made trousers of the "knockabout" class to southern merchants. Coats generally came from the factories outside of the region.

The ante bellum suit trade was supplied by special tailors. Ready-made clothes in the local stores were practically unknown, and when a man bought a suit, it had to be made especially for him. Following up this custom, storekeepers kept huge sample books of New York, Baltimore, Cincinnati, and Chicago tailors lying around on their counters, and they encouraged customers to look through them and select patterns which they wished to order. It was in this way that much of the more particular "Sunday" clothiers trade was supplied. Likewise, this was an added source of income for the merchants.

The stores catered to undiscriminating field hands and local dandies alike. Surprisingly, some of the stores carried sufficient stock of an ephemeral nature to outfit the most meticulous gentleman. A blade in the Lower South informed a neighboring merchant, "It may be that I'll be called upon to go to the dance this Evening & after looking over my wardrobe I find I'm very short on some little things which please send by Mose & I will send money for them tomorrow. I want a standing collar and neck tie suitable for the occasion, also a heavy pair of black ½ hose— P.S. you can please send me 3 boxes of shells, no. 8 shot. Send Bill." There were scores of other orders which reflected the nature and condition of the times. J. A. Stewart of Fairfield County, South Carolina, had to travel dirt roads, and he wished to keep as much of his native soil as possible from settling on his shoulders. He was in the market for a duster. In his note he instructed a storekeeper to "let Luke have a duster I want it to be as cheap a one as possible. One that does not cost more than a dollar. Do not give him the one he saw when he was there before and if the eggs do not pay for one Please send word how much I owe you, you can put it on a paper and give it to him. I send seven dozen eggs. Give Luke five cents worth of candy."

Most complicated of all the fancy-dress trade, however, was that of supplying "Sunday" shirts. A sadistic stylist conceived of a shirt as being a thing of many complicated parts. It was a body, a set of cuffs, a detachable front, a high collar, a pair of collar buttons, and cuff links. It was not enough for the ordinary man with thick, clumsy fingers to struggle through the ordeal of buttoning an unreasonably high collar under his chin, but he had likewise to attach his shirt front, and fasten securely a pair of long starched cuffs. The whole scheme of putting a shirt on a man's back was one of making the task as difficult as possible. In many instances it was practically impossible for a man to put his shirt on by himself.

The detachability of the several parts of dress shirts was purely a matter of weak subterfuge. There was a belief that the body of the shirt could be worn indefinitely, but that its component parts had to be cleaned with some degree of regularity. Fronts could be detached and laundered, and so could collars and cuffs.

Most popular of collars were the cheap paper ones which came packed a dozen or more in a box. The theory back of their use was that they could be destroyed after each wearing, and that it was reasonable to maintain a clean collar supply. There was a distinct drawback, however, to the whole system of shirt assembly; in the South, where the weather was extremely warm, fronts, collars, and cuffs melted within an hour. Men who were accustomed to working in the field and who perspired freely spoiled their clothes before they could leave the house.

Sundays were unhappy days for the average church-going southerner who dressed up for the occasion. Sitting through a long sermon with a stiff shirt on one's back taxed human endurance, but to sit in church with one's best girl added considerably to the discomfort. It was practically impossible to keep up an appearance of dignity when a shirt front let go from one of its moorings and was curling up toward the chin, or, if it remained in place, it was rapidly becoming as limp as a dishrag. Too, chins that were unused to high stiff braces such as were the stylish collars for forty years, put an insufferable strain upon the back. It is little wonder that agonizing customers wrote, "Please let me have a plaster to go on my back and I will pay you for it when I gin I am down with my back."

Buying men's clothes was a twice-a-year job. In the spring light shoes, suits, ties, and hats were generally in demand. Just as the leaves were coming out and the dogwood was in bloom, the stores expected their biggest business in men's and boys' clothing. This was really the season for getting set for at least seven months of the year. It was the beginning of frequent church meetings, political campaigns, and picnics. Usually a dressed-up country-church crowd in June presented a remarkably scrubbed appearance. Men reddened by the hot spring sun were freshly shaved, and their hair was combed back in long dampened or oiled roaches. Shoes were dabbed with oil polish, and there was a peculiarly ill-at-ease atmosphere in every assemblage. New clothes on the backs of both sexes were in keeping with the freshness of the spring season. There was the loud composite smell of cheap suits, freshly laundered shirts, shoe polish, the sizing in the cloth of new dresses, spring flowers, Hoyt's colognes, tobacco, and rugged humanity in the air.

Merchants bought items of clothing in dozen lots, and sometimes a single store would sell dress outfits to nearly every individual in a community. In this way the merchants became both arbiters of styles and forces in creating a deadening monotony of taste. In isolated communities, when a man was bored with a sermon, he could sit in church and establish a price for the clothing which every person wore because he either had the same kind on his back or had examined it in the neighboring store. This was, without a doubt, one of the most active forces in helping to create in the South a distinct sense of provincialism.

Where merchants anesthetized a local sense of variety in their customers, they partly compensated with loud colors, especially in shirts. In the late nineties the average Sunday shirt had about the same combination and tone of colors as were seen on the backs of the successful contemporary comedians. A popular selection was described by one distributor as being "Open front and back, fancy colored stripe, all overlaundered bosom shirt, with an extra long bosom and the proper width, in a very beautiful combination of striped pattern effects, full shoulder yoke, double stitched curved armhole, sleeve facing, cloth gusset, stayed bottoms, rolled seams and supplied with one pair of detachable cuffs." Collars for these shirts were in keeping with the graphically described "shirred" shirts. As for trade names, there were the Dixie, Gloucester, Tango, Dante, Zarko, and Congressional. The Zarko was described as having two-and-a-half-inch points, one-and-seven-eighths-inch band. Ties ran to stripes and plaids, except for the conservative black strings which had a Congressional flavor about them.

Like the sale of pants, shirts, and shoes, the hat trade was a profitable one. Southern men, unlike their wives and daughters, could buy hats of a fairly staple quality and style. Right after the end of the war the broad-brimmed gray semi-Confederate was a prime favorite, but gradully it was supplanted by the broad-brimmed black planter's hat. Most popular was the sober "staple-shape," which had a six-inch crown and a three-and-a-half-inch brim, and was sold wholesale for as little as seventy-five cents. In competition with the "staple-shape" were the planter and the broad-brimmed western styles. Most of them were doleful black in color and gave to their wearers a characteristic lantern-jawed, red-necked appearance.

The average wide-brimmed high-crowned country-store hat, like the famous splint bonnets, became a symbol of a kind of simple but raw agrarian dignity and respectability. Along with handle-bar mustaches and long sideburns they characterized the largest single political and economic group in the South. Politically most of the wearers of this kind of headgear were known as the "wool hat boys." It was they and their popular leaders who helped to stir up much of the bourbon wrath which filled long newspaper columns for three decades prior to 1900. Even as late as 1920 this "staple" black hat was still a favorite with men above thirty-five years of age.

Contemporary with the antiquated hoop skirt and the

bustle was the hard-plated derby which rivaled the "planter's favorite." It was a dashing Sunday hat for young men who were courting, or for landlords who sensed their importance and aped the urbane traveling man in dress. Many a two-dollar country-store derby and a cheap bargain-house Prince Albert coat gave southern males their only moment of feeling the slightest bit sophisticated. Among the more youthful wearers the derby-hat period in their lives was in fact a break between pulsating adolescence and complacent maturity.

Bearing little kinship to the wide-brimmed planter's hats and derbies were the cheap palmettos which were sold by the millions each spring. In parts of the South a hot April sun forced the purchase of these broad hats, and they were worn until the latter part of October. The art of their manufacture came from Portugal and Spain, but the products themselves came from the Philippines, Mexico, South America, China, India, Spain, and Portugal. Following pretty close to the course of the Mississippi River, the straw-hat trade moved northward and was finally localized in St. Louis. From this center there have gone out each year carloads of these sun breakers, which became important as a part of the southern agricultural tradition.

Almost as formal as the fancy "boiled shirts" were the raincoats or mackintoshes. The motif of pomposity and frills gave the raincoat of the eighties and nineties a general appearance completely out of keeping with the country-store trade. Wholesale houses produced pictures of stern males dressed in mackintoshes which were similar to the austere figure of Prince Albert printed on the sides of tobacco tins. For as little as one dollar and fifteen cents a North Carolina farmer clad in a long coat and cape could drive a pair of muddy, half-drowned tobacco mules away from a store with all the formal appearance of a French actor.

Clearly this type of coat was impractical. Distributors described it as having a "large detachable cape, black diagonal wale surface. Scotch plaid lining, with pure gum layer between. This garment is of superior make, cut full, is double stitched, and has patent cut pockets with tape around the seam to prevent same from tearing down, faced coat and cape." From the start the cape proved unsatisfactory, and it was laid aside. In the laying aside of the cape, however, there was a sentimental story. Sunday morning in the southern country was a time for fetching out mackintosh capes and stacking two straight chairs together preparatory to a siege of haircutting. Capes were hooked tightly under chins, and heavy-handed home barbers went into action with scissors and combs. Here was the native source of the famous "soup bowl" haircut which gave a bit of comic variety to the general pattern of southern life. Perhaps few customers ever looked at racks of mackintoshes between the late sixties and 1910 without shuddering. To them the dangling capes meant, not stormy weather, but long sieges of sitting in hard chairs while amateur barbers cut, slashed and pulled off enough of their hair to keep it from growing down their shirt collars. It was not until World War I that the "feather edge" haircut done with clippers came into popular style.

After 1900 a revolution occurred at the men's clothing counter. Overalls and jumpers made of blue denim finally took the place of jeans and coarse cassimere. Ready-made shirts or blue chambray piece goods crowded out the trade in cottonades and calico. The machine age caught up with the southern farmer, and in it his clothing, like his plow tools, came to him ready for use.

Blue denim overalls, brown duck pants, and khaki shirts of the post–World War I period have very nearly comprised the dress of the rural southerner. Piles of these types of clothing lie on open display upon the store counters. Where once men conceived of trousers being made of heavy jeans and carefully lined with unbleached domestic, they came to think of them in terms of material, dye, and shrinkage. Industrious advertisers have made the region conscious of certain qualities by publicizing new methods of processing cloth. A frugal backwoods customer adequately sized up the complications of the "sanforized" era in men's clothing when he sauntered into the Harbour Pitts store at Cerro Gordo, Tennessee, and asked a lady clerk to show him a pair of overalls. After a close examination of the garment he eyed her with a knowing look and asked naïvely if "these britches has been circumcised."

13

THE HALT, THE LAME, AND THE BILIOUS

SAMUEL HOPKINS ADAMS in 1904 wrote in *Collier's Weekly* a series of effective articles attacking the patent-medicine trade. He, along with the crusading Edward Bok of the *Ladies' Home Journal* and the American Medical Association, was preparing the end for "The Great American Fraud." Two years later the Pure Food and Drug Act was passed, thus ending one of the most highly imaginative periods of lying and swindling which the country has known.

Proprietary medicine makers found ready customers by the millions in the postwar South. Booming crossroads stores and villages became profitable outlets for a vast stream of tonics, pills, ointments, liniments, and dry-herb mixtures which poured out of "laboritories" in the larger distributing cities.

Three years after the Civil War the manufacturers of Plantation Bitters boasted that below the Potomac they were selling five million dollars' worth of their product each year. It was a profitable business to whet the South's indifferent appetites and to prod its sluggish colons. Alcohol-laden bitters of various types were regarded as fine conditioners for the former Confederate system, and country merchants lined their shelves with them. This was commonplace merchandise which required little or no selling, and only a slight portion of profits went for advertising.

Manufacturers were quick to sense the changed political condition of the South. Through the columns of the *Carolina Watchman* of Salisbury the makers of Kookman's bitters advertised their medicine and their political spleen in the same box. When Hinton Rowan Helper was replaced as Republican postmaster by a more subservient rival, the medicine men gloated. "This gentleman [Helper] is not radical enough to please his party and has been removed as postmaster at Salisbury—use Kookman's Bitters."

But the bitters trade was to move on to new fields. Country-store ledgers in Mississippi tell a long story of moral crusading against the use of liquor. To drink liquor was one thing, but to take a generous "dose" of port wine or alcohol in bitters was altogether different. Some of the stores' customers became so decrepit that they were forced daily to replenish their stock of "medicine." Long before Edward Bok and the Massachusetts Board of Health discovered the high alcoholic content of bitters, country-store customers in the South knew the secret, and not from laboratory analysis!

Gallant compounders and distributors of bitters made a brave fight to keep their ancient formulas before the public. They first played upon local political prejudices and then turned to the new age of industrial expansion for catch phrases and names with which to give their products a timeliness. In Chicago, H. E. Bucklen and Company gave their powerful medicine the name "electric." For a time it caught on and was a big money-maker. Even though the New South was in a period of economic and political prostration, it was far too rich to be handed over to the unimaginative bitters trade without keen opposition. Within ten years after Appomattox, trees, barns, and country stores were lined with garish ads offering peace and health to all who were in pain. It mattered not where nor what the pain was. The southern country was now free, and the "sky limit" was high.

From behind fierce "professional" whiskers, doctors of every description smiled benevolently and scientifically upon the bedraggled and aching humanity of the crossroads. These doctors bobbed up from Chicago, St. Louis, Louisville, New Orleans, Memphis, Atlanta, Baltimore, and Savannah, and some from as far away as France. They were first of all masters of a bewildered humanity's psychology. If a man did not know he was sick, then it was up to them to tell him that he was. Symptoms had to be described so vividly that the healthiest man in the country would at once feel hollow-chested and weak-kneed.

These bushy-faced savants knew the names of all the ailments which beset man with their devitalizing grips; but, most important of all, they had accurate notions of the loneliness of much of southern life. They knew it was a real joy for many southerners to have a pain and a bottle of alcoholic medicine to break the tedium of their environment. Men suffered a series of pains in the stomach, in the chest, or in the limbs. Women complained of continuous backache from bearing too many children or from their "peculiar female troubles," or from a combination of both.

Diets of fat meat, corn bread, hot biscuits, molasses, and white gravy week after week clogged the whole physical system with poisons of constipation. The skin broke out in sores. Teeth decayed from lack of care. The breath was bad. Backs gave out. The memory grew weak. Piles preyed upon most southerners like dread ghosts from the pine-hill graveyards. Appendixes ruptured in the night, and one victim after another was carted off to be impounded in the tight clay of the countryside.

Worn store customers, like John Holder who traded at Bill Nixon's place in "Possum Trot," Alabama, dragged themselves home with bags slung across their backs containing mixtures of groceries and medicines. John started the spring work with purchases of baking powder, salts, soda, coffee, calomel, quinine, and headache powders. It was a pitiful bill of goods, but the liberal assortment of drugs told a dramatic story.

Holder's Alabama neighbors were in the same predicament. Young women early lost the bloom of beauty and became crescent-shaped accessories of the washtubs and dishpans. They early reached the point where their husbands could scarcely live with them. Their children were cowed, and the happy home they had hoped for was lost in their eternal sufferings. It was to these helpless victims that the sanctimonious disciples of Aesculapius with their father-confessor methods of advertising appealed.

Mailbags, dragged down from the backs of sweating mules before crossroads stores, were crammed with bundles of dulcet messages of health. The saviors of womankind located in all parts of the country were energetic in distributing their mauve and pink advertisements. Dr. McLean in St. Louis offered strengthening cordials, volcanic oil liniment, vegetable conditioning powders, and a horrific compound labeled "tar wine lung oil." In New England that "benevolent" lady, Lydia E. Pinkham, with a properly bloused shirtwaist and a motherly soul, created a formula which was a boon to all females and to many males. In the South she was a strong competitor for Dr. King's New Discovery and McElrees' Wine of Cardui. Jones' Mountain Herbs brought health and good cheer, and from the byways letters of praise poured in to proclaim its saving grace. Mollie Ray of Lyonsville, Alabama, found it "a first-class medicine for ailments peculiar to any sex." From Nashville, Tennessee, there came a lifesaver called Coussen's Portaline or vegetable liver powder, which quickly developed an army of highly partisan letter writers who gave out profound literary and scientific observation on the power of this conditioner.

The liver, stomach, muscles, and reproductive organs were easily reached. Nature, so it was said many times, had paved the way through its plants, and all that remained was for the golden touch of a natural man of medicine to blend them into the perfect combinations. For diseases of the nervous system the remedies were far more complicated. Real study was necessary before a doctor could announce the astounding fact of his discovery that the nerves in most cases were in an advanced state of debility due to abject starvation. As a result, many wonderful neural foods in bright-colored packages found their way to the market. Among the host of discoverers of nervous starvation was Dr. I. C. Shoop of Racine, Wisconsin, who took great pride in showing his patients pictures of himself, his great pharmaceutical plant and his commodious, pillared mansion. Candidly, he was a prosperous man. His ingenious restorative was able to reach inside the nerves and to relieve the pressure of illness. This adroit scientist had evolved a theory of the "power nerves," and by treating the victims of nervous failure with food, he quickly restored them. In nearby Chicago, Dr. J. A. McGill profited by the same theory and placed upon the market nerve-food powders which he advertised in country stores by distributing tiny sample packages.

Just as southern women were beset with their "peculiar ailments" and their eternal headaches and backaches, southern gentlemen likewise were subjected to perplexing ills. Many wonderful remedies were concocted to smooth their paths. When the merchants of Baltimore co-operated in the eighties in preparation of an elaborate book containing a mercantile directory and a bit of Chesapeake Bay history as a compliment to the trade of South Carolina, they included an advertisement from John B. Hurtt and Company, distributors of various proprietary medicines. One of these was a nostrum prepared by the eminent French physician, Dr. Francis Boudalt. He had begun selling to the American public a medicine which was "endorsed by all physicians," and in 1876 the Republic had awarded him a gold medal at the Centennial in Philadelphia. His was truly a medicine of great power. It cured "weakness of memory, difficulty of recalling names or dates, inaptitude for business or study, lameness, weakness, weakness in the back or loins; weakness of the organs, with deficient, feeble powers; langour, easy fatigue from mental or physical labor, loss of nervous power and general tone of the system, weakness from loss of vital fluids at the stool or during urination, involuntary vital losses at night during dreams, weak or failing powers and threatened impotence, prostration and debility from overwork or mental effort."

It seems that the postwar male was the victim of a disease for which the bushy-faced doctors invented the name "spermatorhea." Among this new school of scientists of impotence was Dr. Culverwell who offered no medicine, but a little book which he sold through the country stores. It was he, perhaps, who popularized the name for the disease. He guaranteed debilitated males that he would aid them to marriage and happiness ever afterward. Drs. Culverwell and Boudalt had their competitors, and the increase of their advertising indicated something of the spread of venereal diseases in the southern region.

A continuous stream of letters, written on cheap green-striped pieces of nickel tablet paper, poured into the "confidential medical advisers" and told intimate tales of suffering females. Women wrote vivid descriptions of either their "private ailments" or those of their daughters. The unctuous solicitations of the county paper and almanac "doctors" gave rural woman hope of deliverance from her ills and loneliness. Their letters gave away their most intimate secrets and at the same time told of harrowing stories of indigestion, constipation, crying spells, spots before their eyes, kidney trouble, torpid livers, and complete loss of appetite.

There were the skinny females who were victimized by promises of flesh in abundance. Many of them hardly dared show themselves in public for fear of causing a sensation. But a few bottles of Phyto-Gingerin, Oxien, Kodol Dyspepsia Cure, Dr. King's New Discovery, Dr. Pierce's Favorite Prescription, Electric Bitters, half a dozen brands of sarsaparilla, McLean's Strengthening Cordial, Jones' Mountain Herbs, Herbs and Iron, McGill's Nerve Food Powders, Dr. Shoop's Restorative, Parker's Tonic, Howe's Arabian Tonic, Peruna, and a host of others restored them to shapely proportions. In many cases these compounds were found to have a high alcoholic content mixed with anise, opium, digitalis, senna, golden seal, oil of cloves, and water. An analysis of Dr. Pierce's Favorite Prescription furnished the *Ladies' Home Journal* in 1904 by Dr. Samuel W. Abbott, secretary of the Massachusetts Board of Health, showed that it contained tincture of digitalis, tincture of opium, oil of anise, and about 17 per cent alcohol. Even the famous female preparation of Lydia E. Pinkham of Lynn, Massachusetts, came under the ungallant analysis of the Massachusetts Board, and it was found to be at least two times as potent in alcoholic content as the same amount of Schlitz or Anheuser Busch beers.

In some instances nervous women drove their husbands to the point of despair. There was the famous Kentucky matron who shook so badly in her bed that her spouse had to move away from her side. One bottle of an "exotic" herb preparation restored her to a state of nervous equilibrium and improved health. Once again her bed was a place of quietude and rest. Her grateful husband returned to her side from his nocturnal couch of solitude. He was thankful indeed for the cure which had been effected; but, with more appreciation for his wife's cure than for the propriety of his language, he wrote a testimonial in which he said his wife was at last quiet enough for anybody to sleep with her.

A large measure of the success of the patent medicines upon the southern country-store shelves depended upon the advertising which they received. A note written in a scratchy, half-illiterate hand praising the results of a medicine was a fair start. The writing of testimonials, however, was work for a master psychologist. It was not a matter of making a simple statement that a certain doctor's vegetable conditioner powder or liver and kidney tonic cured a patient. A patient's ailment had to be described in vivid and all-inclusive language; in fact, the illness of one patient had to be that of thousands. In turn these testimonials found their way onto handbills and into almanacs and county papers. When a wholesale house accepted a proprietary medicine for sale among its customers, it did so with the promise that the manufacturers would conduct a vigorous advertising campaign.

Astounding testimonials were written about the curative powers of the medicines which lined the country-store shelves. It was a matter of great pride among the merchants themselves if one of their customers had his testimonial published. Such an honor placed the store, the testifier, and the community in the public notice. A country merchant in Tennessee wrote a note saying that two bottles of Dr. Roc's Rheumatic and Neuralgic Cure had done the wife of one of his customers more good than five doctors who had been waiting on her at a cost of $200. Over at Toisnot, North Carolina, W. B. Bott's wife had suffered with a running sore for fifty years, but Dr. Roc's medicine cured her within a few weeks. This was a marvelous medicine indeed; it cured headache, fullness in the head after eating, dizziness, dots before the eyes, shooting pains through the body, dyspepsia, and constipation. It was composed of "exotic herbs" suspended in a generous quantity of alcohol.

Joseph Shumaker and Company of Hamilton, Ohio, distributed through the country stores a folder advertising their miraculous rheumatism cure. It had the celestial name of Angeline, and it could be taken internally. The company submitted numerous testimonials, one of which came from a rheumatic who had been confined to his bed for years without hope of recovery. When he did move around it was on his knees with the aid of short crutches. The first bottle of Angeline got him out of bed, seven more put him on his feet, and four more put him astride a wheel in a bicycle race. Angeline had cured "the worst chronic case [of rheumatism] on record."

Merchants were bombarded with boxes of handbills, folders, almanacs, and calendars with their names printed on them. Trees, barns, and fences soon were lined with brightly colored, posters calling attention to the medicine. Sample bottles and packages were placed on store counters for customers to try. Wholesale distribution offered "free goods" with each shipment, and the merchant was put in a position to make nearly a hundred percent on his investment plus the clear profit of the "free goods."

Perhaps Fletcher's Castoria, which in time storekeepers came to regard as a "standard," was the most common of all the proprietary medicines. Advertisements showed babies with outstretched chubby arms screaming for the great soother of childish pains. Trained medicinal service for children was almost nonexistent, and many a harassed mother turned to this patent medicine which was so profusely advertised on trees, fences, barns, and store walls. Little thought was given to the contents of the slender vial of childish delight. It was comforting enough for a mother with a worn and exhausted body and frayed nerves to know that the baby was asleep.

Walking the floor of a lone farm house with a child choked with croup was an anxious experience for parents. A dozen folk remedies were nearly always available for just such an emergency, but these were slow in acting. It remained for a miracle to bring instantaneous relief. Tacked on the sides of stores and on posts and trees were streamers printed in bold type bearing the caption, "LITTLE GIRL ATTACKED." This bold heading brought many a prospective customer up closer to read that "Little Ones are the sunshine of every home. If you have children of your own you will be interested in the story of a night attack on the life of the young daughter of C. B. George of Winchester, Kentucky." George's story was of how he had saved his child's life with a few doses of One Minute Cough Cure. Another favorite was to raise in bold black type the caption, "DIED OF EXPOSURE," and then explain in fine type how lives can be saved with the "One Minute Cure."

Almanacs and samples were trade getters. One dose was equal to a good toddy, and a victim with an aching stomach found that a single spoonful of the medicine lulled his pain and sharpened his appetite so completely that he was able to eat everything in sight. Sitting before their hearths, ravenous victims showed neighbors their almanacs and calendars and told them of the medicine, and soon there was a good trade.

The so-called tonics were the best money-makers. So firmly was the idea of seasonal conditioning established among the rural people of the South that spring was ushered in with a round of medicine for nearly every individual. This was so true that the very name tonic symbolized a well-toned physical system. These tonics presented the greatest possibility for the highly imaginative compounders. Ability to achieve four major results was a necessary criterion of any tonic. It had to ease pain immediately, give a cheerful warming glow to the whole body, taste strongly of herbs, and move the bowels. Equally as important as the therapeutical immediacy of the medicine was a fetching name. Actually many of the tonics were manufactured by the same agency and sold to distributors who put their own names and brands upon them. This practice likewise applied to price. A wholesale house distributed a medicine with a label on it but no price mark. In their advertising they attracted customers from among the country-store merchants by telling them that they might establish a price which they thought their trade would bear. Such a medicine was Phyto-Gingerin, "the great Southern tonic." Spurlock-Neal of Nashville advertised this tonic to merchants as "a most powerful, efficient and pleasant remedy for all diseases arising from an impure state of the blood. *Nothing better for a general appetizing tonic.* Put up in 14 oz. round bottles, $4.00 a doz. No price is marked on bottle, therefore you make your own price. We are advertising PHYTO-GINGERIN extensively."

Next to the tonics for the country-store trade were the ointments. They were easily compounded and easily sold. In many communities a majority of the customers were cursed with running leg sores, which resisted all home-remedy efforts to cure them. It took powerful medicine to check these sores, and the patent ointment makers knew this fact. Patriarch of the salves was the famous Gray's Ointment, manufactured in Nashville, which antedated the Civil War. Early invoices from drug houses contained generous shipments of this salve. There was a general belief in the rural South that a strong-smelling, greasy ointment could reach deeply into the seat of pain and that it had "sure-fire" curative power.

Actually many of their preparations were little more than a mixture of petroleum jelly, cheap perfume and carbolic acid. Their curative powers amounted to nothing more than a temporary disinfecting and glazing over of stubborn ulcers.

Dr. King's New Discovery cured leg sores, abscesses, and consumption. This was a godsend in a country where leisons were such a factor in human welfare. Especially was this true among the large colored population, where leg sores were almost as common as legs themselves. The manufacturers of Bucklen's Arnica Salve made extreme claims for curative powers. Down in Rome, Georgia, J. M. Norris in 1885 was saved from an early grave by a combined "course" of Electric Bitters and Bucklin's Arnica Salve and Blood Purifier. From elsewhere in the South this combination robbed gaping graves by saving lungs, legs, arms, and faces.

Clever advertising in local papers and in the tons of seductive folders which passed through the mails called attention to the effective cures which could be expected from a score of medicines. A company in Atlanta sold a compound named B.B.B. which was a wonder. Spreading the name of Alexander H. Stephens across the top of a column of print in bold letters was an eye-catcher for their advertisement. However, it was not "Little Aleck" who had experienced physical salvation from the use of B.B.B. but a remote cousin. Since 1868 this railway-clerk relative had suffered from a ravenous cancer which spread over his face. He finally discovered B.B.B. just in time, and between February and April he cured the cancer. In proof of this fact the advertiser printed a testimonial from the editor of the Athens *Banner-Watchman* saying that James A. Greer was an honest, upright citizen. In Atlanta the good work of B.B.B. went on with success. James Clemmons' wife was saved from a cancerous death when both of her breasts were healed.

Down in Paris, Texas, there was great excitement. By melodramatic accident, samples of Dr. King's New Discovery and New Life Pills found their way to the deathbed of J. E. Corley. He was bedridden with consumption, and many doctors had shaken their heads in confusion and despair. Two boxes of pills and a couple of bottles of New Discovery saved his life. Everywhere in the South aged consumptive and cancer-ridden citizens spoke with ancient authority in favor of Electric Bitters, McLean's Strengthening Eye Salve, Swift's Specific, Tar Wine Lung Balm, Dr. Bull's Golden Eye Salve, DeWitt's Witch Hazel Salve, and Mark's Carbolized Gum Herb Salve. These were used nearly always in cases where the doctors had given up and backed away.

The ointments had other functions. Gray's Ointment particularly was an effective means of delousing a family. Wherever there was a country school, there was certain to be a rapid spread of the socially outcast head crawlers. A generous application of ointment mixed with sulphur and a fair degree of social isolation usually restored a squeamish family to its place of former dignity. This same mixture was highly useful in holding other social diseases reasonably within check.

Pills have ever been common stock-in-trade with the rural stores. Entries on almost every page of account books tell stories of thousands of pills reaching the consumer. Pharmaceutical houses rolled a brown sugar-coated mass which they correctly labeled "compound cathartic." This common pill was an important product of the trade, and at the same time it was a powerful purgative. The pharmacists who rolled millions of pills of all colors and sizes must have had a keen Irish sense of humor. Among brands advertised from every country-store door were the "big five," names which are virtually suggestive of the crossroads trade itself. These were Ramon's, Tutt's, Doan's, Carter's Little Liver Pills, and DeWitt's highly volatile Little Early Riser's.

The pill makers kept careful track of their victims. They never doubted what results the pill takers wanted, but there was a substantial difference in attitudes toward the sizes and shapes of pills which they would swallow. Some customers measured pill values quantitatively, while others were more of a qualitative turn of mind. Carter's and DeWitt's products catered to the trade by producing two sizes and left the matter of selection up to the storekeeper, who was depended upon to know the general sensitivity of his customers. Carter's early advised the bilious public that "If you are taking the large old fashioned griping pills try Carter's Little Liver Pills and take some comfort. A man can't stand everything."

Pills were potent remedies. As an example, it was claimed that one Smith's Bile Bean a day would "cure biliousness, sick headache in four hours, prevent chills, relieve neuralgia, cure fever, a sour stomach, bad breath, and clear the skin." About the time in the spring that turnip greens were ripe to pick and crops were ready for planting, entries in account books contain a generous sprinkling of pill orders. For twenty-five cents a countryman could purchase a box of pills for a "round" of spring medicine which would ease his tradition-burdened conscience.

Swamplands of the South sent customers piling into the stores seeking cures for wracking chills and fevers. Medicine drummers struggling along the miry country roads which crossed the barren pine lands took time to nail tons of bright yellow signs to trees, barn sides, and even the fronts of dwelling houses. These signs proclaimed the virtues of scores of chill tonics. They were 666, King of Malaria, Rich's, Wampole's, Kodol, Grove's, Johnson's, McLean's, Gross', and others. On every side the southerner was reminded by signs that his land was beset with devitalizing malaria. Chill tonics returned almost as much money as the cotton crops. There was an eternal fight against the insidious germ which broke down the red corpuscles and brought on body-wracking quakes. This was a fertile area for the tonic exploiters, and they worked it with diligence. Boats floated up and down southern rivers loaded with chill tonics, and salesmen disposed of them in large quantities to riverside merchants. Spurlock-Neal, the big drug house in Nashville, sold Rich's Tasteless Chill Tonic on the basis of "no cure, no pay." This product was put up in "the neatest package and largest bottle on the market for the money. It is so pleasant to taste, that the *Young, Middle Aged,* and *Old* all enjoy taking it." It was sold for forty-five dollars a gross, less 10 per cent in four months and plus twelve dollars' worth of "free goods" in other family medicines. The merchant was guaranteed a profit of 118 per cent.

Distributing free samples of new brands as sales attraction was a practice followed particularly in the sale of medicines and tobacco. The country merchant nearly always disposed of his extra goods at a clear profit to himself and without ever letting his customers know their origin. It was the custom for many purchasers to ask the storekeeper to prescribe a medicine for them, and he could always recommend the medicine which he received free.

Country-store shelves were also piled with the nonproprietary remedies which were regarded by the storekeepers as "standard" merchandise. Calomel and castor oil were in strong competition with the proprietary pills. An aching stomach was a sure sign that the sufferer needed a purgative, and the stronger the purgative the more effective was the job which it performed. There was a general notion among the medically uninformed country trade that the reason for stomach disorders was the fact that the intestines had something in them that should be forced out. It seems never to have occurred to them that their troubles might be organic. One of the mortal diseases of the South was "cramp colic," and many a southerner found his way early in life to the graveyard because he tried to relieve his abdominal pains with large doses of calomel, salts, or castor oil.

Before the passage of the federal narcotic laws in 1911, laudanum, opium, morphine, and paregoric appeared regularly on drug invoices and among the items listed in personal orders and accounts. Loneliness of the surroundings of the rural South preyed upon the minds of temperamentally unstable persons, and eventually they resorted to the use of whisky or narcotics to break the tedium of life. Victims sat night after night on front porches or on rickety doorsteps with nothing to do but listen to the call of whippoorwills or to the monotonous rasping of "July" bugs. Or during the winter months they remained cooped in ill-smelling, cold shacks, where they became as bored with life as caged animals. Soon diseases, either real or imagined, began to plague their bodies. There was one quick way to cure loneliness and disease.

An eighth of an ounce of P.&W. morphine sold at wholesale for about 26 cents, and it retailed for as much as 75 cents; a half-ounce retailed for about $2.70. That once-a-week entries for morphine appeared in so many books is proof enough that addicts were numerous. Time after time on the credit side of the ledger there would appear the price of a hen or five dozen eggs, and in the debit column a vial of morphine or laudanum, showing that customers kept themselves supplied with narcotics from their chicken yards.

Medical service was inferior, and often completely untrained doctors solved their therapeutic riddles with a dose of morphine, laudanum, or opium. These drugs brought quick relief, and frequent use of them over a period of weeks kept the patient quiet until nature could intervene and effect a cure. In cases of acute illnesses, ignorant doctors were quick to use the most active sedative available. So general was the use of these agents that the rural quacks themselves eased their own troubled and befuddled minds. Storekeepers kept local doctors supplied with narcotics, and an army of rural drug fiends are to be found upon the debit side of both the merchants' and ill-prepared doctors' ledgers of life's misdeeds.

Morphine was a fairly gentle palliative which eased its victims into a happy frame of mind. Its gentleness, however, tended to wear away after a brief period of use, and the habitual users began to show signs of nervous disintegration. But seldom did the habitués of morphine reach the violent nervous state of those hardened "laudanum drinkers," factious wild men when they were in the threadbare stages of desire. Frequently they tore into stores and snatched at ounce bottles of the liquid, drinking it in a maudlin frenzy in order to restore some measure of stability. At other times it was with a certain degree of pride that luckless individuals sat by the stove and drank their vials of poison. They would hold the bottles up to the light and brag to their neighbors that the contents would kill half a dozen ordinary men.

Opium in a less violent form than laudanum was cut, bit by bit, from large gum balls. Wholesale houses distributed it either in the form of gum or as a powder. Its effect was practically the same as that of its liquid form. Gum seems to have been the more popular form among the rural users. It was sold at the rate of $3.10 an ounce in gum or at $4.00 in powder. Wholesale houses always listed it as one of the standard necessities for the drug shelf.

Paregoric, a milder form of camphorated tincture of opium, came distinctly within the classification of painkillers and baby pacifiers. It was more frequently used than any of the other forms of opiates. A user of opium or morphine could find momentary solace in an overdose of this mild camphorated mixture, but generally it was reserved for nursery use. This medicine was a competitor on the long lists of bottle goods which were placed on store shelves with no more definite description than the general one of "colic cures." These were brewed for the specific purpose of making a baby forget the infantile pain which started a crying spell, or of making an adult forget the fact that between his head and heels there was a considerable yardage of feverish intestines. It seems that colic cures were created for the particular intent of heading off the excruciating pains of an unruly appendix until gangrene could complete its fatal work.

King of the "standards" was turpentine, a product of the tidewater pine forests. On every mantel board, be it ramshackle Negro cabin or pillared mansion, turpentine occupied a place of medicinal leadership. It was the universal medicine. Long before Louis Pasteur established his germ theory, southerners were combating infections with turpentine and pine resin. Everything from a cut finger to worms, backache, kidney trouble, sore throat, rheumatism, croup, pneumonia, toothache, and earache was treated with this cheap native antiseptic. Children with smothering colds gagged at heaping spoons of sugar dampened down with it. Turpentine had three important medicinal requisites: It smelled loud, tasted bad, and burned like the woods on fire. Southern kidneys paid a heavy price for its frequent use.

Rows of castor-oil bottles standing in solid phalanxes on the shelves of the country stores caused the entire trade to shudder. Like turpentine, the castor-oil bottle stood in the front line of the medical ramparts. This greasy purgative which slid down throats and left behind it a nauseous film was a major item on the drug invoices. For a merchant to be without castor oil was almost as ridiculous as for him to be without sugar, salt, soda, or matches. No extravagant claims were ever made for this commonplace cathartic. Old-timers knew it was a bowel mover, and that was testimonial enough.

Major purging was work for calomel and its running mate, Dover's powder. Spring was not only a time to clean house, fence rows, and ditch banks, but likewise the season of cleaning the intestinal tract and of a round of tonic.

A round of calomel was an ideal physical hyphen between winter and spring. For unclogging the human system, said the wise folk-practitioners, there was nothing like it. It was just the conditioner to prepare for the approaching season of fresh vegetables and half-ripened fruits. Stores carried this drug in large quantities, and almost always the merchant or one of his clerks had to measure the correct portions for the purchasers. This mercurial drug was given in "rounds" of broken doses, and thus it was that measuring calomel in a country store became an art requiring some degrees of exactness. At best, however, the amount of the dosage was purely guesswork, and the results were equally irregular. It was in the selling of opiates and calomel that the country stores perhaps made their most serious medicinal mistakes. Addicts found the cheap and readily available stocks of narcotics a godsend, and many a rural user came to a tragic end because of this. But the indiscriminate use of calomel was more generally harmful. It always injured its victims because they were totally ignorant of its dangerous powers.

There were scores of other medicines, such as Epsom salts, saltpeter, copperas, sulphur, and bluestone, which were looked upon as staple goods. Salts were bought in large quantities and sold in smaller amounts for nominal prices. But, like turpentine, these medicines were regarded as being mild and necessary to rural well-being.

Aside from the miraculous elixirs of new life and the forthright purgatives on the drug shelves, there were preparations for the more vainglorious and fastidious. Well-advanced southern male and female candidates for matrimony, conscious of their ripening years, fought valiantly, if with faulty weapons, against gray hair. Spurlock-Neal and Company offered Spurlock's Quick Hair Dye and as a special inducement included a free brush with each bottle. This was a precious item and caught the eye of the trade. Purchased at wholesale for $1.75 a dozen bottles, it was retailed at the merchant's economic discretion.

For those whose locks were not traced with gray, there were the pomades of a hundred different brands. One of the quickest ways to make a small fortune in the South after the Civil War was to manufacture and distribute a reasonably satisfactory hair straightener. Any pomade which could withstand with fair success the entangling influence of wet weather assured a handsome profit. The pomades removed from the head of the colored female the tight string-wound rolls of hair and gave her fluffy locks instead. Plain petroleum jelly, one of the first patent straighteners, was soon pushed into the background by more elaborate mixtures in gaudy tin cans and wide-mouthed bottles. Elaborate labels vividly portrayed long, waving tresses of a negroid belle—or, sometimes, the long, wavy hip-length crown of a fairer daughter. For twenty-five cents a rural woman, white or colored, could buy a tin of highly perfumed jelly which would give her a pliant head of hair for twenty-four hours at least. Even the southern males found the pomades a useful aid in giving their hair and mustaches a "fixed" appearance.

The drug shelf was thus a place of both physical and spiritual solace. Sooner or later every member of the community made of it a place of call. Literary men of a base, but exceedingly clever, stripe popularized it by filling the "patent" columns of the local papers with advertisements and testimonials of the most seductive nature. Nearly every store became a dazzling proclamation of biliousness and nicotine. Roadsides were given the air of "civilization" by myriad signs, some of these as sensitive to regional lines as the southern Democratic party.

Even the sanctity of the home was not spared from the insidious literary and artistic triflings of the great "scientists of the age." Walls were covered with calendars which were remiss in art but eloquent in claims for the curative virtues of their medicines. Underneath a lithographed painting of rearing horses towering over the scantily draped body of Achilles, Dr. McLean proclaimed extravagantly the powers of his volcanic oil liniment. Other artistic morsels were available to break the monotony of drab bedroom and parlor walls in exchange for the privilege of conveying messages of health. Among these degenerate Victorian masterpieces of the lithographer's stones were such subjects as "Day Dreams," "Little Barefoot," and "Pharoah's Horses." This inside medicinal advertising dealt southern artistic taste a deadening blow from which it has never fully recovered.

The literary aspects of medicinal advertising of the post–Civil War period were perhaps the outstanding achievement of a vast army of restored humanity in the South. A veritable flood of little memorandum books poured into the stores. One side of their pages bore a combination of testimonial and descriptive matter of the medicines which they advertised and the other was a ruled page for notes. Writing testimonials was a matter of high literary attainment for many people. One of the surest ways of getting one's writing into print was to prepare a glowing testimonial for a medicine. Too, it was possible to get one's picture published in a memorandum book, if real effort was exerted in preparing a fetching letter describing one's diseases and speedy cures.

The more original the source and the more sensational the use of a medicine, the better the chances of publication. From Ranchero Grande, Texas, J. E. Pierce sent the cheering word, "The cowboys carry Simmons Liver Regulator with them and take it when they feel bilious. They use the dry powder, taking a pinch of the same and washing it down with a little water, it having a satisfactory effect." Surely it was pleasing to malnourished customers of country stores in the cotton belt to read that they could take the same medicine which performed such wonders for the cowboys of the wild and wooly West. It was downright heartening to know that Judge Roy Bean, Andy Adams, Wyatt Earp, Doc Holliday, and the Clanton Gang were all saved from bilious attacks by swallowing generous pinches of Dr. Simmons' Liver Regulator. Biliousness was not all it cured. The cowboys did not go around with "a diseased stomach, which had a morbid longing for something to stimulate and excite it. . . ." "Solomon," wrote the medicine men, in all his wisdom had said of liquor, "I will seek it yet again." He would "seek it yet again" if his stomach was "depraved." "A man with a *pure stomach,* a clear skin and an *unclouded* brain has no desire to be a drunkard—Simmons Liver Regulator produces this effect by arousing the *torpid digestive organs* to healthy action, counteracting the desire for more drink, thus *promoting* the cause of temperance in an *effective* manner."

Selling medicine and moral purity was, of course, not confined alone to cowboys and drunkards. There were the ladies, "God bless them." A poetic script writer broke into sentimental verse:

If your wife is weak and ailing
And has trouble with her Liver,
And you want to make her happy,
What's the best thing you can give her?
You might give her a nice new bonnet,
But her profit will be much greater
If you give her a bottle or two
Of Simmons Liver Regulator.

In line with these tender thoughts, an army of benevolent "doctors" labored to make woman's life ever a happier one. They strove manfully to lighten the yoke of womanhood, and triumphantly a host of their patients wrote of their miraculous recoveries. Miss Ellen Otey of Bedford City, Virginia, was troubled for three years "with female weakness." "I had," she wrote, "two physicians but neither did me any good. . . . I thought I would die with pains in my back and stomach. I also had chills. I could not get up without fainting. One of my friends told me to write to you, so I did without delay. I took three bottles of Dr. Pierce's Favorite Prescription and two of his 'Golden Medical Discovery.' I am glad to say I do not have any pains at all and I am in better health now than I ever was in my life."

In the thriving country store village of Oakfuskie, Alabama, Mrs. J. T. Smith lay in her bed daily and expected the cold cadaverous hand of death to lay hold of her. She "was afflicted and suffered untold pains and misery, such as no pen can describe, for six years," but she was saved in the nick of time by a great "female regulator."

Using the normal fears of approaching motherhood, the medicine men printed tons of booklets and handbills giving unctuous advice and assurance that there was no need of fright, provided expectant mother followed instructions and used their tonics. For instance, the "Favorite Prescription" was a mother's dearest friend, "for it makes child birth easy by preparing the system for parturition, thus assisting Nature and shortening 'Labor.' The painful ordeal of child birth is robbed of its terrors, and the danger thereof greatly lessened, to both mother and child. . . ."

One after the other the "medicine books" distributed through the southern country stores described the region's diseases, and then proceeded to produce testimonials to show that there were wonderful cures. One of them said in 1898 that "*mal-aria* signifies 'bad air.' It is generally understood that malaria poisons are absorbed into the system from the atmosphere. The fact is, there are always liable to be more or less unhealthy infectious conditions in the atmosphere; it is absolutely impossible to prevent malarial germs from entering the system, but it is altogether possible to prevent their doing harm after they get in." This was a statement which attracted attention. In the South "mal-aria" signified not only "bad air" but likewise untold suffering and debility. A man with malaria was willing to take a chance with any medicine which promised relief. It was a fact that there was a belief that chills and fevers came from the air. Generally people living in the South believed night air was bad for the health, but that swamp air especially was bad.

From throughout the South there came a steady stream of letters bearing glad tidings of cures. Most of these notes of cheer were boring because of their similarity. Exceptions to this were those notes which came up from Texas. The tall men there never did things in halves. When a Texan was chronically ill, it was not a matter of five or ten years. Picture the horrible plight of Mr. Shields of Oakwood, "who had piles for forty years. He had utterly despaired of being helped by medical aid, abandoned all labor, and the past year was subject to fearful spasms, by which his body was drawn into contortions. Mr. Shields also had convulsions almost daily. On one occasion of his sufferings Col. Manning, a friend and distinguished citizen, happened to be present, and having heard of C. C. C., sent by express for the medicine, and it was afterwards applied, giving instant relief." Within a week this victim was able to attend to business as a free man.

In all of this literature of healing three facts stand out. The medicines advertised were for the common man. At least 95 per cent of the testimonials originated in the tiny villages. It was the rural man and woman who took the medicine and then wrote about it. Sometimes salesmen driving through the country solicited testimonials and pictures as a part of their business. There was ever a conscious effort to discredit local doctors and occasionally other patent medicines. On one occasion Dr. M. A. Simmons warned: "Beware of 'Black Draught'; 'Simmons Liver Medicine'; by J. H. Zeilin and Co. when sold as 'the same' as 'Dr. M. A. S. L. M.' "

This medicine business was a major reason for crusading for a Pure Food and Drug Act in the first decade of the present century. One by one the *Journal of the American Medical Association* exposed the famous doctors' humbuggery in its column "Propaganda for Reform."

Edward Bok and Samuel Hopkins Adams would have given

up in despair had they appreciated fully the efficiency of the country store as a dispenser of the medicines they so heartily condemned. It was in these stores that the medicine manufacturers had their most important sources of income. They catered to people who were ignorant of proper medical care and without adequate trained medical service.

14

THE FARMER AND HIS ALMANAC

FROM ONE END of the South to the other, two familiar proprietary medicines have had a constant sale. Wine of Cardui and Thedford's Black Draught have been as well known in the store trade as sardines and cheese. Wherever a southern store opened its doors after 1879, these medicines were among the first articles placed on its shelves. Both medicines were made from original semifrontier folk formulas concocted in the 1830's. Black Draught was compounded by Dr. A. O. Simmons, a Tennessee frontiersman, who first commercialized it in 1840. Sixteen years later ownership of the recipe passed to his son-in-law, J. H. Thedford, and in that year, according to data on the packages, the M. A. Thedford Company began large-scale manufacture and sale of this vegetable laxative.

Contemporary with the introduction of Thedford's Black Draught was a new medicine produced by R. L. McElree which he called Wine of Cardui. It was designed especially for the ailments of women. From the beginning this medicine has used the basic ingredients of alcohol, blessed thistle, golden seal, and black haw, and throughout its existence it has rivaled its laxative counterpart in sales. Within a decade manufacture and sale of these medicines reached considerable proportions.

Perhaps no business enterprise in the New South has had a more representative history of the postwar period than has the Chattanooga Medicine Company. When the Civil War ended, two Federal soldiers, Z. C. Patten and T. H. Payne, were mustered out of the army in Chattanooga. They formed a partnership for selling paper, blankbooks, and miscellaneous stationery supplies. Business in Chattanooga was in a disorderly state because of the chaos caused by the war, and the rapid surge forward of business reorganization. Soon after its formation the Patten-Payne partnership acquired control of the debt-laden Chattanooga *Times*. This fortunate deal perhaps inspired Z. C. Patten to favor a program of expansion, while his more conservative partner wished to hold on to the property which they already owned. Patten, however, gave rein to his expansive ideas and bought the formulas of Thedford's Black Draught and McElree's Wine of Cardui, and organized the Chattanooga Medicine Company for large-scale production of these medicines.

Fourteen years after the end of the war Chattanooga had practically recovered from the rigors of reconstruction, and was rapidly becoming a prosperous city of the postwar South. Falling under the spell of southern progress, Adolph Ochs of Knoxville, an enterprising lad of twenty, began his illustrious career with the struggling Chattanooga *Times*. He was offered the paper for the modest price of $800, but, even with the aid of his friend Colonel E. A. James, he was unable to borrow more than $300 on his note. In two years, however, the youthful publisher had increased his paper's business to such an extent that it cost him $10,000 to complete the purchase which was originally offered him for $800. The lack of $500 cost him $9,500. Before Ochs became owner of the paper, a negotiated sale was necessary to clarify its final disposition. Through this deal, arranged by Z. C. Patten, Ochs became indebted to the drug manufacturer, and the two later developed a warm friendship.

Doubtless it was because of this friendship that Adolph Ochs was tempted to violate a rule of publishing ethics which he upheld so rigorously in his later years as publisher. In addition to his responsibilities in the management of his paper, he became the second president of the Chattanooga Medicine Company. Thus it was that medicine making and newspaper publishing in Chattanooga were intimately linked for a brief time. Ochs, however, in later years went on to bigger things in New York, and Z. C. Patten's medicine company concentrated its attention on the rich medicine trade of the New South.

Sticking rather faithfully to the territory of the former Confederate states, with Kentucky, West Virginia, and Missouri added for good measure, the Chattanooga Company sought business at every crossroads store. Publicity was the soul of the business, and salesmen were instructed to see that the name of the two medicines became household words in the region. Freely they wielded the tack hammer and paintbrush. The only paint used on many barns and buggy sheds in the South was that which proclaimed in black and yellow the inseparable names of Black Draught and Wine of Cardui.

In 1884, when the Pure Food and Drug Act was unknown and the lid was off, a medicine manufacturer's ad writer was constrained by no inhibitions when it came to boosting his products. Of Wine of Cardui, a newspaper ad said, "This pure wine is a simple vegetable extract without intoxicating qualities, and has proved to be the most astonishing *tonic for women* known to medical science."

Twenty years later when Samuel Hopkins Adams published his "Great American Fraud" articles, he mentioned the advertising of the Chattanooga Medicine Company as not being suitable reading material for a family gathered around the breakfast table. In keeping with this reformer's cryptic remarks, some of the Cardui ads do constitute a revealing chapter in medical publicity. Somewhere in the periphery there seemed always to be a literate husband who was anxious to testify to his mate's suffering and final cure. "My wife," said a well-known gentleman, "has been in delicate health for fifteen years. She suffered fearfully every month with pains and excessive menses. Doctors could do her no good. One bottle of McElree's Wine of Cardui restored her health, and she gained eighteen pounds of weight in two months while taking it." This was good stuff, but not good enough, and being a little carefree in the wording of his sentences, the copy writer took his lead from the enthusiastic husband. He said, "McElree's Wine of Cardui is recommended as a tonic for delicate ladies. It was tested in 7000 cases and *cured* 6500 of them. Its astonishing action mystified Doctors, delighted sufferers, and restored thousands of suffering women to health and happiness." Obviously a batting average of 6,500 out of 7,000 cases was enough to mystify the doctors and delight the sufferers. Likewise for a puny and failing wife to gain eighteen pounds from taking one bottle of Wine of Cardui explains why Z. C. Patten's friends sometimes chided him by asking whether his "female preparation" was "a beverage or a medicine."

Interestingly enough, in sixty years of ad writing, the man at the copy desk has grown considerably more conservative. He has become exceedingly skeptical of the word *cure;* in fact, there is no such word in his glossary, and he will not let a grateful patron become so exuberant in praise as to say that she has been healed. Illustrative of this was the moderation with which Mrs. John A. Bailey, R.F.D. 2, Arab, Alabama, wrote in 1941 that "my use of Cardui dates back to my mother's home, she would give me Cardui when I needed it and it always *seemed to help me*. I have used it since, when needed. Cardui is the only *tonic* I have ever used."

Even Samuel Hopkins Adams' gentleman of the Victorian breakfast table would find practically nothing in the new-style advertising to offend his sensitive womenfolk. Frankly Thedford's Black Draught has become a forthright laxative containing, in its liquid form, "extract of senna, rhubarb, cinnamon, clove, nutmeg, and annis." In powdered form the formula is essentially the same. Even more interesting is the candid warning which appears on the back of the traditional yellow pasteboard packages. "Some people," say the manufacturers, "have a tendency to rely too much on laxatives, which, if continued a long time, may lead to too much dependence on them. Medical authorities advise against this." This admission within itself constitutes a significant chapter in American social progress which perhaps explains why Black Draught has been able to enjoy a rich market for so long a period. Neither Wine of Cardui nor Black Draught was involved in any of the major analytical "line-ups" of the proprietary drug offenders listed by the public health boards until 1914.

In 1914 a series of articles appeared simultaneously in the *Journal of the American Medical Association* and *Harper's Weekly Magazine* which made an ill-advised attack upon John A. Patten and the Chattanooga Medicine Company. This resulted in three libel suits which dragged on for two years in the courts. Finally in 1916 two of these suits were decided in favor of the Chattanooga Medicine Company, and the personal suit brought by John A. Patten was abated by his death before the case was finished. These famous lawsuits grew out of a strange bit of social journalism which came at the end of the stormy period of muckraking. The editor of the *Journel of the American Medical Association* believed that this suit was "by far the most important of its kind that has ever been tried." It might be that it did serve as a source of clarifying the state of contention which had long existed between the American Medical Association and the proprietary medicine industry.

Literature and advertising material of the Chattanooga Medicine Company until the time of the world war indicated that the business was largely southern in nature. It was not an important factor in the highly competitive medicine trade outside of the cotton and tobacco belts. With the advent of the war, however, the population of the South underwent a significant change. Southerners moved away to the large industrial centers in the North and took with them their demands for regional foods and medicines. This was especially the case when southern automobile workers poured into Detroit. They began demanding Black Draught and Cardui, and the Chattanooga Medicine Company expanded its business in this direction, with the result that in the last twenty-five years this business, which was built upon the New South, became a factor in the age of the new American industrialism. Likewise, southerners filtering into other centers like New York and Chicago have increased the demand for these medicines.

Significantly the expansion of the sales area of the Chattanooga Medicine Company is indicative of the change which has taken place in the South itself. Some of its population has moved away to other areas where economic opportunities have been better, but in this moving the southerners have taken with them their regional tastes and demands. A large proportion of emigrants from the South have carried with them their country-store tastes, and in some instances have helped materially to shape the pattern of merchandising in northern communities where they have lived.

The clever merchandising of the Chattanooga Medicine Company has certainly claimed a big portion of the southern drug market. By some means Black Draught, especially, became practically a folk remedy. It was used for everything. When a man had a boil on his leg, he made a poultice of the powder. When a hornet stung him, he dampened a pinch and applied it to the infected spot. Characteristic of Black Draught's popularity was the testimonial of Andrew Jackson Flippen of Alief, Texas. He said he was named for General Jackson because his father once had seen the General, and since 1860 he had taken Black Draught, which he bought at "a little settlement store called Yegua in Washington County." Merchants themselves came to consider Wine of Cardui and Black Draught as "standards." When a customer wanted a purgative, or when his ills sounded as if he could be relieved with one, the storekeeper sold him the laxative. Likewise, he recommended Wine of Cardui for every ailment of womankind, and sometimes he sold ailing men customers bottles of it on the elementary assumption that it tasted enough like medicine to do good. In fact, some male users were ready to testify that they had been benefited by its use, even though the *Viburnum prunifolium* and blessed thistle found nothing in their systems upon which to react.

Equally as universal as the medicines, and more generally popular, were the indispensable pair, the *Ladies Birthday Al-*

manac and *DeVoe's Daily Weather Forecast and Calendar.* The *Birthday Almanac,* first published in 1890, rapidly became a southern institution. From its first issue it contained tables of the chronological cycles, the seasons, holidays, fixed and movable festivals, eclipses, time of rising and setting of sun and moon, and the signs of the zodiac arranged about the disembowled figure of a man. Each month was listed separately with two pages of detailed weather and seasonal information. The monthly chronology was arranged so as to give weather signals, zodiac signs, standard time changes, and birthday and Biblical proverbs and references. At the foot of the column was the DeVoe weather chart presenting a general over-all long-range weather prediction for each month.

Mixed in with the weather forecasts were proverbs and bits of miscellaneous historical information. On page two there was an anniversary table which served the purpose of a short chronological encyclopedia. For instance, almanac users were told these facts: "April 1, April Fool's Day"; "April 13, Thomas Jefferson's Birthday"; "May 13, Settlement of Jamestown, 1607"; and "June 3, Birthday of Jefferson Davis. Confederate Memorial Day in Tennessee." Scattered through the book were words of ancient wisdom—"Plant your taturs when you will, they won't come up until April," "Till April's dead change not a thread," "Whatever March does not want April brings along," "The more thunder in May, the less in August and September," and "Be sure of hay 'til the end of May." Added to these folk proverbs were daily scriptural references in keeping with the season.

Weather predictions and chronology of both the *Ladies Birthday Almanac* and the weather chart were the work of Professor Andrew DeVoe, an amateur meteorologist of Hackensack, New Jersey. Professor DeVoe made weather a profitable hobby. He worked out a system by which he believed he could make successful long-range weather predictions by the relative positions of the earth and sun. Weather, he felt, was governed by the angles of the earth because they in turn determined the eclipse. That he was successful in forecasting weather events was attested by the fact that he predicted both the Galveston Flood and the Florida Hurricane. These forecasts brought the almanac and weather-chart maker much newspaper publicity and established him as something more than an amateur in meteorology.

"The Cardui Calendar and Weather Chart" was equally as famous as the almanac. Professor DeVoe transferred his chronology and weather forecasts to the shoulders of the large calendar face. Figures of the calendar were in bold black-face type inside large red-lined squares containing sufficient blank space for miscellaneous notations. Smaller red script lines underneath the numerals gave notices of religious holidays and sun and moon changes. But of equal interest was the fact that many significant anniversaries in southern history were recorded. These included arbor days, famous southern battles, the birthdays of southern statesmen and military figures, and days on which there was to be no rural free delivery.

The large blank spaces around the bold black letters of the calendars became places for making notes of all sorts. Breeding records of livestock, the setting of hens, and the births and farrowing of calves, colts, and pigs were recorded there. Often purchases from the stores were set down in the squares on the proper dates. Time records of wage hands were written on the calendars. Women sometimes used the squares for the purpose of keeping check on their menstrual periods. For those who dreaded pregnancy the calendar's stories became a mild sort of torture. For those who became pregnant the notes kept the date of the expected confinement in mind. Because of these business and intimate personal data, the DeVoe Weather Chart and Calendar was often left hanging on living and store room walls for several years at a time.

Calendar headings were cut so that specially printed cards bearing merchants' names and business legends could be inserted. From choice of stereotyped headings, merchants selected one which suited their business, and it was inserted in the calendar. In 1904 the calendar manufacturers advertised that a single merchant the year before had ordered seven thousand. "Business men," said the circular, "have for years sought in vain for such a Calendar [*sic*]. We now put it in your easy reach." Storekeepers were told that "you can find no better investment than to put out as many of these calendars as possible. Do so and each one will be making you friends and customers every day in the year.

Calendars were published and sold to storekeepers at ten cents a single copy, without business cards, and for four and five dollars per hundred for quantity lots with cards inserted. Historically calendars and almanacs have been a part of both the store and medicine business. The Chattanooga Company, growing out of a stationery store, has since 1890 maintained a considerable printing plant in which its advertising material has been prepared. In 1915 the company had approximately thirty thousand store outlets, and each of these ordered calendars and almanacs in fairly large quantities. Thus the medicine company's printing business has been in its way comparable to that of the two famous newspapers developed by its second president.

It might be much easier to arrive at a notion of the economic and social influence which the two medicines have had on the South, than to determine that of the almanac and calendar. Perhaps Professor DeVoe's weather charts have been more influential between 1890 and 1920 in determining the planting and cultivating of crops than have been many of the southern county agents. In matters of agriculture where the exact date was a factor, the DeVoe chronology was always at hand. Many farmers depended upon the changes of moon and sun time, especially moon changes in planning their planting and harvesting activities. Realizing that the almanac was a factor in farming, the editor advised farmers that he could not devise a chart of plantings of a sufficiently simplified nature to make it practicable, and he advised them either to consult their county demonstration agent or write their congressmen for information. Even though the almanac has lacked a planting guide, it has remained a farmer's handbook. It told him approximately when he could expect rain, and when the weather would be fair. Cotton farmers watched anxiously for the clear signals and indications of late frost before planting their crops. Later in the season these same farmers looked frantically at leaden gray skies with one eye and scanned the almanac with the other, hoping for rain. Dr. DeVoe's information was not always encouraging. In July and August, when the weather was hot and dry and crops were wilting to the ground, the blank little signal flags on the "Wine of Cardui Calendar and Weather Chart" were ominous.

For the stores themselves, the almanac and calendar were the most important means of cheap advertising. The surest way to keep a store's name before its trade was to make use of the red and white trade cards clamped into the cut-out portions of the calendars, or to have its name printed on the cover of the *Ladies Birthday Almanac*. Both of these hung usually above the mantel, and the green-backed almanac swung by its traditional pink string from a nail off to one side.

For more than sixty-five years Thedford's Black Draught and McElree's Wine of Cardui have been retailed in the South, and during this time few people have known the correct pronunciation of either name. Customers have called for "Black Drawft," "Black Drot," "Black Drawght," and, correctly, "Black Draft." Wine of Cardui became, instead of "Car-du-eye," "Wine of Cardooey," and "Wine of Car-du-we."

Customers' letters, in their humble way, trace the history of proprietary-medicine advertising for five decades in the United States. In the earlier years of the history of the Chattanooga Medicine Company happy customers wrote that they were cured by Cardui or Black Draught, and their enthusiastic letters found their way into the almanac. At the time muckraking was at its height, the Chattanooga Medicine Company was blithely laying claim to positive cures. On the face of their packages and in the almanac, there appeared the figures of a white woman standing beside a kneeling Indian maid. The latter pointed dramatically to a stalk of blessed thistle, while saying to her ailing sister, "Take and be Healed

—The Great Spirit Planted It," and then the medicine company added the encouraging by-line, "A Certain Cure for Menstrual Disturbances of Women."

Forty years later the Indian maid is still kneeling before the blessed thistle, her finger is still pointing steadily toward the plant, and the same white sister is listening attentively, but the pantomime is a silent one. The nonsense about the Great Spirit's horticultural and therapeutical activities has been removed. Today the Cardui package says with terse frankness that its contents are "alcohol 19 % by volume—used as a solvent and preservative of the active medicinal ingredients," which are extract of blessed thistle, black haw, (*Viburnum prunifolium*), and golden seal. Where the old package, in the golden age of American *laissez faire,* boasted "a certain cure," the modern package says "Valuable in relieving Functional Dysmenorrhea (painful menstruation)."

Throughout the history of the New South, the story of the Chattanooga Medicine Company has been intimately tied up with that of the country store. The region maintained a diet closely akin to that of the frontier. Salt meat, hot breads, and a lack of fresh vegetables, fruits, and dairy products contributed to constipation. Dr. Simmons had sought a solution for this affliction in the original Black Draught formula which he passed on to his son-in-law, J. H. Thedford.

Thus it was that constipation and systemic sluggishness of the regional population became a factor in southern big business. In the changing years both chemical and medical science were employed to improve on the Simmons formula. Chain-belt packaging lines were erected in the factory, and millions of twenty-five-cent yellow and black packages, bearing a scene of herb gathering on the side of Lookout Mountain as a trademark, were prepared for distribution. Like constipation, menstruation was an important factor in regional commerce, and trainloads of McElree's formula have passed through the bottling machines at the foot of Lookout Mountain in St. Elmo.

Obscured by more spectacular business developments, historians of the New South have overlooked the rise of the Chattanooga Company. Likewise, regional historians have little appreciated the fact that the big presses in the basement of the Chattanooga Medicine Company have turned out almanacs and calendars in astronomical numbers, and that they have been read more assiduously than most volumes of southern history.

15

DEATH ALWAYS CAME AT NIGHT

IN JANUARY, 1893, Nathan Long of Marengo County, Alabama, with a hand bound down in grief drafted a sorrowful note on yellowing tablet paper to his furnishing merchant. His mother was dead, and Nathan, a dutiful son, prepared to pay a last and dignified tribute to her memory. His humble note was a classic in the simple affairs of death in the South. "Ples send me a cheap coffin and some Bleatching a Bout what you think will Beary a Body in something like a sheet My Dear old Mother is Dead i am Poor But I wants to Beary Her i will need a Bout 6 yds to mak a sheet for Her and Charge them to me." In a postscript the affectionate Nathan summed up the morbidity of death in his isolated community. "Ples send me a par stocking to Put on Her feet."

A wrinkled, weary old soul had found the upswing of winter too hard for one of her years and had given up the struggle. It was difficult for Nathan to start the spring under the handicap of added expenses, but he wished to extend the last full measure of filial devotion. A simple coffin "on the credit" cost ten dollars. Six yards of shoddy bleaching for a binding cloth cost seventy-five cents, and a pair of grayish-white stockings for the aged, calloused feet which in life had seldom known such comforts was twenty-five cents more. The total cost of the old lady's funeral was not great, but even so, in the panic year 1893, it required half of a big bale of cotton to pay the bill in October.

Scattered among the pine hills of the rural South are the

sprawling graveyards. They epitomize a gaunt, struggling death which gives a grievous ring of truth to the psalm of finality that "from dust thou art to dust thou returneth." Broken tombstones deeply etched with fragmentary biographies and trite phrases and verses of solace and hope bear mute testimony to the closing phases of a way of life. Fruit and stone jars half-filled with stagnant water and shriveled flower stems, sea shells cankered with clay and sand, and rows of odd-shaped and colored glacial stones outline an infant grave over which a drowsy, ill-shaped lamb keeps heavy-eyed watch. Native stones mark heads and feet of nameless mortals who succumbed to the obstacles of life or who lived on borrowed time long beyond the allotted space of threescore and ten years, and wasted away in a soft but befuddled rocking-chair twilight.

Straggling gnarled cedars, pines, oaks, broken and frostbitten Cape Jessamine, crepe myrtle, and gangling mimosa compete with rapacious honeysuckle for life from the starved eroded soil. Once each year, where members of families remain in the community, the graveyard is scraped bare of crab grass, blackberry and "saw" briers, Johnson grass, and sassafras bushes to give them a "cared-for" appearance. Here and there blunt marble blocks or stone slabs raise their stained heads above their neighbors, and the names chiseled across their tops are those of family sires who lie lordly in death as they lived, with their get about them. It is here in these neglected plots which stand off to the sides of ancient church houses that the changing fortunes of southern health are nobly documented.

This inanimate document coupled with vital statistics, and the history of disease prevalent in the region reveals an important facet of the picture of rural southern life. Death has ever been a subject of primary interest in the region, and around it has developed a huge volume of folk history. In the confused years of the late sixties plans for the decennial census of 1870 provided that the published findings should contain an extensive section on life and death which would go beyond the highly formalized statistics of earlier reports. Long categories of diseases were given for the states, and deaths were catalogued by newer classifications. Diarrhea, enteric and intermittent fever, measles, whooping cough, childbirth, croup, consumption, skin diseases, scalds, burns, cholera infantum, malaria, and general debility were given high places among major causes of southern deaths. Out of the chaos of the times and the gross inaccuracies of the census takers' reports there comes a pattern of some significance. In graphic varicolored charts, disease and pestilence were spread forth on the face of the national map. Many of the areas of the Confederate states were stamped in heavy colors to indicate that pneumonia, malaria, croup, measles, consumption, and debility were fatal.

For the succeeding decennial reports, planners of the census gave careful attention to the state of health in the nation. Decade by decade the picture was made more intelligible by expanding medical knowledge and more detailed classification. There were not only the old stand-by causes of death listed in 1870, but destructive newcomers isolated from the older ones by progressive medical technique were added. Deathly fears of enteric fevers, typhoid, dysentery, consumption, skin diseases, debility, cramp colic, brain fever, and scores of others of the older generalized classifications were lessened considerably in succeeding decades. Parisitic infections, devitalizing pellagra, tuberculosis of many kinds, and general malnutrition soon occupied important positions at the top of the list of life-destroying diseases.

Spread across the face of modern charts and pictoral maps of health reports and vital statistics was an ever changing picture of the status of life. With cringing disgust visitors to the South watched people gathering and eating lumps of clay, and rushed away to write horror stories of what they had seen. As the influence of the land-grant colleges and their schools of agricultural and home economics began to be felt, attention was focused upon living conditions of rural people. *Bête noire* of the domestic scientists, pioneer state health departments, and home demonstration agents was the "white diet," which took its heavy annual toll in a dozen different ways. Scores of bulletins, reams of letters, and voluminous books and special reports contained long outpourings of criticism against the average daily diet of the southerner.

Store invoices are graphic major sources of information concerning the undernourished. They catalogue exactly the materials which comprised the evils of the "white diet." There are molasses by the thousands of barrels, salt meat by trainloads, cooking oil, flour of a dozen inferior grades, and bolted meal by thousands of tons. The myriad orders told more eloquent stories of malnutrition than did the public-health laboratories with fantastic displays of chemicals and bubbling test tubes.

Ten years after inquisitive census takers had labored indifferently in reconstruction and disorganized South Carolina to make sense of their fragmentary reports, E. P. Mobley of Fairfield County wrote a sordid answer to several of the causes of the state's 7,380 deaths. In an old-style handwriting in which the tail of the first double *S's* came below the line, he asked that one of his tenants be supplied "a gallon of molasses, 12 lbs Bacon one Bushel of meal on his Liean 10 cts worth Tobacco." This is a random order; from 1865 to 1920 an incalculable number of such missives reached the country stores, and the reaction from the monotonous and harmful diet which they asked for was mirrored in the lengthening rows of vital statistics.

In the midst of the formidable phalanx of diseases which swept thousands of southerners into the arms of their fathers is a catch-all classification entitled "debility." Behind the deaths from this cause, however, are the exceedingly human stories of shriveled and worn bodies which withered away more from living too long and too hard than from the blight of a specific disease. Like an ancient and stubby shovel sweep which had been dragged through too many long furrows, the force of life in these individuals was gradually blunted and worn away. Palsied hands fluttered and dropped uselessly at sides and quivering arm muscles gave up the struggle to lift them again. Outwardly debility was the only cause of death, and so it was explained in vital statistics. Surprisingly the list of deaths from debility was long; life with its many treacherous hazards and ineffective diet spared a large number of persons to enjoy a peaceful and leisurely old age of chewing tobacco and dipping snuff on porches and under shade trees.

There were actually few customers for coffins in the rural South prior to 1910. Death like birth was pretty much a homemade affair, and because of its eternal element of misfortune the burden was spread out to as many people as possible. Neighbors contributed to the financing of the costs of materials, and making coffins was almost always a labor of charity. A tenant farmer's child took sick with the "summer complaint" and within a day or two it was dead. Crops were "in the grass," help was scarce, and the moment was the most unfortunate one of all for a child to die. The father had no money, and the margin of credit on his lien note failed to take into consideration the certainty of death. Thus it was that burying the dead in a majority of cases became a community responsibility.

Fixtures were bought from stores and carpenter-farmers spent hours shaping oblong, hexagon, or curved-end boxes into caskets. The ends of death were served with the most careful workmanship possible. Hour after hour hot water was poured over pine, walnut, and oak boards, and triangular slits were cut halfway through to facilitate the bending. The monotonous pounding of the bending hammer was heard on many a sultry night. Blinking lanterns lighted the activities of the cabinetmakers as they moved around from one detail to another. Laboriously the handmade boxes took form to receive an army of victims of consumption, pneumonia, croup, measles, skin diseases, fevers, and debility. Long steel tacks were set in place. Heavy screws with ornamental heads decorated with classical designs of cypress and garlands marked the bends and joints. There were other nails in the shape of crosses which held the lining in place, and sometimes were driven into a line of beading around the lids. When they were set in place against a background of black cloth and dark stained woods, they presented a striking and dolorous appearance of funereal adornment.

Coffin hardware was sold wholesale by distributors located in the larger centers. Wholesale houses like Belknap in Louisville supplied fixtures in completely assembled bundles. There were four handles and a plate bearing the legend "At Rest," "Our Darling," or "Our Babe." Sometimes the handles bore imprints of lambs at rest against a background of Elysian fields, and the lid screws were leaden roses in a half-blown stage. For adult coffins there were various designs. There was the legend "Mother" for married women's coffins; the inevitable square, compass, and "G" for the Masonic fraternity; the open Bible and letters I.O.O.F. for the Odd Fellows; and the rugged lengths of tree trunks and axes for Woodmen of the World.

At Whitakers, North Carolina, Hearne Brothers and Company specialized in supplying stores with a large assortment of hardware. Their large illustrated catalogue was a graphic document of burial artistry for the years following the Civil War. Page after page portrayed designs of varying types of fixtures, and every one of them conveyed an intensity of sorrow. The last four or five pages were devoted to tools and equipment for merchants who wished to become undertakers.

The Hearne Brothers' catalogue was of more than ordinary interest. For the boys sitting around the stores it furnished a fearful diversion from the usual course of idle conversation. Perusing its pages was in fact a theft of a surreptitious glimpse at the face of life's greatest inevitability. These catalogues sometimes figured in folk beliefs. Many persons believed that looking at such things as coffin fixtures was flirting with death itself. Especially was this true of the weary colored customers who timidly pushed up to the stove or eased up to the porches to take a moment of ease only to have a coffin book opened in their faces. The realistic illustrations of coffins and fixtures sent half-frightened customers home to ponder such things in their subconscious minds and to awaken at night in the midst of dreams of death. The belief was strong that to dream of coffins and open graves was to be in imminent danger of a dreadful accident.

Underneath the shelves where the boxes of casket hardware and tacks were packed back out of sight in the stores were the rolls of crinkled gray, white, and black lining which was sold by the yard for the better boxes. Even when cheap factory-made coffins were sold to the stores and stacked away upstairs in the storeroom, many of them were without trimmings and inevitably finishing them was a task for the late hours of the night. It was always necessary for either storekeepers or their clerks to crawl out of bed and spend an hour cutting and fitting a lining into a frail box.

Such a case was that of making a coffin to receive the weary and bedraggled body of Dora Richardson Clay Brock, formerly child bride of the aged Cassius M. Clay. Dora died in poverty in one of the shacks atop a phosphate dump at the mines of Woodford County, Kentucky. Her tragic life was at an end. Once she had known the luxuries of splendid White Hall in Madison County as the wife of its famous master, and then she had gone away to meet the trials of life among people of much lesser social stature. The years had been cruel to her, and finally, in a moment of one of her bitterest downsweeps in the winter of 1915, the end came. The wife of the proprietor of McKinivan's country store lined a coarse pine box for a coffin with unbleached muslin and placed padding and a pillow in it to give comfort to Dora's emaciated body in her last earthly adventure.

Everywhere in the South merchants tacked down their funereal black, gray, and white linings with leaden cross-shaped nails, or they rolled off yards of black calico and unbleached domestic to be used in covering up faulty places in the jerry-built boxes. One of the important factors in life was unbleached domestic. It was, perhaps, the commonest of all the cotton cloths, and for this reason was the most universally use. It was symbolical of the whole process of cotton production, and throughout life it was a useful fabric. When a hard-pressed cotton farmer or a member of his family died, the body was wrapped in unbleached cloth in the ancient style of Lazarus. Thus it was that many a lifeless body enshrouded in six to ten yards of unbleached cloth was jolted away for burial in a cotton wagon through acres of cotton fields. In final judgment these postwar Jeremiahs of the Lower South will arise and stand before their Maker in the coarse, unfinished raiment which was bought for them of country merchants.

Burial customs in the rural South in the postwar years were closely patterned after the spirit of the times. Funeral directors were unknown. When a person died, he deserved better treatment than to fall into the hands of unctuous and patronizing professional undertakers even if he had possessed the money to pay burial costs. The corpse was "laid out" by neighbors, local carpenters and cabinetmakers made the coffin, a nearby store supplied the materials, and friends kept the wake and dug the grave. In all the thousands of hapless victims recorded in the vital statistics of the census reports before 1915, a remarkably small percentage of them were carried to their final resting places by anyone other than neighbors. The only charges ever made in death were those which found their way on to the ledgers as entries for fixtures, linings, and shrouds. Between 1865 and 1915 it was not unreasonable from a financial standpoint to die. Seldom did an ordinary casket cost more than five to twenty-five dollars, graves were dug by obliging friends, there was seldom a hearse, and the wake nearly always turned out to be a semisocial affair.

There was a commingling of sorrow and joviality in the "sitting up" parties of the South. For members of the corpse's family sorrow was genuine, but among the neighbors there were definitely mixed emotions. The tedium of a long, weary night of sitting up with a neighbor was often broken by pranking and drinking. A dozing barefoot brother suddenly came to life with all the wrath of hell burning between his toes where cotton had been stuffed and then set on fire. At other times long vigils at the side of a corpse turned into feasts of eating and drinking, but always the wakes were neighborly affairs.

Pallbearers of the postwar years approached their tasks with a formal reverence in keeping with the cold finalities of the occasion. Clad in their best clothes, with white gloves and, sometimes, mourning sashes, they were ready to extend their last gracious respects to a departed brother. White gloves were almost always necessary, and they were lent by storekeepers, who kept four pairs constantly on hand to accommodate funeral parties. In instances where the gloves were thrown into graves by fraternal orders, they were purchased from the stores.

Graves were dug in light clay or deep sandy loam by volunteer laborers. They were usually four to six feet deep with a narrower pit the size of the casket. Lowering a coffin into the grave was always a mechanical problem. The most common practice was to use buggy lines with buckles stripped off so that when the casket came to rest at the bottom the straps could be pulled out from one side. Then there were the patent straps which hooked into a bracket on the side of the boxes, and once the box rested on the bottom of the grave, the straps were slackened and the brackets were released. Often stores kept these straps and lent them throughout their territory for use.

Once the casket was in place, the boards were placed over the shoulders and the grave was ready to be filled. Throwing the first shovels of dirt into the box was a heartless operation. Always there was an inhumane maliciousness in the monotonous rumble of dirt over the boards. This was, without exception, the most morbid of all the experiences of human life in the South. As one shovelful of dirt after another poured down on top of a vacuous coffin, and the sound rolled back in a hollow roar, the very emptiness of most of life in the region itself was echoed in its starkest degree of depravity. The rising sound of fresh dirt over a grave was in reality the last full measure of the bitter sting of death.

If the departed one were a Mason or a member of another fraternity, his connection with the store did not come to rest by simply lying among surroundings of unbleached domestic and sateen trimmings beneath heaping mounds of auburn earth. Lodges of sorrow in which a postwake ceremonial took place were held over the stores, and again the cheap resources of mourning goods were tapped. The Caldwell Lodge number 82, in Abbeyville County, South Carolina, bought of the Longmore store two pieces of gilt braid, postage stamps, ten yards of linen, a quire of note paper, sixteen balls of tape, and four pieces of crepe. Every year the lodges held their sessions of mourning, and overhead in the stores the gloom of a year of dying was revived for a night.

Death became a chapter in the ledgers and journals of daily store transactions. Tucked away in an inside cover of the Reed Brothers' ledger for 1882 was a characteristic itemized burial account. This miscellaneous order consisted of "1 Bx for Coffin, 1 yd print, 1 bx tack, 1 doz. screws, 1 # nail," and involved a cash outlay of ninety cents. A more formal entry inside the ledger included a goods box for a coffin, a dozen screws, a pound of six-penny nails, two yards of calico, and a box of tacks. Near by at Eagleville, the estate of W. T. Puchell was charged with four and one-third yards of cassinet, one pair of black pants, one yard Italian cloth, one spool silk, one spool of black thread, one and one-half yards of bleached domestic, a yard and a half of prints, half a dozen buttons, and a pair of socks. In all the bill was $11.25, and this customer was buried in grand style.

While the carpetbaggers and scalawags were playing havoc with domestic peace in Mississippi and the famous Kemper County War between native sons and scalawags and carpetbaggers was in progress, E. F. Nunn and Company at Shuqulak sold James F. Lundy an order of burial goods which consisted of two yards of bleached domestic, half a yard of flannel, a pair of hose, three yards of velvet, three additional yards of domestic, a dozen coffin lags, three and one-half yards of ribbon, a dozen coffin screws, and a loan of ten dollars in cash. Elsewhere in the Nunn books there are entries for similar funeral supplies.

Everywhere there was a shocking casualness in the purchase of merchandise for burial purposes and in the commonplace everyday method of making entries in account books. Closely akin to the constant business of selling meat, meal, flour, shuck collars, and plowpoints was the sale of screws, lining, shrouds, and hardware for coffins. With characteristic credit business methods, A. C. Calloway asked a Faunsdale, Alabama, merchant to "please let Elizza Thomas Have one coffin for $5.00 to Berry her daughter, and Charge to my account." A South Carolinian asked T. G. Patrick to supply his tenant, Boler, with enough "cloth to cover and lining for a coffin and three yards of sheat stockings and gloves two papers of tacks, a pair of pants."

One after another the "coffin notes" came to the stores. R. A. Jones of Marengo County, Alabama, gave instructions that Jake George was to "have some cloth for shroud for his nephew (boy 4 yrs old—) & if he needs any other material for covering coffin & lining it let him have it cheap as you can." At White Oak, South Carolina, a cotton farmer attempted to escape the unexpected financial burden of death by ordering "2 yds cheap bleaching ½ doz. 2 in. screws (wood) ½ doz coffin screws." Two notes from the Williams store at Eagleville, Tennessee, illustrate the businesslike art of dying. H. E. Campbell asked the merchant to let "Scott Jordan have a cheap burial suit and I will see it paid." His neighbor, J. G. Demmanbrane, informed James Williams that "Mr. J. H. Harper will get some burial clothes and I will see you paid."

A little more adequate preparation was made for funerals for persons in better financial condition. For these individuals there were numerous purchases of white and black goods. One note requested "4 yds of white flannel, 5 yds of nice bleached Domestic 4½ yards some albatross of some sort of goods suitable for a burial robe for a child, if single width it will take 7 yards & ball or something to go on neck. Shoes or slippers No ones black stockings 2 spools white thread one 40, 1 no 50." Carrying on the "white" tradition was an order for "5½ yds white woolen dress goods double width or 8 yds single width,

2 yds white lace, 2 yds white ribbons three inches wide, 1 pair white hoes, 1 spool of thread no 60, 3 yds white flannel. All white if have it—if not all cream."

With monotonous regularity accounts appeared in ledgers telling of the sad end of neighbors. "Spring sicknesses" killed the babies and heavy winter weather thinned the ranks of the old folks. C. B. Summers made frequent entries in his daybook at Earls, Kentucky. For $2.97, a customer purchased "3 yds of velvet, 3 yds black domestic, 2 pa. tax, 1 doz screws, 1½ doz coffin screws, 2 lbs of nails, 3 yds coffin fringe, 1 child's wool hat." A $15.00 funeral consisted of "9 yds of alpaca, 9 yds of bleaching, 1 pr. shoes, 1 pr. gloves, 1 pr. hoes, 1 calico skirt, 2 yd. Ribbon, 155 ft. lumber, 6 yds. of velveteen, 6 yds. ribbon, 8 wood screws, 8 coffin screws, 1 paper of tax." Stores not only supplied the needs of their customers in the stringent time of death, but they likewise gave aid in other ways. "Please send by bearer—5 yards of bleach cashmere (if double width) or 8 if single, 4 yds of black silk 2 inches side—six yrds black calico —3 yrds white flannel for skirt—1 net skirt—& 1 pr. drawers (Ladies) 1 yrd suiting (white)—1 pr-low cut shoes—No 6— Signed John H. Clark and William Clark. Telephone to James Joyce send word to Beasly." Already the storekeeper knew what had happened to the Clark family, and it took no prodding for him to call James Joyce, and he sent word to Beasley by the first passer-by. In fact, merchants took up where the doctors left off, and they continued to serve the needs of a family long after the doctors were gone. There was a lot of humanity in their services, even if their goods were cheap in price, gaudy in appearance, and shoddy in quality.

Thus it was that the stores in death as in life were sources of supply for all human needs. For many they were the beginning and the end of things. There was a sort of complete story of life in the fact that there were long entries for furnishing supplies from month to month for a long span of years, and then without warning there appeared an entry for burial supplies. When this occurred, that name disappeared from the books and a change in community personality was inescapable. There was Matthew Brown, who traded for a score of years with Ike Jones at Black Hawk, Mississippi. His account became a permanent fixture in the Jones books. Its itemized listings of commonplace merchandise played hide and seek in and out among similar entries of fellow farmers. In a sprawling "post-office" hand Ike Jones extended week by week Mat's humble list of purchases. His was a perfect story of a man whose annual income was often less than a hundred dollars, and his purchases were fairly well within keeping of his income. In 1911 at cotton-planting time, when Mat's services were most vitally needed, a member of his family closed his account at the store by purchacsing a ten-dollar coffin and a few "little extras." Mat would be unable to finish his crop, but already he had produced his quota of cotton. In the midst of the long, ruled ledger sheet Ike Jones posted in his bold hand a final entry for his faithful customer. He brought his affairs to a close in debt for two months' supplies and a cheap coffin. Unlike Elisha, this faithful country-store customer was not going forth to eternity in a chariot of fire and blaze of glory but in a cotton wagon and a humble winding sheet of unbleached domestic grown on the meager cotton acres in the Lower South.

Mat Brown's account in 1911 practically saw the end of the custom of neighborly burial and of buying funeral supplies from the country stores. After this the business of death became far too delicate to be handled by such unskilled persons as neighbors, merchants, and graceless cabinetmakers. Here was a golden opportunity for the oily professional sympathizers of the age of impersonal commercial transactions. No longer was it proper for a man to return his body to the clay in a country-store coffin lined with bleached domestic on the inside and trimmed on the outside with balls of fringe held down by leaden rose-beaded tacks of the hardware store. Burial associations were organized to insure hearse funerals of stipulated prices worth more than three cotton crops, and for which individuals pay annual fees, ever hopeful of cashing in on the investment before the last installment is paid. In this way death never comes unexpected as it did to Mat Brown—instead, it is ever kept a live subject by periodic arrivals of notices that another "nominal" installment is due on a $300 funeral.

16

HEAVY GOODS IN THE CORNER

SPRING IN THE SOUTH has ever been a time of promise. When willows and maples along the streams began to "green" and dogwood and wild bush honeysuckle buds were ready to burst, and a long roll of log heap smoke obscured the heavy setting of a lazy reddening sun, it was farming time. Almost overnight farmers sprang into action. It was a time for taking an inventory of harness and tools and of piecing out last year's equipment with new supplies.

Such were the duties of Waverly Fitts of Marengo County, Alabama, early in 1898. This impatient farmer took time from his field work to inscribe an important note in southern social and economic history. As he drew his blunt pencil across the crude piece of scrap paper before him, he documented the story of one-horse farming from 1865 to 1915. Wave was preparing to start a new crop in true cotton-belt style. He hurried his boy off to John C. Brown's general store to get "2 yds osnaburg [for backbands], two trace chains, 30 yds rope [for plow lines], 4 shuck collars [sewed with twine], one double bar [doubletree], two singletrees, one small 10¢ clevice [for buckhead] & .05 cts worth teall thread. P.S. also send one lap ring."

The next day Wave's boy was back at the store with another note which said, "The collars you sent yesterday are too small for my mules & I send two of them back to exchange for larger ones. Be sure & exchange them for me, as I need them right away—also send me 1 galon K- oil."

Thousands of southern farmers wrote for collars, plowlines,

clevices, backbands, grass rods, plows, and heel bolts. Seldom did their orders ask for a mechanical device more complicated than a patent coffee mill or an improved cotton or corn planter. Scarcely were the fall cotton trade and Christmas goods out of the stores before the aisles were crowded with plow tools and harness. Center and rear passageways were blocked with piles of iron plows, rolls of plowlines, plow stocks, bundles of singletrees, breeching, and bridles, collections of backbands, and boxes of hoes and axes. Ceiling joists swayed out of line with loads of leather and shuck collars, bundles of bridle bits, whip racks, trace chains, well buckets, and plow handles. This was a season when the "heavy hardware" trade flourished, and likewise a composite smell which made lazy men uneasy.

As characteristic of the store ceiling as fly specks were whip racks which swung down with their captivating display of shiny oilcloth-bound stocks and rawhide crackers. For seventy-five cents an owner of a horse and buggy could purchase six feet of factory-made whip with which to trim his dashboard and prod his lazy nag. Prices ranged upward from thirty-five cents for the cheap short oilcloth "reminders" to four and five dollars for the fine tight-wrapped buckskin articles with inlaid stocks and long lively crackers. Near by was a row of detachable sockets which gave dash to a fancy courting buggy. These receptacles, like the whips which they held, ranged in quality and price from the cheap little turned wooden sockets to those of more imaginative design.

There was genuine attraction and interest in the whip and fixture displays, but without a doubt the oil-brown saddles hanging from rows of hooks by single stirrups was a greater one. Saddles bespoke horses, and southerners generally depended upon horses and mules to transport them from one place to another; too, there was the spirit of the cowboy and adventure in the saddle. Plow hands saw themselves mounted on cantankerous bronchos galloping off after Indians and steers. They admired the fancy tooled fenders, the bright yellow tie strings, the high pommels and the slender horns.

Most of the country-store saddles, however, were of the

modest narrow-pommel and unadorned types. They came from Harbison and Gathright in Louisville. This firm began manufacturing saddles and harness the year after the Civil War ended, and their goods were found in almost every place there was a hook on which to hang them.

The Harbison-Gathright saddles had a heavy claim on the southern trade. Josiah B. Gathright rode away from Kentucky in '61 with Morgan's command as a first lieutenant in the 8th Kentucky Cavalry. Later he was detailed to the quartermaster's staff under the command of General Adam R. Johnson to take charge of the manufacture of saddlery. In 1866 he formed a partnership with a cousin, John T. Gathright, a Federal veteran who had fought before Vicksburg, and the two former soldiers turned their attention to the South and its need for saddlery. That they succeeded is borne out by the hundreds of their invoices found among store records.

In a corner of the country store hung the slender buggy harness. There were tiny narrow-faced collars which scarcely touched a horse's shoulders. Heavy buggy traces which were almost as suggestive of punishment for freedmen as of transportation were looped into slender iron hames, and these in turn were buckled onto bright oilcloth-trimmed saddles and heavily stitched breeching with their soft rounded cruppers. There were dainty driving lines of narrow strap leather and special blind bridles with their single-check reins. One set of harness was suspended on top of another in a perfect maze of straps, hames, rings, and buckles.

Carriage harness was the superlative in the "gear" trade. Its insecure straps and driving lines stood out in contrast to the commonplace rows of shuck, canvas, and reinforced leather collars which formed a robust phalanx around the ceiling. The horse-collar trade was a constant money-maker for the merchant, but for most of the customers it was a matter of major capital outlay. Customers usually sized up the job which their mules had to do and bought collars accordingly. A fifty-cent shuck collar was good enough for an ordinary plow mule, but a sturdier collar was desirable for heavier work. There was also a matter of social consciousness in the type of collar one's mule or horse wore out in public. A farmer driving into town with his mules equipped with shuck collars advertised his backwardness to a degree that was embarrassing, but for three decades after the Civil War machine collar manufacturers contended with shuck weavers as important competitors. Merchants bought shuck collars in winter and spring months for a very cheap price and retailed them to their trade for a substantial profit. Several stores had regular customers who made their living by this method of home manufacture.

Interspersed among ceiling and wall displays and in the invoices and ledger entries were huge bundles of trace and breast chains, canvas backbands, bridle bits, bridles, hames, and hame straps. For less than five dollars a farmer could equip a gaunt mule with essential harness from the ceiling of a store. Nowhere else in the United States were standards of necessary plow harness so low. Equipping a mule in February for the plow was a simple matter of making a few purchases at the store. John M. Gayden, a South Carolina farmer, drew an accurate picture of average farm conditions when, on February 17, 1886, he ordered his spring supplies. He bought three sides of bacon, two gallons of molasses, one plow stock, two pairs of trace chains, two backbands forty-two inches long, one paper of seed peas, one package of beans, one quart of onion sets, two papers of turnip seeds, a paper of drumhead cabbage, and two pairs of plowlines. For less than three dollars his pair of mules were ready for work.

More frequent were orders for rope. Generally it was considered that a mule and a plow stock were approximately thirteen feet long and that twenty-six feet of cotton rope would make a pair of lines. Spools of rope were ordered in December and arrived for sale in late January. They were put into position along the counter bases where boxes of oranges and barrels of apples had stood during the Christmas holidays. These rolls of triple-twisted rope were symbolical of the whole pattern of southern cotton and tobacco production. Rope lines were as much products of the southern cotton fields as were antiquated shuck collars. Much of the raw material which was shipped out of the cotton-growing region for processing was shipped back as a finished product with a steep added manufacturing, distributing, and freight cost. A pound of plowline in the spring required nearly eight pounds of lint cotton in payment in the fall.

Plowlines in reality were connecting links between men and mules. They were stout bonds which forced the two to move across hot sandy fields in unison. A philosopher who annually stood by a store stove and watched clerks reel off twenty-six feet of cheap Yankee manufactured cotton put his homely thoughts in writing. He spoke in profound sincerity for all those whose wrists were scarred by a continuous sawing of heartless dust and dew-laden cotton reins. "Over a hill," he philosophized, "trailed a man behind a mule drawing a plow. Unexpectedly the plow hit a root, the mule stopped, and the man began to grumble as he fixed the hames: 'Bill, you are just a mule, the son of a jackass, and I am a man made in the image of God. Yet here we work hitched up together year after year. I often wonder if you work for me or I work for you. Verily, I think it is a partnership between a mule and a fool, for surely I work as hard as you, if not harder. Plowing or cultivating we cover the same distance, but you do it on four legs and I on two, therefore I do twice as much as you.

" 'Soon we will be preparing for a corn crop. When the corn is harvested I give one-third to the landlord for being so kind as to let me use a small speck of God's earth. One-third goes to you, the rest is mine. You consume all your portion, while I divide mine among seven children, six hens, two ducks and a storekeeper. If we both need shoes, you get 'em. You are getting the best of me and I ask you, is it fair for a mule, the son of a jackass, to swindle a man, the lord of creation, out of his substance?

" 'Why, you only help to plow and cultivate the ground and I alone must cut, shock, and husk the corn, while you look over the pasture fence and heehaw at me. All fall and most of the winter the whole family from baby up picks cotton to help raise enough money to pay taxes and buy a new set of harness and pay the mortgage on you. Not a thing, you ornery cuss do you have to do. I even have to do the worrying about the mortgage on your tough, ungrateful hide.

" 'About the only time I am your better is on election day, for I can vote and you can't. After election I realize that I was fully as big a jackass as your papa. Verily, I am prone to wonder if politics were made for a man or a jackass, or to make jackasses out of men.

" 'And that ain't all, Bill, when you are dead, that's supposed to be the end of you. But me? The preacher tells me that when I die I may go to hell forever. That is, Bill, if I don't do just as they say. And most of what they say keeps me from getting any fun out of life.

" 'Tell me, William, considering these things, how can you keep a straight face and still look so dumb and solemn?' "

Definitely there was an affinity between the solemn mule and the man who trailed him. A plow was rammed tightly underneath a stump, and this accident had set off the soliloquy about the mule's favored position in the scheme of one-horse farming. The plow itself was an antiquated contraption. Its clumsy beam and foot piece came from the near-by woods, its handles came by way of the country store from Louisville, Lynchburg, Chattanooga, and Moline plow factories, and the clevice and grass rod came from Belknap's. The heel bolt and plow came from Birmingham, Cincinnati, or Louisville. At best it was a poor rig. Frankly, these plow stocks would not have been entirely strange to Naomi and Ruth, and certainly the yeoman farmers of Arthur Young's England would have understood their working. Washington and Jefferson would have been familiar with their construction. Only one improvement was noticeable—these plows had iron points.

Piled high around the foot of the counters among the nail and horseshoe kegs were the so-called "plow irons" or the detachable shares which went with the homemade or shop-designed iron "Georgia" stocks. These heaps of pressed and stamped plows were interesting studies in sectional variations within the Solid South. In only one respect was there unity, and that was in their general degree of antiquity. Sandy regions required plows which did not go so deep, but which turned wide furrows. Here was a depository of southern agricultural experience exhibited in its most primitive sense. By colloquial designations the various strange shapes were known to the trade as sweeps, shovels, scooters, twisters, half-shovels, muley twisters, half-sweeps, bull tongues, buzzard wings, scrapers, and subsoilers.

Entry after entry in ledgers is descriptive of the prevailing type of cultivation which took place in the South following the Civil War. While heavy Oliver, Deere, and International Harvester gang plows were beginning to turn up the sod of the plains and northwestern alliance and granger conventions were rampant with criticism of the plow combines, the South remained steadfastly devoted to its archaic equipment.

Ledger descriptions of plow purchases do not tell the full story of sectional variations of types of cultivating tools. A sweep in Georgia was not a sweep in Mississippi, nor was it identically the same in Virginia. There was a remarkable regional sensitivity governed sharply by the varying consistency of the soil in the several geographical regions. In the friable sandy soil of Mississippi it was possible to use sweeps with a wingspread up to twenty-two inches, while in the tight "pipe clay" lands of Georgia a narrower and sharper-pointed plow was necessary. The heel sweep, a slender secondary plow which was attached to the foot of the stock behind a keen pointed narrow bull tongue served the purpose of a spreader. It pushed the soft fresh-turned soil up to young cotton and tobacco plants without actually breaking the surface of the ground. Local inventors spent much of their time trying to improve on this fragile implement. One of these was the Wilson patent sweep manufactured by M. and J. R. Hines of Milledgeville, Georgia. This plow was a curious contraption with a stout brace to hold the wings apart.

For the clerks in the stores it was not enough to have to remember the names of all the different types of plows but there were numerous special attachments which were always in demand. There were buckheads, clevices, heel bolts, grass rods, cutting colters and bands, single and doubletrees, and stretcher bars. Likewise, these terms varied from one region to another, so that a buckhead in one section was something else in another. But with all the multiplicity of terms and variations of usage, one thing was absolutely essential. Every merchant and his clerks had to know the name and use of every plow part in stock. If a greenhorn clerk had sent a cutting colter for a grass rod, he would have become the laughingstock of the community and perhaps would have lost trade for the store. Certainly the local wags would not have let him forget it for weeks to come. Yet it was often a matter of wonderment to a farmer that a man who wore "Sunday" clothes through the week could distinguish between plow parts carried in stock.

In the warerooms or crowded along the aisles in the stores themselves were the assembled implements such as middle busters, turning plows, side harrows, spring tooth cultivators, corn and cotton planters, and bone-dust distributors. These plows marked the major invasion of the new age of industrialism into the tight conservatism of southern agriculture before 1918. Carrying out the refinements of Thomas Jefferson, Charles Newbold, John Deere, James Oliver, and others, the "buster" and "pony" turning plows were made fairly efficient implements.

Two southern manufacturers, T. E. C. Brinly and Benjamin Franklin Avery, captured a major portion of the post bellum plow trade in the South. Almost from 1865 to date their plows have been southern standards. Brinly began the manufacture of plows in 1825 in his blacksmith shop in the tiny Kentucky village of Simpsonville. Occasionally he sent a load of plows into Louisville and traded them for supplies, and just before the outbreak of the war he moved his shop to the Ohio River town and prepared to supply the cotton country's need for plow tools. Fortunately he made distributive arrangements with W. B. Belknap and Company who were just then seeking southern patronage.

The war halted the Louisville plow business, but just as soon as it was over, Brinly enlarged his manufacturing plant, and wherever a Belknap drummer sold goods, his plows found purchasers.

Brinly had an understanding of the southern trade, and he catered specifically to it. He understood the eccentricities of his regional customers, and it was a matter of great personal pride that he was able to enlarge his southern sales. Making plows for the former Kentucky blacksmith was more than a cold matter of business. Between 1865 and 1900 he must have plowed up every fairground in the region from Austin to Richmond. In thirty-seven years of proudly demonstrating the work of the Brinly plows he won trophies in eight hundred plowing contests.

Competing with the tremendously popular Brinly plows were those manufactured by Benjamin Franklin Avery and Sons. This firm was founded by a long-whiskered Aurora, New York, "Yankee" who followed the agricultural frontier westward to the Falls of the Ohio. At Louisville he and three stalwart sons began the manufacture of plows for both the cotton lands of the South and the stubble lands of the West. Like Brinly's firm, Avery and Sons were delayed in development by the war, but during these lean years they improved their organization and prepared for the lush postwar market. Once the channels of southern trade were again open, B. F. Avery and Sons were foremost of Louisville merchants to understand the importance of the crossroads customers. They knew the secret of making a cheap plow stock for the cotton fields, and their stamping machines and forges were kept busy preparing shovels, sweeps, heel sweeps, and twisters. Competing with the thrifty pioneer Brinly, they entered the market with their famous "hillside" turning plows and their "bat wing" middle busters which lightened the task of ripping up tobacco and cotton stalks in the spring. Likewise, these busters were used as a kind of extreme unction to snatch a foundering crop from the grass in a wet spring. Benjamin Avery's Yankee ingenuity was to take him into new fields of implement manufacturing.

He introduced the Louisville planter, the Avery mower, and a wide-range hay rake. For years these were the most complicated machines, except cotton gins and sawmills, in the rural South. In the nineties when farmers were experiencing hard times, the improved Louisville planter was sold wholesale in carload lots to merchants for seven dollars apiece, and were retailed on the credit to farmers for twelve to fourteen dollars. Carload lots of these machines rattled southward over the Louisville and Nashville Railroad to compete with similar implements coming from manufacturers in Chattanooga, Lynchburg, Moline, South Bend, Richmond, and Baltimore. Circulars boosting the Louisville planters crowded the buggies of mail carriers all over the South. Many of the farm records were made in the Avery memorandum books, and store walls everywhere bore the famous five-pointed device spelling out the name of the Aurora plowmaker.

The Avery planter competed with the antiquated Gantt Dow Law cotton planter which was manufactured in Macon, Georgia, and used wherever mules pulled cotton plows. This native machine was a clumsy contraption which consisted of a double frame, a wheel, a side arm, a tricornered hopper, and a drag mounted on two strips of steel. The arm worked a ratchet inside the box which poured a roll of seed in a continuous wasteful stream. This planter was as primitive as the homemade wooden plow stock, yet for seventy years it was used to plant a major portion of the southern cotton crop. Modern planters did not distribute a wasteful roll of seed, but there was always fear that their steel swords would go too deep. Changing a Dow Law user over to an improved planter was almost as impossible a task as converting a southern Democrat into a Republican postmaster. "Sword planter" drummers and dealers fought an uphill battle which they did not win until the second decade of the present century.

Always hotbeds of conservatism themselves, the stores and their owners did practically nothing to change modes of cultivation, or to force manufacturers to improve their implements. For everybody concerned, life remained much simpler if no radical changes were made in types and uses of plow tools. Clerks did not have to memorize new names and applications of implements. They did not have to build new bins, nail up new brackets, or clear away fresh space on the floor. Heel bolts and grass rods remained in the same place throughout the life of a store. Plow handles, beams, iron feet, ground slides, shares, clevices, and buckheads were always to be found lying on the same spot or swinging from pegs where the first ones were put in stock. Because of this ultraconservatism, clerking became largely a matter of instinct.

Drummers and blacksmiths likewise conspired to keep the southern plow on a traditional basis. It was a simpler matter for a drummer to come around and take a stock order for conventional parts than it was to drag catalogues of new machines around and debate the merits of new tools with every merchant in his territory. Blacksmiths did not have to learn new repair methods, and they could spend much of their year preparing for the early spring rushes. Some of these craftsmen were less picturesque than their counterparts in New England poetry. It was they who were continually encouraging farmers to use primitive tools. When cotton crops failed, farmers took up again the use of homemade or blacksmith-made tools as the least expensive method of recovering their economic feet.

Most opposed of all to changes in plow tools were the southern farmers themselves. Farming methods in the postwar South were largely conditioned by factors encompassing soil types, weather expectations, experience, and precedence. A middle-aged farmer flaunted himself in the face of progress and used a scraper to prepare cotton for chopping and a twister for "dirting" corn, because "Pa always did it that way, and Pa always made cotton and corn when he had the Lord with him." Likewise, he used a Brinly turning plow or an Avery middle buster or a Gantt Dow Law because these were the tools "he was raised with," and a change-over to more improved implements at best was irksome, and, possibly, threatened the loss of an entire crop.

This resistance to change noticeably flavored the porch and

stove conversations. The sight of an Avery turning plow or a Louisville planter touched off the Farquhar and Brinly partisans. Hour after hour an aroused farmer discussed the merits of one plow over another. It was not actually a matter of proved superiority because all the plows did practically the same type of work; rather, it was strong traditional religious and political contentions carried over into the economic pattern of rural life. It was the "Solid South" justifying itself in the way it plowed its cotton.

Brinly, Avery, Oliver, Deere, Farquhar, Chattanooga, Lynchburg, and scores of minor plow works fashioned a one-horse way of life for the rural southerner. Alabama sweeps, Florence shovels, Hartsville twisters, Brinly turning plows, and Georgia bull tongues were vital tools of the cotton and tobacco systems. Yet these manufacturers in decades following World War I sped farmers on to a mechanical revolution. It was a quiet revolt which took place on store and warehouse floors. Disk and section harrows, spring-tooth and riding cultivators, check-row planters and sulky plows began to appear in stock. In some sections barefoot plowboys began to lose their "plow legs" when they crawled aboard riding tools once declared useless in the South.

Most remarkable of all the revolutionary implements which began to appear in stock were reapers and binders, hay bailers, pea threshers, and transplanting machines. It is an irony of historical fate that a southern boy was one of the first to conceive the idea of a mechanical reaper, yet his section was the last to enjoy its advantages. In May and June of each year invoices appeared among store records indicating the purchase of cradles, cradle blades, spare fingers, and handles. Kindred bills were for scythes and grindstones to be used in sharpening the long heavy blades. There was the famous "Josh Berry" grain cradle, for instance, which was thirty pounds of back-breaker, sleep-getter, and morale builder.

Many a harvest-weary southerner sat in a flimsy church house on Sunday morning and heard a perspiring parson repeat tender stories of Biblical gleaners with far more understanding and interest in the fact that they were gleaners than that they were examples of brotherly and sisterly love. Gleaners of southern oat fields went to their task on the shady side of two o'clock in the afternoon full of buttermilk and blackberry cobbler, and two hours later sprawled panting in the thin shade of a persimmon bush wondering why God ever allowed them to be born. They were truly unimaginative southerners in the age of McCormick and Appleton bending their backs under the weight of antiquated scythes from the age of Ruth and Naomi. This primitive method of harvesting is one reason why the South has compared unfavorably with the rest of the country in basic bread production.

Backwardness in one aspect of southern economic life was accurately reflected in another. This was true of the comparable machines of the furrow and the road. Country merchants specialized in the sale of shiny red and yellow wagons. They rolled away from the stores bearing traditional black stripes, green beds, and high spring seats and side body panels with dealers' names stenciled on them. Few things for many customers were more joyous than the purchase of a new, freshly painted wagon. No implement ever had more eloquent salesmen than these vehicles. Literally hundreds of blacksmith-wagonmakers turned out their bright wares under romantic names. In fact, a southern town was of no consequence at all if it did not have at least one wagon and carriage maker giving fancy names to his product. Even crossroads were often important because honest smiths fitted axles, skeins, hounds, tongues, and bolsters into wagons which were sold all over the South. Thousands of Weber, Florence, Tennessee, Salisbury, Chattanooga, Old Kentucky, Old Hickory, Milburn, Studebaker, Avery, Love, Lynchburg, and Piedmont wagons were dragged uncounted miles over rough southern roads.

Around the stores, churches, blacksmith shops, and picnic grounds, boastful owners claimed that they had such excellent wagons that they could pull them with a single hand. They sat before their wheels and admired the delicately dished effects or followed behind them and pointed out the accuracy with which they tracked. They argued by the hour over the relative virtues of dropped tongues and breast yokes as opposed to the newfangled "stiff tongues" and breast chains. Broad tires versus narrow tires created enough conversation to have filled a volume of the *Congressional Record.*

After 1918 these same arguments were in process, but the partisans were proclaiming the ease with which their Fords and Chevrolets went up hills and through sand beds in high. It was they who drove their "Detroit buggies" through loose dirt and then stopped to admire the clear impressions which their tires made, or blew their horns and slammed their tin doors to prove the quality of their machines.

Characteristic of the beginning of the postwar wagon and carriage business was an ad which appeared in 1869 in the Chester (South Carolina) *Reporter.* An outspoken German carriage maker of decided Confederate leanings aired his sentiments on the business of carriage making and frailty of human character. He sought a blacksmith, a wheelwright, and an industrious man all in one person. His notice said that he "wanted a good body-maker or wheelwright no matter what color. If white, not a person who occasionally gets drunk, or who works five or six hours in the twenty-four, and three days in the six, curses the poor man's fate, boasting that the world owes him a living, when he at no time has done anything for the world to be indebted to him. If a colored man when the shop is crowded with work, he at the sound of the fife and drum, with a blue scarf around his herculean shoulders, Mexican spurs on his heels, a cavalry sword dangling at his side, mounted on the skeleton of a horse imagining himself 'William the Conqueror on horseback' riding hellwards, Such is not wanted. I want trained muscle and bone. The drafting and brain I will furnish myself."

Making and selling wagons was only one aspect of the vehicle business. Long before the Civil War the South was a rich market for carriages of conservative design and price. Persons below the big-planter class traveled about in light rigs, and it was this stable middle-class demand which supplied a profit to ante bellum carriage makers. After Appomattox and the age of the grand carriage there was a growing demand for family surreys and single buggies. The surrey was in itself a bedrock of conservatism. Like the derby hat, the Prince Albert coat, the shirtwaist, and the bustle, it was a thing of unquestioned virtue and dignity. A family surrey with its dainty fringe on top mounted on four slender iron standards bespoke marriageable daughters and family honor, the matronly authority of mother, and the position of father as the natural family head. It was symbolical of all the formal aspects of southern society. The fringe top was an inseparable part of camp meetings, weddings, funerals, and barbecues. Church grounds were always crowded with these four-wheel matrons drawn by pairs of matched horses and mules. Even store grounds on Saturdays had a sprinkling of family surreys pressed into a workaday service of fetching away flour, fat meat, molasses, and tobacco.

Wherever gentle womenfolk traveled, there were the surreys. Bewhiskered and wrinkled "britchied" patriarchs occupied drivers' seats with great dignity as they jogged frisky teams off to meeting, and many of their innocent journeyings wound up in mishaps which became a part of the folklore of communities. There was that dignified Mississippi Methodist steward who checked his panting team in the midst of a spring branch below the church house to give it a drink. The team became frightened and turned around too shortly, spilling the good brother and his dressed-up family into the water. The steward's heavy britches and round-bellied coat were soaked and his high-top shoes were filled with sand and branch water. Floundering to the bank, he surveyed the wreckage with extreme disgust. Then with rising anger he sought permission of his spouting wife to make just one fitting remark, whereupon he rolled out a lusty and unstewardlike benediction of "damn it to hell."

Typical of all the fringe tops was the luxuriant "Atlanta," manufactured and distributed through the stores by the Brighton Buggy Company of Cincinnati. It was a fine carriage with stout wheels and graceful running gear. Patent-leather fenders covered the rear wheels, and there were elegant brass-rimmed kerosene lamps on either side of the front seat. It was upholstered in leather or whipcord, and was shaded by a neat square top trimmed with fringe and balled cord, overlaid with a heavier scalloped woven trim. This was the epitome of fine carriages, and it was a popular choice of discriminating "family men" who had a flock of shirtwaisted daughters to convey about the country side.

More varied and daring in design were the buggies. After 1865 the southern trade was well supplied with numerous types of single rigs. Everywhere carriage makers turned out fancy "dazzlers," "landaus," "coupes," "Bretts," "barouches," "cut unders," "rockaways," "phaetons," "Texas concords," "runabouts," and "heavy duties." These came with and without tops, and bespoke every degree of moral impulse of the American people. There were the heavy and clumsy two-horse models with unwieldy fabricord tops and side curtains. Then there were the dazzling light, topless runabouts with slender bodies, fancy stick seats, whipcord upholstering, and loud-colored running gear. These were, in fact, the iniquitous vehicles of gaiety and shotgun weddings in the first five uncertain decades of the New South. In reality they were the convertibles of their day. A young man rigged out in a semi-frockcoat, a heavy stock, a stiff shirt, high collar, patent-leather shoes, and a runabout drawn by a fast-stepping buggy mare was a great threat to the patient teachings of southern motherhood. Perhaps a gay-colored runabout, a reliable horse, a pretty girl, a level stretch of road, and a reasonably bright night was the nearest the postwar South ever came to fulfilling the "moonlight and roses" tradition.

While snappy runabouts whirred about dangerously at breakneck speed in the daytime and dawdled shamefully at night, there were the vehicles of more conservative travelers which clamored over the roads. Country doctors dozed through long drives behind trusted pairs of horses or flailed panting nags into wild gallops on hurried calls. Fat city drummers rocked back and forth under heavy derbies with catalogues and trunks of samples to sell everything from Carter's Little Liver Pills, fat meat, and Wisconsin cheese to kerosene oil. Interspersed in this parade were tired farmers who traveled at a steady gait with their long, bony left legs swinging down outside of buggy beds to the tiny oval steps. All of these could have told you that at best the problem of moving about the countryside was difficult, but that buggies and surreys offered the maximum in comfort.

Selling buggies was a pleasant business. The literature was colorful, and like the automobile folders of a later date, buggy catalogues and circulars flooded the storekeepers' mail. From the Banner Buggy Company in St. Louis came beautifully lithographed folders showing in seductive colors the wares of that firm. Then to give the prospective customer a more intimate view of the problem of making buggies, there were cuts showing the four or five departments of the complicated factory. These gay nineties assembly lines were marvels of a rapidly expanding machine age. Here top and curtain makers were cutting and sewing tops, there in another corner mechanics were forging axles, and across the way wheelwrights were putting tires on delicately fabricated wheels. It was, the prospective customer was told, an age of specialized business.

At Cincinnati the Brighton Buggy Company directed its energies toward the southern trade by naming its various models after southern cities. Their fringe top was the "Atlanta," while the "Augusta" was a gaudy little four-wheel harlot with spindle seat, arched axles, and gaily painted trim. The "Macon" was a conservative vehicle with a heavily padded back which sacrificed slenderness and color for comfort.

Hundreds of buggy and surrey makers clamored for southern business. Among the popular brands were the Brighton, Globe, Banner, Murray, Hugger, and scores of others. In thirty-five years the flourishing southern buggy-manufacturing business went to the larger centers, and by 1915 it was showing signs of disintegration. Once in a downward trend, the designers began appealing to modern tastes by advertising new models with latest-style auto seats, arched axles, rubber tires, and electric lights. This, however, was a dying gesture; soon buggy sheds were used to house automobiles, and buggies, harness, and carriage fixtures disappeared from the market except in southern Louisiana and the low country of the Carolinas and Georgia. After 1918 a single buggy maker in Indiana supplied the trade of the South. The Cajuns of the Bayou region of Louisiana clung tenaciously to their traditional language, food, folk customs, and buggies. Lined up daily under the spreading oaks outside of the Judice store at Scott, a dozen ponies drowse between the shafts of their ancient buggies. Not far away is the gray warehouse which delivers up an occasional new vehicle which comes down from Indiana.

Agricultural and transportation equipment was not to crowd out other important goods of the coarse, heavy type. Every year from September to January in the cotton South millions of yards of coarse jute bagging and thousands of bundles of slender steel ties were sold to cotton farmers. The huge rolls of jute gave off a pleasant, woody smell while the steel ties dripping with coal tar had a heavy, acrid aroma which gave the stores a distinctive cotton-picking flavor.

Despite the conservativeness of hardware stocks in the stores, an occasional element of progress crept in almost unnoticed. While hot disputes raged over local stock laws, manufacturers of barbed and net wire sent their wares south through such houses as Watkins, Cotterill and Company of Richmond. By the late eighties General John Bratton was fencing his Farmington acres in South Carolina for the purpose of keeping his purebred livestock at home and his neighbors' scrub stock away. Once the advantages of wire were known, the picturesque rail fences which were forever toppling over in a wind disappeared. It was a strange phenomenon of human prejudice that the staked and ridered rail fences disappeared without anyone's knowing exactly the date, but with their going fence laws became practically inoffensive.

Thus it was that a meaningful chapter of southern economic and social life was formed from the disorderly piles of hardware which cluttered aisles and warerooms. Here was an open story of the hesitancy with which southern one-horse farmers accepted new ideas and new machines. Shuck collars had long been adequate for plow mules, and there was no reason to change. Cultivating southern soil, it was argued, was purely a task for crude hand and horse tools, and manufacturers like Brinly and Avery were slow to introduce new implements. Limited cash returns from cotton, tobacco, and sugar culture did not permit experimentation and radical change. As a result, the three generations of farmers who grew up in the South prior to 1916 were, except for blacksmiths and mill operators, unmechanical in their outlook on life. It was the cheap, simplified Ford automobile with all its mechanical eccentricities that got southern farmers interested in machines. This fact was perhaps more influential than the passage of the Morrill Act and the founding of land-grant colleges, and the Smith-Lever Act of 1914 and its county agents, who began to destroy the caste system of agricultural methods.

As gasoline pumps crowded themselves up to store doors and top buggies became antiquarian curiosities, a new generation of southerners was born. Orders for backbands, trace chains, lap links, buckheads, and buggy antirattlers were now changed to requests for spare engine parts, gasoline, oil, heavy plowshares, drawbars, and extra disks. Tragically for the stores, this business went to the garages which supplanted the blacksmith-wheelwrights or to special agencies in the larger towns. This is the reason why an old-fashioned North Carolina merchant sat on his store porch on a hot cotton-chopping afternoon, spat a generous quid of tobacco into a rusty pile of outmoded plows, and observed with feeling, above the roar of a passing Standard Oil truck, that "we have a different kind of people now. Since 1921 they have been going to hell on the run in an automobile or a-straddle a tractor." This old-timer knew as he fingered the raveled end of a practically fresh coil of rope that no longer was there a specific affinity between a one-horse farmer and a long-eared plow mule.

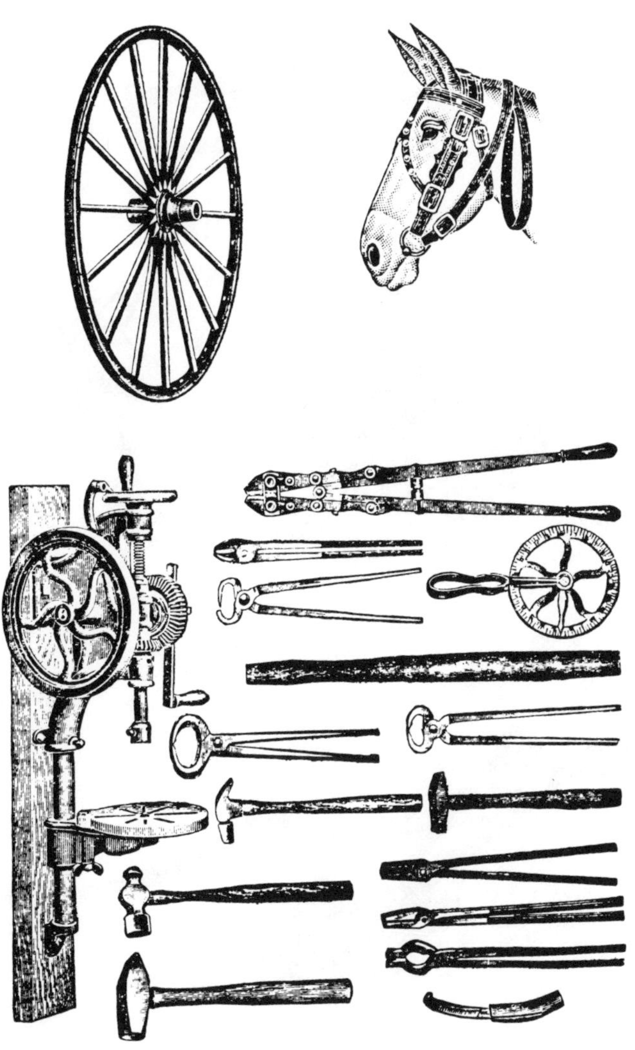

17

MONEY CATCHERS

Conveniences of southern rural life consisted largely of the little things which could be bought at the stores at moderate prices. Spirit and culture of the South was rather accurately reflected in the disheveled piles of sundries strewn on counters, shelves and in the glass cases of the general stores. One of the most attractive features of country merchandising was this curiosity-shop character. There was something extremely alluring about shelves laden with shoebrushes, rolls of fiddle-strings, black-head mourning pins, lamp burners, calf muzzles, coffin screws, fishhooks, padlocks, handsaw files, and scores of other articles.

Every item in the sundries stock had a specific meaning in the everyday affairs of the people which went deeper than the mere matter of its price and sale. For instance, life was made far more endurable for James McDonald, a south Alabama fiddler, because of his order for "one set of the best violin strings, and one E string extra. I want 2 E strings in all." Much of the southern musical taste was robust, and enterprising merchants quickly capitalized on this fact by stocking locally favored instruments and accessories. There were calls for fiddles, guitars, banjoes, and French and Jew's harps. A fiddle without strings was a major social calamity, especially when a community dance was impending. Hundreds of customers, like James McDonald, ordered extra strings for their fiddles, guitars, and banjoes. McDonald's request for an extra E string indicated the heavy use which he gave his violin. Fiddles were community institutions, and their owners sawed out interminable dance tunes such as "Granny, Does Your Dog Bite," "Hell Broke Loose in Georgia," and "Sugar in the Gourd." Ledgers everywhere carried entries for instrumental strings. Vigorous Saturday-night frolics nearly always produced demands for new sets with a few extras for safety's sake.

It was possible for merchants to stock a "good shaped instrument, red shaded, common [fiddle], put up in paste board box" for as little as $0.68. For a more discriminating trade there were classical models. A "Hopf" of "dark brown, good quality, plain inlaid edges, lined and backed, cost $1.50." "Stradivarius," "Maginis" and "Vuillaumes" climbed upward in price. A "Stradivarius good enough for anybody, dark finely polished, fine instrument, ebony finger board, well made, put up in paste board box" sold for $2.80. This was excelled only by the "Magini" at $2.92 and a "conservatory" Stradivarius which sold for $3.65, and a $5.50 "Vuillaume" which was "specially adapted for professional and solo use.'

Banjoes ranged in price from the plain little seventy-five-cent cotton-field numbers to the expensive ones which sold for $7.50. According to nostalgic tradition, much of the southern population was entranced by the strumming of these stringed calfskins. In fact, the banjo was a regional instrument of distinction. It was quite common for goods in the stores to bear lithographed labels of grinning Negroes stroking lightly the strings of their banjoes. In close competition with the banjo was the guitar. For as little as $1.95 merchants could stock a "Spanish model with patent head, maple wood, red shaded, varnished sound board, good quality in a paste board box." There were other and more refined models which sold at prices up to $5.00, and which produced a softer and more appealing chord. Among these were the Banner, Brooklyn, Star, Rosedale, and Spanish. The last had an inlaid center down its back and a series of pearl position dots on its neck. Its strings gave forth soft tones which blended perfectly with the sounds of the night, and made an overpowering don of its owner.

The guitar appealed to the joyous heart of Negro customers. Almost by instinct they knew the feel of a guitar's neck, and many of them were able to run the scale as naturally as they scratched their heads. Within a remarkably short time the youthful field hand learned to play the simpler tunes, and from thousands of cabins on the edges of cotton and tobacco fields cadent yodels of day's end harmonized with the soft undertones of country-store guitars.

Equally as popular as stringed instruments was the French harp. Those who were unable to make music with their fingers could at least make a series of musical sounds on their harps. The first thing a harpist learned to do was to lose himself in musical revery by imitating the sounds of a train gathering motion punctuated frequently with blasts of the whistle. Many a country dance was enlivened by the music of harps, which emphasized even the tones of fiddles and guitars.

Musical supplies were only incidentals in the prosperous sundries trades. Scattered in with these items were razors, razor straps, tooth soap and brushes. Packed in their slender black cases with telescope covers were the thin steel blades or somber bone-handled weapons of home barbers and social frolics. A good razor for the more meticulous male was a thing of great joy. Too, it has been said that they were great conveniences for those who were more versatile at getting into trouble than at fist fighting. A favorite make was that manufactured by Wade and Butcher. Their most popular number was advertised as being "full hollow ground, highly polished," and "too well known to need further description." There were several makes which attracted the trade, and nearly all of them sold for less than a dollar wholesale. These razors had important missions to perform, and the more vigorous heads of households held theirs as inviolate pieces of property. Occasionally children got hold of them and sliced fingers or gapped them in whittling. Sometimes an irresponsible wife forgot herself and used her husband's razor to slice fat meat and caused an unusually bitter family quarrel. But in the face of all these mishaps the razor trade in the stores remained constant. Along with the razors were the straps which were used for whetting dulled blades. Merchants displayed these in bunches, and there were frequent calls for them because of the recklessness with which they were slashed in two.

Crowded in among the fiddles, strings, razors, and straps were other articles of vanity. There were combs of half a dozen types: tucking combs for maidens with long hair, fine combs for those whose heads needed more detailed attention, long straight combs for high roached masculine pompadours, and especially designed half-circular ones, listed in invoices as "nigger combs." The latter was used for straightening and combing hair which had become entangled in tight bunches. This type was a ready seller and was always kept in stock in reasonably large numbers. Potentially every person in a community was a purchaser of a comb, and many customers bought combination combs and brushes. Characteristic of customer demands was an order from Mrs. Anne Terrell of Alabama which read, "let me have a Comb and Brush for my wavy 'Lock' and 50 cents worth of meat."

Mirrors were a third party with the comb-and-brush combinations. Guessing what kind of lookingglasses their trade wished to buy was an idle pastime for many merchants. Wholesale houses offered a variety of types. There were the famous cheaply priced squares of silvered glass, framed in flimsy, beaded strips of wood, which hung just above the washstands on back porches. Then there were the inexpensive circular ones bound in celluloid with either the heads of girls or advertising on their backs which allowed a user only a partial glimpse of himself. The larger the glass and the more ornate the frame, the more important the family. A full-length mirror often denoted a family of well-being and dignity.

A more intimate article of personal hygiene was represented by the toothbrush. Storekeepers kept small stocks on hand for more refined customers, but generally they were little in demand by the trade. Significantly few orders appear either in invoices or on ledgers for brushes, and their appearance in cases with miscellaneous goods indicated they were minor factors in southern life. Teeth were woefully neglected, and early in life many mouths were as badly gapped and eroded as were neighboring hillsides. Coupled with the trade of thin little brushes was that of bottles and boxes of tooth powder.

Long before the day of unctuous radio advertisers and the slick-page magazine horrors of bloody toothbrushes and nauseating and insidious gum diseases, country storekeepers were selling Raymond's tooth powder, which was "fragrant and refreshing." It cleaned teeth and was, as a matter of course, "recommended by the dental and medical profession." But most captivating of all was Tappan's Sweet Bye-and-Bye powder, which was highly recommended because it came in "beautiful oval bottles with polished nickel screw caps, cannot injure the enamel of the teeth, gives the breath a delightful fragrance and hardens the gums."

Even though the Sweet Bye-and-Bye tooth powder, like many of its modern counterparts, promised much and gave little, it attracted few customers as compared with the assortment of tawdry jewelry displayed alongside it. Every store was in the jewelry trade, stocks ranged from small handfuls of essential items to wide cases filled with elaborate displays of baubles and "cheap john." Although jewelry caught the fancy of both races, actually it attracted the Negro trade more. Bar pins, finger rings, earbobs and rings, stickpins, fancy hairpins, combs, buckles, metal buttons, necklaces, charms, and lapel buttons were ready sellers. Too, there was a constant demand for fraternity jewelry, and since stores and lodges were often in the same building, it was natural that there should be a profit in selling emblems.

Not only was there jewelry for sale in all of the stores, but likewise watches and clocks, which bore direct kinship in this more select trade. Keeping up with the time in the Lower South, however, was not always a matter of great importance. Rural southerners relied more upon the mark of the shade of a tree and the position of the sun to tell them the time. As in the case of frontiersmen of an earlier period, the exact hour for most farmers had little meaning until they came into possession of watches and clocks. Then time meant everything. They became conscious for the first time of the length of workdays, and from breakfast to noon was an interminable space of time. Country-store watches were of many different styles and degrees of accuracy. There was R. H. Ingersoll and Brother's famous stem-wound Yankee which retailed in the nineties for a dollar. Other timepieces bore the familiar marks of New Haven and Waterbury on their dials and were offered at moderate prices. From the seventies on, America became extremely conscious of the "exact time." Railroads established official schedules, even though they were seldom able to keep them. Engineers and conductors became wedded to their watches, and this feeling spread. Thus in order to give questionable watches a seal of quality, manufacturers stamped prints of locomotives on the back covers of their wares. This favorite design was interchanged with those of the "noble stag," the head of a horse, and the fleur-de-lis. For stores the trade in watches was often a profitable side line. When a merchant sold a watch, he created a market for both a chain and a charm. If the purchaser belonged to a fraternity, he bought the emblem of his lodge. Younger customers and Negroes were fond of novelty charms such as dice, skulls and crossbones, girls' legs, monkey wrenches, pistols, and bird dogs. Even when these things were not carried in stock, they could always be ordered, and numerous invoices indicate that this was done.

Of all the timepieces handled by the general stores, the famous carved-wood mantel clocks are best remembered. They became the postwar grandfather clocks and were symbols of peaceful family firesides. Among the many types, the Oriole, described by one wholesaler as "our famous 8-day, ½ hour strike, oak and walnut assorted, dial 6 inches, height 22¾," was characteristic. Everywhere these were standard home timepieces. Sitting in their places of honor on family mantel boards, they ticked away the hours, their lazy pendulums swinging back and forth. Their hollow metallic chimes sounded the passing hours with resounding smashes. They announced hours in numbered strikes, and half hours in single strokes. These three-dollar clocks were not timepieces alone, but likewise hiding places for small change, prescriptions, recipes, and important papers.

For those individuals who wanted more dash and variety than were offered by the conventional mantel clocks, there was the model of 1899 with Teddy Roosevelt astride a charger sitting perpetually in the midst of a high jump over the instrument's dial. Where the political implications of Teddy's roughriding was not in favor, there were nonpartisan elephants, cupids, dogs, and pot-bellied knights who strained away at holding up their ticking burdens of springs, cogs, faces, and revolving hands. In all of these timepieces merchants had a pleasant trade which gave their customers both reasonably good service and a vast amount of sentimental entertainment.

Jewelry was a steady year-round seller, and the volume of profit from its sale in many stores was considerable. But as fascinating as this trade was, it had a businesslike rival in fishing tackle during the early spring months. When merchants put garden seeds, onion sets, plowlines, and straw hats on display, they likewise filled showcases with bright red- and green-striped floats, boxes of fishhooks, spools of line, and bags of split buckshot. Hardly was the last bit of winter chill out of the air before store loafers were crowding around the tackle case buying hooks and lines. "Please send me 25¢ of fishing hooks & lines send some Buck shot to put on them. I will settle soon" wrote an optimistic southern fisherman in February 1893. Already other entries had appeared in the ledgers, and farmers were giving way to an impulse to spend their time along the creeks.

Fishing in the South has ever been the common man's sport, and every spring an army of customers expended considerable energy trying to inveigle mud cats, perch, and bream onto their hooks. The excitement had started in the stores. Tackle displays suddenly converted more than half the population into primitive men once again searching for food and sport in neighboring creeks. There was something tempting about the colorful displays of fishing tackle which lowered sales resistance, even of those who disliked fishing.

For merchants the sale of fishing equipment was both profitable and unprofitable. When credit customers showed too much interest in sitting on the creek banks, there was grave danger that they would let the grass run away with their crops and would prove poor credit risks. For the cotton and tobacco farmer it was one of those unhappy perversities of nature that grass grew most luxuriant during the best fishing season of the year.

Other sports competed for the store's trade with the universally favorite pastime of fishing. Baseball was a general favorite. The craze took hold after the Civil War, and merchants stocked balls, bats, gloves, and masks and supplied the local teams with equipment. In this latter trade, however, the stores functioned both as places where sporting goods could be bought and as central points for participation in ball games.

By nature southerners were extroverts, and they took to athletic games with a relish. During the Civil War, Confederate soldiers learned to play baseball. Twenty years before, General Abner Doubleday of Cooperstown, New York, had expanded the ancient sport of "One Old Cat" into a three-base game along with a set of rules. Southern soldiers in federal prison camps learned how to play this game and introduced it into the Confederate Army. After the surrender veterans took the idea and rules home with them and organized community clubs.

As community centers, hitching grounds about the stores were scenes of most of the baseball games. Continuously there were fights between farmers and ball players because of runaways caused by stray flies. One of these irate customers, airing his views in the Shelby *Guide,* accused roughnecks of Columbiana, Alabama, of ruining the village. They were galloping up and down the road catching fly balls, running all over the hill encircling the bases, scaring horses, and raising sand in general. Taking a characteristic postwar view of things, this sorehead concluded that the game was a moral detriment. "It does not," he wrote, "recommend gentlemen who play the game." Despite this criticism, the boys went on batting out Texas leaguers in the vicinity of the stores, and many a southern boy learned the art of pitching the kind of curved balls which have so badly confused batters since 1850.

In Georgia nearly every store had its baseball team and brass band. Scores of old nesters recall the proud days when "we used to play ball right out there before the porch and the band played the hottest music in the country." It took three surrey loads to hustle the Fork Flyaways and their noisy band over to Greenville to cross bats with the Pop-and-Go Team. The Paoli Blues of near-by Elberton challenged all comers and occasionally ventured across the Savannah River to the South Carolina villages.

On one occasion a South Carolina team went over the river to meet Georgia competition and they took a Negro band along to make the music. South of the river the colored musicians infuriated the home band, and they were forced to grab up their horns and drums and wade home.

A thrifty ball club was organized in 1876 at the Patrick store in White Oaks, South Carolina. On the opening pages of the store's ledger there is an itemized account of the income and expenditures of this organization. Twenty-four members paid $12.65 in dues. Balls cost $1.60 apiece, bats were $0.50, iron pins, $0.30, a water carrier received $0.25, and a weed cutter was paid $0.15. Absent were charges for gloves, masks, chest protectors, and shin guards. Baseball was a man's game, and men caught balls barehanded, sometimes disjointing their fingers in the effort.

Actually the sale of general merchandise or "racket" goods went far beyond articles for entertainment, vanity, and sports. The list of goods carried in stock was long, and seldom was it more orderly on invoices than it was on shelves and counters. Shipping and billing clerks mounted on high stools in wholesale houses inscribed long lists of merchandise which included currycombs, rattail files, coffee mills, hatpins, candles, paint, monkey wrenches, butter molds, rivets and burrs, spectacles, shoe lasts, tacks, half soles, padlocks, scissors, writing papers, washboards, pegging awls, hog rings, bridle buckles, coffeepots, wire staples, rat poison, tortoise-shell hairpins, matches, window shades, sifters, rubber nipples, nursing bottles, mousetraps, churns and dashers, graters, lampwicks, comic post cards, gun tubes, mucilage, worm candy, trunks, suitcases, strainers, calf muzzles, Jew's harps, lamp chimneys, shoe polish, whet and grindstones, writing pens, molasses pitchers, watch chains, pocketbooks, spurs, cowbells, sadirons, thimbles, axle grease, dinner bells, palmetto fans, dice, plush-lined albums, black-head mourning pins, and many other articles which made living in southern households for the past eighty years a little more pleasant.

Included in the long list of goods which poured into the stores were furniture, china and tableware, stoves, and kitchen utensils. One of these lists included plates, saucers, cups, platters, bowls, pitchers and tumblers for the dining table. Another listed stoves, stove parts, fire shovels, tin pipes, frying pans, bakers, bread pans, cast-iron kettles and dishpans. Furniture invoices were filled with entries for housekeeping essentials—bedsteads, cane-seat straight and rocking chairs, tables, and safes with perforated tin fronts.

Distributors like the Marietta (Georgia) Manufacturing Company; the Hoy Furniture Company, Decatur, Alabama; Home Furniture Company, High Point, North Carolina; Stowell and Warrick Company of Athol, Massachusetts; Myer, Bridges Company, Louisville; J. Leopold and Company, D. E. Haynes and Company, Baltimore; and Phillips and Buttorff Manufacturing Company, Nashville, shipped millions of pieces of furniture, chinaware, and stoves to southern merchants.

The succession of life in the region followed a fairly routine pattern. Young couples were married, and ledgers of a neighboring store recorded more intimate stories of their starts in life than did the local newspapers' flowery accounts of their weddings. Housekeeping in the rural South was a highly simplified matter. All that was needed in the beginning were from two to six cheap cane-bottom "straight" chairs, a rocker, an iron bedstead, springs, a mattress, a bureau, a safe with tin doors, a cooking stove, a few pots and pans, a set of cheap dishes, a water bucket, a washpan, and a mirror. These, of course, were the bare essentials for housekeeping, but historically bare essentials have constituted the equipment for a large proportion of homes.

Utensils and dishes were all that remained to complete household needs. A characteristic family purchase is to be found in a Williams store entry headed "Samuel B. Taylor, per self and lady." Their list of goods included "1 sett knives & forks, 1 dish, 1 wash pan, 1 coffee mill, 1 coffee pot, 1 molasses stand, 1 oven and lid, 1 sifter, 1 sad iron, 1 coarse comb, 1 qt. coal oil, 4 lb. coffee, 1 Box matches." The only thing of consequence missing in this order was a set of plates.

Sprinkled through all of the invoice and ledger books are orders for tableware and china. A "sett" of bone-handle iron knives and forks sold at retail for $2.50; a set of cheap plated spoons cost another $1.50, and for three times this price one could buy either Brazilian silver or Rogers' plated ware. Setting table for some country-store customers was literally a repetition of the story of the *Arkansaw Traveler*. Many a slightly embarrassed hostess re-enacted in her own kitchen a scene comparable to that where the squatter's boy told his pa they lacked enough knives to set the table, to which the old-timer replied, "Like to know why there ain't! There's big butch and little butch, and short handle, and corn-cob handle, and no handle at all, and if that ain't knives enough to set any gentleman's table, I would like to know."

Volumes of long invoice slips clearly indicate that the business of supplying the hardware trade was not alone a matter of carrying in stock the heavy goods of the farm. There was an endless demand for miscellaneous hardware items listed in the catalogues as "shelf goods." Among these were hinges, hasps, staples and fasteners, screws, bolts, washers, tacks, springs, rivets, brads and burrs, padlocks, mousetraps, currycombs, hog rings, speying needles, files, and harness snaps. These articles were always in stock, and seldom if ever were they purchased before there was an immediate need for them.

Orders were always in the nature of emergencies. Corn was ever scarce, and there was grave danger that thieves would raid cribs if they were left unlocked. A customer ordered "a cupple of pad locks 2/-locks will answer." Another wanted "2 good padlocks, for my corn crib worth-about 25¢ Each." Then there were orders for other shelf goods. On a rainy day an amateur cobbler ordered a shoe last, a "barrel" of shoe tacks, and a pair of half-soles with which to mend his brogans. Harness makers bought strips of leather, buckles and brads, and made bridles, breeching, and wagon lines. An old sow grew restless in her barren pasture and rooted down the fence. A rider went scurrying away to get "hog rings" and a ringer with which to stud her nose with steel so as to keep the ravenous beast a long-suffering but subdued prisoner.

Womenfolk enjoyed the advantages which the varied stocks of household supplies offered. Seamstresses needed shuttles, needles, hooks and eyes, thimbles, and scissors, and they could always get them at the store. Their notes were highly domestic. Characteristic was a friendly request from a housewife saying, "Will you please take these needles back—They are not the size I wanted. Tell him [Chesley Williams, Eagleville, Tennessee] when he gets in his no. 1 to send me 2 of them & one ½ I have got big needles enough to run me until Gabe blows his horn. Will be ever so much obliged."

Perhaps there was no elementary human need which could not be satisfied at the store. Everything from stove bolts to spectacles was to be found in stock. Many stores actually carried on the quackery of the last five decades by stocking inferior spectacles to be sold to customers whose eyesight was failing but who were unable to pay for specialized optical services. Far too many customers for the public good were fitted with country-store glasses. In Atlanta, Kellam and Moore claimed to have "the only lens grinding plant in the South." They assured their customers that "no goods were sold to peddlers or street vendors at any price"; they reserved their trade strictly for the storekeepers. In order to attract trade, and to give their wares a semiprofessional stamp, company letter and bill heads carried the profile of a bewhiskered eye doctor tinkering with a "scientific" instrument which he used to test both eyes and lenses in the same sleight-of-hand operation.

Kellam and Moore enjoyed exclusiveness in the South only by reason of the fact that they had a "grinding plant." There were likewise competitive Yankee spectacle-grinders who showed real concern for southern eyesight. The famous counter catalogues all offered specs for sale at remarkably low prices. One famous list included spectacles of a dozen different types, and optometers which merchants were supposed to use in fitting the glasses. Glasses were available at ridiculously low prices. Steel-framed spectacles with convex lenses could be bought for as little as forty-six cents a dozen. "Scenery spectacles, for beautifying landscapes, views, etc., with extra long bows" were offered to merchants serving hard-pressed southern farmers for eighty-eight cents a dozen. There were many other types which ranged upward in price to as much as $3.65 a dozen. For instance, a weak-eyed farmer could give himself the general appearance of a county editor with a fifty-cent pair of cork nose specs which dangled at the end of a black ribbon.

In the showcases at least, specs and art went together. Perhaps the scenery spectacles were intended to encourage the sale of country-store art which consisted of framed pictures of all kinds. Drab plank walls of combination bed-living rooms were enlivened with such brilliant lithographed subjects as "St. Cecilia," "The Madonna and Child," colonial kitchens, waterfalls, sheep grazing in rich green pastures, the inevitable cottages by romantic creek banks, snow scenes, and, occasionally, pictures of sad-eyed girls who bespoke chastity in every line of their lithographed faces and bodies. These cheap pictures were expressive of a desire of rural customers to break the monotony of their daily lives. They put them over mantels, in parlors, in family bedrooms, and even in their smoky kitchens. Both white and colored customers had a fondness for pictures. Where the trade was unable to purchase the finer framed goods, merchants were able to supply gaudy prints which could be tacked to walls in order to give them color.

Country-store art after 1880 took on an exceedingly conservative tone, on the one hand, and a sickening smart-aleck flavor on the other. Much of American society was just reaching a stage of self-consciousness when people were showing off. Nearly every store had its racks of comic valentines and post cards. The cards had such clever captions printed on them as "To fall in love is simply awful—to fall out is awful simple," or, in commenting on kissing. "Some furniture house will make a sale," or "Something we can all afford." The artistic taste carried over into the manufacturing and sale of jewelry and notions. Ladies' garters were offered for sale by wholesale houses with naughty gay-nineties inscriptions, "Forget Me Not," "Stop Your Kidding," "I'm a Warm Baby," and "Private Property." When these goods found their way into the hard-boiled channels of workaday trade, they were listed on invoices as "fancy novelties."

This was all a pleasant part of the country-store business. Sometimes there was comical incongruity in the sale of commercial fertilizers, turning plows, heel bolts, garters with thermometers on the buckles, comic cards, razors, fiddlestrings, butter molds, and curling irons. But back of it all was the sage mercantile philosophy that storekeeping was in reality a business of self-sufficiency. Before 1920 there were few competitive specialists who holed themselves up behind bright red store fronts which sported their names in huge gilded letters and snatched greedily at a trade which belonged to the crossroad merchants.

18

AN OUGHT'S AN OUGHT

IN THE YEARS immediately following the Civil War former slaves, feeling the pressure of "free" economics, composed a little settling-up ditty which expressed their attitude toward the credit system. It went:

An ought's an ought
And a figger's a figger
All for the white man
And none for the nigger.

Actually the sentiment of this uncompromising little ballad meant more than racial discrimination. It implicated everybody who depended on credit, and most southern merchants estimated that this included approximately 90 per cent of their trade. The country stores were agencies of credit, and it was through them that the new agricultural South scrambled slowly to its feet.

Scarcely a single phase of life was left untouched by the influence of the merchant. Behind the whole business of storekeeping after 1865 was a dramatic story of people seized by panic and of their hunting a solution for their future. There were two parts to the story; one was of slaves who became freedmen with their economic destinies in their own hands; the other, of farmers who lacked capital and were dependent upon merchants for credit to make a crop. It was this feeling of panic and frustration which caused southern legislators to pass lien laws so farmer could give unplanted crops as collateral for supplies. Back of the passage of these agricultural lien laws was the influence of northern and southern merchants, little farmers, plantation owners, carpetbaggers, scalawags, and freedmen. Each was motivated by the hope that a year's credit would help the South produce a single crop and re-establish its economic order.

Perhaps in this army of proponents of the lien laws was someone who could visualize it in operation ten years later, but this is doubtful. Storekeepers were glad the bills were passed, and asked no questions of the future. They could secure liens on crops, discount them to wholesale houses and banks for goods, and build a thriving business on no more than hope for the success of the next crop. New stocks were piled into stores helter-skelter, new account books received their first entries. Packed away safely in new iron safes were the first of rapidly growing packets of lien and mortgage papers, and for the first time records became a major factor in storekeeping. Now that wholesale houses, and even Wall Street, were interested in the affairs of the southern crossroads merchants, it was necessary for them to keep a careful daily check on their sales.

Country boys began studying business forms, the writing of business letters, and the art of penmanship. Business colleges sprang up in the larger towns, and heavy-handed bookkeepers learned the fine, graceful touch of the Spencerian hand by scribbling over and over, "The pen is mightier than the sword." They learned to keep track of daybooks, journals, ledgers, invoice books, cotton-gin reports, cotton-sales books, guano accounts, and long strings of cash orders. The system was not too complicated, and there was room for personal variation in method from one store to another. It mattered not whether they used single- or double-entry systems, or whether they itemized their sales in their journals and transferred the prices to their ledgers, or observed other rules, so long as they could make sense of each year's business.

Every store had its "books." For most customers, however, the activities of the bookkeepers were beyond human comprehension. A remarkably large number of them could neither read, write, nor cipher, and for them the intricacies of determining interest was an unfathomable mystery. It could be done as far as they knew only on the basis of gross approximation. Early each spring these unlettered debtors drew wavering cross marks between their given and surnames, and were told by merchants, for instance, that they could trade up to $75.00 worth for the year, but the amount was to be divided into seven monthly allotments of $10.50 each.

For freedmen, this economic servitude was almost as binding as slavery. White farmers began to taste the bitter fruits of economic enslavement. Readily they would have agreed with the editor of the Elberton (Georgia) *New South* that "Either farming is the most profitable of all callings or Georgia farmers who borrow money [or operate on credit] are on the road to ruin." All over the South editors singled out the merchants for special abuse. Miles of editorial columns bemeaning the money-changers for charging outrageous prices and interest were poured into the presses. Every man who wrote a book or special magazine article on the economic affairs of the New South used up considerable space discussing the evils of store credits.

Actually neither the methods of credit granting nor the lien system of giving security was a product of the New South. Cotton factors who had supplied ante bellum planters, and who continued in business for a decade or more following the war, had relied upon a similar type of crop-chattel mortgage for security. But once legislators, after 1865, gave this method of credit granting an almost universal application in the South, it began to attract editorial attention. Prices in the stores were pushed up to the maximum level. A barrel of flour in 1894 sold wholesale for $3.47, but before it reached a customer's table the price was at least $7.00, or 100 per cent increase. Thus it was that country merchants were charged with usury in its grossest form, and on the strength of individual cases they were guilty as charged. The customer not only paid a published interest charge of 12.5 per cent, but a mark-up of

25 per cent and more for credit price plus a profit charge of 10 to 50 per cent. Interest rates were always based upon a period of twelve months, or, as one merchant said, "from gin whistle to gin whistle." Actually the carrying period seldom averaged longer than seven or eight months.

When customers depended upon stores to credit them for everything they bought, liability for merchants was great. A general crop failure promised ruin for the store and certainly bankruptcy for the customer. The sudden disappearance or death of a customer was a blow to a storekeeper's business. If he remained in business, he had to spread his liabilities to all of his trade. A hundred credit customers who religiously settled their accounts at the end of each crop season were often forced to pay the accounts of another hundred who did not. Perhaps the principle of this type of credit granting was open to serious question by those who would set the South's economy in order, but the ethics, in the eyes of the merchants, was not. Both merchant and customer were clear on the point that good risks had to be responsible for the bad ones. Storekeepers learned that they could not operate very long if they did not follow this practice.

"Paying out," however, was shrouded in mystery for the debtor, even though merchants in the great majority of cases kept honest books. But the great discrepancy was the sliding level of prices and the poor quality of goods carried in stock. They were bought at the cheapest wholesale listings and were sold at maximum retail prices. Thus "paying out" was little more than 50 per cent of the ledger record. Few customers ever had more than the most elementary concept of prices, and they gave little thought to what goods cost in relation to what they had to pay. For them the first consideration was getting them charged to their credit accounts.

Always there was an element of secrecy involved in price quotations. Brogan shoes could be bought wholesale for 75 cents a pair, but they retailed at prices from $1.25 to $2.25. Suits of woolen clothes were bought for $3.25 to $15.00 but were sold for $10.00 to $25.00. Meat was 5 to 7 cents a pound, flour $3.00 to $5.00 per barrel, and sugar from 4 to 6 cents per pound. But before any of these commodities were loaded onto a customer's wagon, the price was practically doubled. Lumbering home in their wagons, purchasers studied the strange marks which the merchants had made on tags and barrel heads and wondered what they all meant. They meant something to the merchant the customers knew because they had seen the clerk examining them. The arrangement of the letters and symbols, however, was senseless. One row read CD2 and the second BD2, and sometimes there was a third row of letters. They were, of course, letters from the code word.

Every merchant selected a Price Symbol as soon as he went into business, and it was made a password to his sales methods. It had to contain ten letters, preferably no two alike, and it could not be too easy to decipher. Some of these were "Baltimore," "Comb basket," "Black Snake," "Prudential," "Cumberland," the first ten letters of the greek alphabet, and special symbols such as those used by the J. D. McGraw house in Louisville, Mississippi, XΦΘΛΛϟZ∠ΛV. Thus markings on goods became " XXZV " or $14.00. Always it was the practice to mark goods with both the purchase and selling prices. If a store did an appreciable cash business, clerks marked the purchase, cash, and credit prices. In this way the trade was unable to keep up with values. One of the favorite pastimes for the few customers who understood the use of code words was that of trying to guess what they meant.

This subject of prices and credit charges disturbed the English traveler, Robert Somers. In southern Mississippi he became acquainted with a Jewish merchant named Solomon who explained in candid terms his concepts of the postwar credit system. Rations were corn meal, first price $0.75, the second $1.50; sixteen pounds of meat, first price $0.13, the second, $0.25; one gallon of molasses, first price, $0.50, the second $1.00. These were arbitrary surcharges, of course. When Somers asked, "But Mr. Solomon, is not 100 per cent of retail profit too much?" he received the answer that "It ish large profith, but it ish profith in de books, not profith in de pocket."

"How so?" queried the visitor. "Why, de white planter is very poor, and de Negro, who sometimes raises crop for himself, ise very idle, and knows no counts. He comes to me and says he will raise crop if he is fed and get clothes. . . ." Mr. Solomon's conversation with Robert Somers covered many features of the store-planter system. "We do a great deal [of riding to inspect crops and credit risks]," said the merchant. "I have three horses riding on saddle—my own, one of the best pacers in de country; and when Sunday comes I say to my clerks, "Go you dis way and dat, and I go de other, and we see how de work is going on. . . ." He said, "De store ish de inside of de plantation. If de Negro wants bacon or molasses, we give him half de quantity or none, and de planter de same. His wife wants silk gowns; we give her a cotton one or none."

The Mississippi Jew gave a faithful outline of much of the store's place in the credit system of the South. Merchants, once they granted a customer credit, were forced to keep track of what he was doing. When a farmer placed a lien on a crop, it became somebody else's. Both the storekeeper and the wholesaler based their business upon crop prospects, but they required a stiff payment for their services. In almost every store, the picture of community finances was locked in the safe.

Regularly each spring a majority of landowners and tenants alike called at the stores to sign lien notes. It was a hard bargain that the printed document prescribed. It provided that the debtor "Hereby gives and grants unto the said *John Doe and Company* a lien on all crops which shall be made by or for him on said plantation during said years. . . . Also gives and grants unto the said *John Doe and Company* a lien upon said crop or crops for all costs and charges which may be so incurred, including Clerk's and Sheriff's costs and incidental expenses, and hereby authorizes and directs the collection of the same in addition to such sum as may be due for advances aforesaid." This embodied the essential elements of the lien law in action. It represented the credit system of the New South in its starkest form.

So common was the practice of accepting lien notes in lieu

of cash that regularly printed forms were available at all times. Characteristic of the credit negotiations is this letter from John M. Allison of the Terrill Place in Marengo County, Alabama. On January 3, 1893, he wrote John C. Brown, "This is handed to you by Frank Prowell who expects to work with me this year. He has herewith a written contract which you will please read to him and take his signature thereby. You will also please let him have five ($5.00) in merchandise, and chge to me for Frank Prowell, so that his acc't can be referred to at any time. His wife Charlotte also intends to work a half patch with me. I am to furnish her a sufficient quantity of land to produce two bales upwards of cotton so that she will be entitled to at least one bale of cotton. Please advance her something on such patch—of course I am responsible. I will be up in a few days and arrange my mortgage for this year. P.S. Let her have 5.00 or 6.00 worth. Charge to her Charlotte Prowell."

Everywhere the system of control was effective. In Mississippi, Louisiana, and Tennessee it was the same story. South Carolina farmers struggling to make ends meet on the poor, leached soils between the Wateree and Broad rivers looked to the merchants for help. Throughout the cropping season they bought goods on their liens, and for most of them there was a credit limit scrawled in red letters across the heading of their accounts. One tenant needed money with which to pay wage hands, but his landlord wrote, "His lien must not Be let go over sixty dollars. What I want you to do is just notify Him that His lein is out and that He need not send any more order to Be Paid off if His lien is not over sixty dollars you can pay off this order if you think it right. I expect His Crop may Pay it." Others requested merchants to clamp down on their tenants with the hope that they could insure their paying out in the fall. As "laying-by" time approached, landlords were less ready to grant their tenants additional credit. One of these cautious boss men wrote an Alabama merchant, "Please limit Noah Collier to amt of four dollars on November's time." Another asked that a storekeeper put Major Blake on a strict ration of two and one-half bushels of corn, a bushel of meal, and ten pounds of bacon, "and please Itemise his account up today I want to see what he has been buying."

There was an endless amount of correspondence over debt. A creditor pleaded with his storekeeper, "Mr. Patrick, Dear Sir, I write you a fewe lines I Did all i could to pay you last year But I could not Doe it Do not think that you will not receive your pay I will pay you if life last I am striving to pay you with all my mite. i will pay you this if i live my crop looks well at this time your Debt is the only trouble withe me hoping you will be satisfied to wait on me. . . ."

This was only one of a continuous stream of notes making excuses for failure to pay. Some were ingenious in their humility while others were pitiful apologies for failure of the land. A North Carolinian explained to his merchant, "Mr. Perry I amed to bin there before crismas but I got horse kict and could not come. I am going to Winston and I will call at your house and pay you. I will be along in a short time. Pleas don't put the paper out I don't want pay no cost on it I will pay off."

Lien notes were worthless if crops did not yield the money. Calling in livestock, produce, implements, household goods, and even the land itself to be sold "at the courthouse door to the highest bidder" was an extremely doubtful method of collecting debts. There was far too much harshness attached to the public display and sale of an unfortunate debtor's goods. Yet many courthouse squares were littered with mortgaged chattels.

Land exchanged hands frequently through the mortgage system, but its exchange was seldom as much publicized as was that of more intimate possessions. Land could not be brought into the county seat and placed on public display. Merchants disliked the idea of foreclosing on mortgages, and whenever it was possible, they quietly negotiated an assignment of deed before obligations matured. But even though they were hesitant about foreclosing mortgages, there were frequent notices that storekeepers were selling their customers' homesteads.

The process of losing possession of farms in the South followed a regular credit routine. Accounts ran hopelessly behind for two or three years with unsettled balances piling up into such considerable sums that lien notes were no longer adequate coverage, then a mortgage was placed upon the land, and the annual deficit continued piling up until it consumed the full value of an unfortunate debtor's possessions. The customer "assigned" his land to the merchant, went through the fiction of making an independent settlement of his account, and then moved away to begin anew as a tenant farmer.

A large percentage of the more progressive merchants became large landowners. Land for all of them was a stable source of wealth. Some stores began on plantations, but more merchants acquired land through the failure of the credit system. Their account books were burdened with red entries at "settling-up" time, and debt for the farmer-customer was a gripping thing. In 1882 the editor of the Greensboro (Georgia) *Herald* estimated that a farmer borrowing and paying back $800 for each crop would within a five-year period pay out $2,800 in interest. In one of the frequent tirades against storekeepers, an old farmer asked a naïve stranger, "Why do you pretend to tell us that you don't know what a cropping mortgage is? Then you are not a southerner."

As the agricultural South became more and more involved in debt to its storekeepers, philosophers tried frantically to find a logical reason which would explain their predicament. With limited views of the true state of their economy they produced various notions of why they were in trouble. One of them impatiently implored the store customers to "quit buying 18 yards of calico for a dress. Tear off the ruffles. Work your women. Turn off the negro cooks. Stop wastage and breakage and stealage. Teach the children to work. Pass a law in Georgia to make everybody work." A neighboring editor looked over the same scene and thought he saw at least one solution of this sort in the offing. He realized that "the day of the Grecian bend and bustle are said to be numbered. The girl of the period dress, with its bunched up skirts and froufrou flounces, is to give place to the stautesque and classical soft flowing draperies over unstarched petticoats will be the order of the day. Hoop skirts have been scorned by fashion for a year or more though they are so comfortable that many ladies will never wear a diminutive crinoline, scant skirts, like those seen in pictures of Josephine and Hortense. . . ."

Far more practical than these droll attacks upon female dress was the statement that "the southern man sells all he can't eat, and the northern man eats all he can't sell. Did you ever see a southern planter who didn't want to borrow money? The more cotton he makes the more money he must borrow. The cotton mania and the credit system are our twin manias." A former Confederate added his voice to the gathering storm of protest and denounced the business methods of the farmer by saying, "All cotton and no corn; buying western corn and bacon and northern hay, running in debt to our factors and merchants, lien receipts, mortgages and sheriffs' sales are the offshoots from the main root."

Certainly these attacks were well within the realm of fact in their criticism of the credit system. Merchants, however, were only functional parts of the whole ineffective scheme of production and credit. In 1866, when postwar stores were getting started, cotton was selling for forty-three cents a pound, and the price remained above twelve cents until 1876. These were formative years for stores and their credit business. What was true of cotton likewise applied to the production of sugar cane, tobacco, and grain. It was much easier for storekeepers to keep track of their debtors if they were forced to grow a single staple crop. Cotton cultivation was ideally adapted to the most primitive methods of tillage and market control.

That cotton led the field in the matter of requiring only a limited amount of equipment was adequately illustrated in the stocks carried by the stores. In 1876 the editor of the Mobile *Register* believed that no man could operate a cotton farm with businesslike methods. In an outburst of self-conscious frustration he singled out the Yankee and Negro for special criticism. He wrote that "any northern man coming South to farm with freedmen and trust everything to them, stands a good chance to break. His money and good business qualifications will not save him even. The working of Negroes on the shares with a good team and a no. 1 rig such as northern men get up have no acquaintance with Cuffy, beats drinking and gambling all hollow. They thought the Negro a colored white man, and when he listened to, 'Boss, you see dat mule standing down dar in de woods, his years set for'ards, his head hung down, wid dat skin place on de shol'der, and no skin on his backbone, wid trace chains, shuck collar, baggin' back band, rope headstall, piece of wire for a bit; dat ol' cas' plow layin' down dar on turning row, an' no other plow, I made five bags cotton. Oh: you bet, wid dat two-hundred dollar mule and leather rig, I can tend dat five and five more and dem ten acres make twenty bags.'

"With this he gets sugar, coffee, molasses, flour, sundry clothes, in all he runs his account up to $400, and his crop makes one and one half to three bales, never more. His $200 mule skinned and scarred all over, at public sale, would not bring over $125. Nothing but a skeleton of that fine rig left. While Negro swindling is going on at one end he is stealing at the other. The southern white man is able to get along for the reasons that he knows him better. He gives the said negro four pounds of bacon, one quarter bushel of meal, and tells him to go to plowing. Cuffy knows who has him and he goes, and next Monday morning he comes again. If he has three or four acres plowed he gets some rations, if not, nothing but a cussing."

Cussing Cuffy, however, did not in any way lessen the evils of the cotton-credit system so far as the store was concerned. Cussing, in fact, was not a tangible bit of property which could be sold at the courthouse door. When the Mobile editor cried out in bitter rage against the Yankee and the Negro, he showed a complete lack of understanding of all the factors involved in his region's agricultural methods. Cotton could always be sold quickly for cash, and the market fluctuations were never too great within a single season. Trends were gradual, and merchants had an opportunity to prepare for changes several months in advance. Nearly every storekeeper was likewise a ginner and cotton buyer. He was forced to buy cotton in order to collect debts, although he maintained that he never made a profit from this trade. Buying cotton was a means by which he kept careful check on his creditors. Sometimes merchants even offered premium prices for cotton which was to be applied in payment of debts by the simple device of reducing excessive interest and mark-up charges.

Cotton and tobacco were commodities most readily adaptable to a fairly complete check and control. Cotton bales were given serial numbers, and they could be traced from the gins to the spinning rooms of cotton factories, and producers were responsible all the way up the line for the contents of the bale. For this reason it was difficult to elude payment of debts by selling crops elsewhere. Cotton early was regarded as a foundation stone of credit, and because of this there was almost a sacred regard for the staple. Cotton, tobacco, and the other staples would pay debts, and merchants sinned greatly by forcing upon the South its unfortunate one-crop system. Almost every account carried in the ledgers from the cotton belt bears testimony both to its importance and to its gradual failure to meet the demands of an expanding regional economy.

After 1870 merchants added another source of income in the sale of commercial fertilizers. As the older lands were exhausted and the demand for cotton increased, artificial fertilization became a necessity. Phosphate was the chief chemical used in fertilizer manufacturing, and some merchants boosted their incomes by manufacturing and selling commercial fertilizers during the winter and early spring months. They purchased phosphatic acids, cottonseed meal, and used stable manure, sand, and loam as a base stock. The product was prepared during the idle season when creditors and the laborers on storekeepers' farms were idle. It was a profitable business until the eighties, when state inspection laws required that each bag of guano bear a tag with a guaranteed analysis printed upon it.

As early as 1870, Robert Somers found the Wando Company of South Carolina developing phosphate from the beds of the low-country rivers, and in its first year of operation it yielded a 30 per cent profit. The Chester *Reporter,* December 9, 1869, said that a home company was being organized for the purpose of mining and selling phosphatic acid to local fertilizer manufacturers.

By the latter part of the decade of 1870, use of commercial fertilizer was almost universal along the Atlantic seaboard. Mixing plants existed in Virginia, in the Carolinas, and throughout Georgia. Everywhere in the old tobacco and cotton belts emphasis was placed upon artificial fertilization to increase the return of exhausted cotton and tobacco lands. In 1877, John Ott, of the Southern Fertilizing Company, Baltimore, wrote W. P. Duke of Henderson, North Carolina, that "our trade is especially fine this season. It is plain that the folks are bent on making *good* tobacco this year, hence our sales of tobacco fertilizer." That same year the Furman formula was developed in Milledgeville, Georgia. It consisted of cotton seeds, ammonia, acid phosphate, kainit, potash, and stable manure. Southern county newspapers published this recipe throughout the South, and it was used by storekeepers in manufacturing guano.

At Baltimore, Richmond, Charleston, and Savannah large commercial guano factories were supplying the store trade along the seaboard. Fortunately for them, cotton prices remained at a reasonably high level until the panic years following 1891. In keeping with the credit practices of the day, guano was sold for both cash and on time. The differential in cash and credit prices varied from five dollars to ten dollars a ton, plus 8 to 10 per cent interest charges and a generous profit for the merchant added.

Merchants served as agents for the manufacturing companies on a commission basis. Each spring they ordered carloads of guano and secured signatures to a special type of credit note which were payable when crops were sold. In this way merchants became important factors in changing the whole complex pattern of tobacco and cotton economy. Here was a new element of business which added to the burden of making these staples pay for their cultivation. As prices declined in the eighties and nineties, the fertilizer burden became greater, and in the succeeding decades the guano trade spread to the newer cotton and tobacco areas.

Farmers became more hopeless victims of a vicious credit system the moment they added the burden of buying guano. Hundreds of hard-luck stories were told. To illustrate the enslaving aspect of that part of the credit business, it was said that a guano salesman in a south Georgia town saw a pair of country boys coming to a store in February to sell cotton. He gave them some advertising literature to read and then wished he had not because the boys would now have to change all of their habits. They would have to pick cotton in October instead of January. Newspapers carried numerous advertisements in the spring offering to sell guano in March and February at the rate of one ton for 450 pounds of lint cotton in the fall. In March, 1882, the editor of the Greensboro (Georgia) *Herald* wrote an epilogue to this practice. He said that all the little farmers had "guanoed" themselves out of something to eat. Those who were "able to dance to the music are hauling it [commercial fertilizer] out by the ton." Guano credit, however, was a treacherous burden. Few debtors could escape its clutches as blithely as did that jocular South Carolinian who answered a notice that his fertilizer note was overdue with the pert message: "Dear Agent; yours received and was glad to hear from you. It found me and my family well and hope this will find you the same."

Merchants' guano books tell a story of profit for the storekeeper, but for the agricultural South it was one of doubtful virtue. Too many times the use of commercial fertilizer was the differential between success and failure for farmers. It, along with the whole credit business of the stores, left its unhappy traces of failure upon the region which can be identified by the one-crop system, tenant farming, lien laws, forced land assignments, and "courthouse door" sales. The big leather books of the stores document the story of far too much of southern rural life.

Out of the story of southern storekeeping has come a fine lot of regional folklore. Bookkeeping for most merchants was a haphazard undertaking at best. Journals were always crazy patterns of miscellaneous merchandise, and one entry had little or no relation to the next in the list. Entries fell into a comical succession of purchases. Bill Nixon of Merrillton, Alabama, recorded a picturesque account of his store as goods and services were sold, and he entered long lists of commodities ranging from Sloan's liniment to crosscut saws. A pair of entries especially bespoke the diversity of his trade. One was a charge for five cents' worth of candy, and the other charged a dollar for the service of his bull.

Some merchants furnished individual account books to special customers, and year after year they totaled the account and presented the books for brief inspection before bills were paid. But bookkeeping for much of the mercantile fraternity was a shot in the dark. For illiterate merchants it was a well-nigh insoluble problem. Yet it was said that one Louisiana Cajun successfully ran a store and kept books without being able to tell one letter from the other. He used symbols for both customers' names and for items in his stock. He used a system of addition based upon counting grains of corn or of moving pegs about on a board which contained several rows of holes. This story doubtless is true, but from stories of this sort have come at least two which are apocryphal, but are repeated over and over as actual fact. One is of the country merchant who kept his credit record on a wall of his store, but while he was away from home, his wife had the inside of the building painted and caused the loss of hundreds of dollars. The other is the ancient story of a merchant who totaled a customer's account and charged him with a hoop of cheese, but when the customer protested that it was a grindstone instead of cheese, the storekeeper recalled that he had forgotten to draw the hole.

Another story of bookkeeping has been told so many times on specific merchants that customers have come to believe it. It is said that a flock of customers arrived at a store on Saturday morning and that in a storm of trading one of them purchased a saddle, but the clerk forgot who it was. After a conference with the storekeeper it was agreed that a charge for a saddle should be entered against fifteen of the house's best customers, and at settling time if they protested, then the charge would be stricken from the book. At settling time, however, only three of the group protested, and the storekeeper received payment twelve times for one saddle. There is pretty good evidence that this story was inspired and used by competitors for the sake of weakening confidence in a popular neighbor.

Store owners were dependent upon land to produce crops with which to pay accounts and to sustain trade. Because of this, storekeepers often branched out into landowning and farming. Too, they acquired other property to such an extent that they were generally the most enterprising men in the community. A story was told of a country merchant who died and went to hell, and immediately the devil had him imprisoned under an upturned washpot. Later a visitor to the lower region was being showed its wonders, but when he undertook to look under the pot, the devil became greatly agitated and shouted at him to keep his hands off. "Don't lift that pot! We have Old Man George Cobb under there and if you let him out he'll foreclose a mortgage on all hell in the first crop season!"

Customers were always of a single mind. They often believed the worst of their merchant, but continued to do business with him in spite of his hard terms. They not only did business with the same house for two or three generations, but they traded with a single clerk. Sometimes a country boy went to work in a store, and everybody from his community would come in to trade with him. There was a feeling that by sticking to the same clerk, they would not receive short weight or poor value. The clerk would see that they got advantage of good cuts of meat and closer prices, and he would understand their peculiar whims and fancies. It was not unusual for customers to sit around the stove for an hour or more waiting to trade with their favorite clerk, or to go home and come back another time if he were away. Buying and selling was always a highly personalized matter, and a shrewd clerk blessed with a good memory and the ability to carry on country small talk was a tremendously valuable asset.

For the customer there were many economic pitfalls, but there were more for the merchant. Storekeeping was profitable, but it was not without its anxieties. By good management it was possible to run a modest sum up to a small fortune. In 1884, T. J. Christian made a gross earning of $16,719.97; thirty years later he was earning $222,040,43 and owned 25,000 acres of land besides. Each inventory climbed. At Lorman in Mississippi, the Cohn Brothers started business in 1875 on a limited amount of borrowed capital, and by 1900 their house was doing a huge volume of business each year. Their influence upon farming in Jefferson County, Mississippi, was of major importance. At Braselton, Georgia, the Braselton Brothers started business in 1887 in a storehouse six-by-six-feet square, with five dollars in cash, a bag of turnips, a bundle of kindling, and a small supply of home-grown peanuts. Twenty-eight years later the tiny store had expanded through a succession of buildings, and around it there were a fertilizer factory, a gristmill and flour mill, a cotton gin and warehouse, a crosstie yard, a bank, and a post office. These combined businesses earned an annual income of one million dollars in 1915, and the Braselton Brothers owned four thousand acres of land.

There were scores of other merchants who had done as well with their businesses as had these three. They thrived in an age when Horatio Alger was telling the American boy that "he was bound to rise" if he was shrewd, industrious, and good. Many southern country merchants had reason to believe him. From modest beginnings, they became men of strong financial security and leadership in their communities.

But the story of country merchandising was to have its dark chapter. As in the ominous line in "My Old Kentucky

Home" where the shadows fell across the path of the happy slave, a shadow fell across the store. Soon after the turn of the century the strange Mexican insect, the boll weevil, crossed the Río Grande and moved rapidly toward the heart of the southern cotton country. Since the late nineties it had moved up from Mexico to Texas, but few believed it would ever reach the South proper. Within ten years it had crossed Texas and was in Louisiana. Before the scourge, however, went wild rumors of destruction and bankruptcy. Both merchants and cotton farmers were frantic. They realized that it was their doom which was creeping upon them. County papers, like the St. Landry *Clarion,* authenticated the rumor that there were weevils at Grand Cane. Eighteen miles below Shreveport the insect had dealt its first blow beyond the Texas border.

In August the North Louisiana Cotton Planters' Association held a called meeting and appointed a committee to devise a plan to prevent the spread of the boll weevil, and to save both merchants and farmers from ruination. A year later the Boll Weevil Convention was called at Shreveport to discuss the calamity. Trained entomologists were hired to catch weevils and to try to discover a means to check them. The panic, however, spread. By 1906 the fate of Louisiana cotton farmers was certain, and at the end of the picking season that year the *Clarion's* editor wrote, "The boll weevil is here. That is equally certain as the sun shines. It is equally as certain that with his advent the farmers must cast an eye in another direction but the focus which has kept it centered from boyhood to King Cotton. The situation is imminent. The farmer *must* make up his mind that it is no longer safe after this season to rely solely on cotton. . . ."

For the country merchant in Louisiana the situation was discouraging. Across the river in Mississippi and Alabama storekeepers observed the fate of their Louisiana brethern with fear. They saw the scourge coming, and they had no patience with the defeated moralists who reasoned that after all the "weevil would be a blessing in disguise." It was for them a calamity unless some substitute crop could be found for cotton. Observers went to Louisiana and Texas to study the credit method used by merchants in the weevil-ridden belt. These came home to advise the development of new crops. Lehman Cohn came back to Lorman, Mississippi, to encourage production of peanuts, cow peas, molasses, grain, chickens, eggs, and livestock as a substitute money crop. In one crop year this house bought fifteen thousand dollars' worth of eggs at seven to twenty cents a dozen. Likewise, it bought and sold every other kind of marketable produce in its territory.

Several favored sections of the Gulf Coast South turned to sugar-cane culture, and the mercantile pattern underwent a revolution. Around the little town of Nashville in South Georgia, the enterprising merchant A. W. Gaskins introduced light-leaf tobacco as a rich source of income for farmer-customers, and this belt soon spread over a large area of south Georgia and north Florida.

Hard years before 1915 wrought significant changes, and no longer did King Cotton economy exactly describe southern economy. Storekeepers began to feel post-World War I deflation; unpaid accounts piled up, and many businesses were in danger of failure. Distressed merchants sat on their front porches and wondered why they had not gone out of business at the end of the prosperous years of 1919 and 1920.

While the boll-weevil scourge swarmed out of the Southwest, another and perhaps greater menace to the country store rolled out of the North. Its fantastic tracks were soon thickly imprinted in the sand beds of southern dirt roads. Newspapers began to advertise the automobile, and storekeepers themselves became interested in the new machine. By 1920 they were clearing away space at the corners of front porches, and the store took on the new appearance of gasoline stations. New and garish petroleum signs crowded the old standard medicine, tobacco, and plow-tool placards into the background. Even mud roads took on coats of gravel and tar. Highway engineers surveyed new routes, and sometimes the roads left the stores off to one side. Thriving towns sprang up around many of the crossroads stores, forcing their owners to become attuned to the new era of industry and business. The twenties and thirties with their changing social and economic philosophies and their jazzy uncertain society were too fast an age for many of the stores. Old-timers who started business in the eighties either trimmed their sails and became more conservative in their business practices or remodeled and departmentalized their houses, modernized their shelves and counters, slapped on coats of bright red and green paint, put up huge electric signs, and went in pursuit of new business. Some gave up the struggle to the chain racket and grocery stores and their plainly marked price tags and cash sales. The old days of secret price markings were ended. Even the old-fashioned lien-credit system was practically through. Pessimistic storekeepers believed the automobile had ruined the people. No longer, they said, "was a man's word as good as his bond." Customers ran off after movies, gas, and tires, and they paid for these things before they settled store accounts. In this sentimental lament, the storekeepers forgot, however, that a man's word had never been his bond in the stores. The promises of some men were good, but printing establishments made good incomes from preparing lien-mortgage forms. Merchants were right in saying World War I had brought a change. Even the New Deal got the federal government interested in the South's credit system. President Roosevelt considered the South's credit system and called the region the nation's economic problem number one. The whole credit structure was changed, new governmental agricultural loan agencies were established, lien notes were forgotten, and the big leather-backed account books became antiques of another day. They were shoved aside by patent accounting records which contained a picture of family expenditures for only a month at a time.

Fortunately, however, not all of the stores were forced into changing their appearances. A considerable number of these stanch old business houses have gone their way without too much concern for the changing world about them. They have grown strong through years of battling. Once the farmer organizations cried out loudly against the usurous practices of the storekeepers. Demagogues even ranted about the crimes of their merchants to their constituents from the front porches of the stores. Farmer customers voted to set up rival co-operative stores, and went so far as to submit bids each year for their supply trade, but before long their secretaries were cutting pages of minute books into tiny strips to be used as order slips for meat, flour, and chewing tobacco.

The boll weevil and falling tobacco prices dealt the merchants a hard blow, and the post–World War I panic sent many of them reeling against the ropes of financial ruin, but still many of them went on doing business. Perhaps an efficient inventory during these trying years would have showed that many a merchant had been bankrupt for at least a decade. They still had possession of the front-door keys, however, and the battered old doors still creaked back lazily on their ancient hinges; therefore, they remained in business.

Although southerners ran after the baubles of five-and-ten and department-store counters and their credit morals were corrupted by gasoline, engine oil, rubber tires, swing music, moving pictures, and installment buying, they still had an attachment for the country stores. The stores were as much a part of the southern tradition as were Lee and Jackson or as boll weevils and mammy songs. Many a successful southerner had clamored out of the confusion of reconstruction and economic panics of later years to expand a country store into a big business. They had first seen what a man with vision and initiative might accomplish as they pumped cans of kerosene, cut off hunks of meat, measured off rods of plowlines and weighed cotton at the warehouses. There was even a sentimental tie for farmers who were forced to give up their land and chattels because of consistent crop failures. The stores were places where they could at least commiserate with their fellows. Certainly they were as vital an institution as were the church and the Democratic party.

BIBLIOGRAPHY

THE MAJOR PORTION of this account of the country store in the New South has been taken from the original records of the merchants. There seems to have been no order in the classification of account books or in the style of bookkeeping. Sometimes the term "ledger" was all inclusive. Occasionally the ledger was only a cash charge and settlement record, and the journal carried the itemized and chronological accounts. Daybooks contain the individual purchases and give an intimate view of the country-store customers and their trading habits. Thousands of scraps of paper, letters, advertisements, pamphlets, almanacs, catalogues, and associated materials constitute choice sources of information which did not get into the store books themselves. Of this latter material there are the records of the merchants' side interests such as post offices' books, doctors' account books, church records, political rolls, school-trustee books, lodge records, turnpike books, accounts of estates for which the storekeepers were executors, and even Sunday-school roll books.

This collection of records represent a fair sampling. There are records in this list from stores in almost every section of the South, and unless otherwise stated they are now a part of the permanent collection in the University of Kentucky Library.

Bibliography

General Business Records

Adkins, W. P., Stephens, Georgia.
Ledgers, 1888, 1890–1916. Cash Books 1892–1917.

Aldridge, W. P., Miller's Ferry, Alabama.
Ledgers 1910–1913.

Barlow, S. T., and Company. Headquarter, Kentucky.
Ledgers 1889–1915. (In possession of owner at store.)

Baynes, R. S., Ruddles Mills, North Carolina.
Plantation Record 1881–1888. Daybooks 1909–1911. Inventory 1908–1909, 1912. Medical accounts 1868–1893.

Bennett, D. C., Louisville, Mississippi.
Private farm account Books 1898–1918. (In author's possession.)

Black and Blackburn, Van Buren, Kentucky.
Ledger 1905–1914. Cash Books 1910–1924. Inventory 1923.

Brice, Calvan and Company (later Patrick and Company), Woodward, South Carolina.
Ledgers 1880–1914. Journal 1875–1907. Daybooks 1874–1891. Cash Books 1881–1885. Invoice Books 1881–1891. Cotton Books 1875–1913. Stock Books 1877–1889. Letter Books 1875–1890. Bill Books 1879–1918. Business papers 1875–1915.

Brice, C. S., Woodward, South Carolina.
Private Plantation Account Book 1876–1879.

Brown, J. C. and Company. Faunsdale, Alabama.
Ledger 1878–1917. Journals 1889–1905. Daybooks 1877–1922. Cash Books 1881–1906. Invoice Books 1889–1917. Gristmill Books 1889–1890. Inventory Books 1889–1901. Trial Balances 1906–1907. Cotton Gin Books 1889–1911. Sunday School Roll Book 1910–1914. Cotton Seed Book 1892–1916. Cotton Picking Book 1889–1903. Rent Book 1904–1908. Stable Book 1905. Cotton Books 1896–1904. Mortgage Books 1901. Gin Books 1906. Order Notes and General Store Papers 1878–1920.

Bush, A. T., and Company. Pickensville, Alabama.
Ledger 1842–1843. (Author's collection).

Carpenter, J. E., and Company. Napier, Tennessee.
Invoice Book 1880–1881.

Carrigan, W. C., Cheraw, South Carolina.
Ledger 1869–1871. (Manuscript collection, Duke University.)

Christian T. J., Northport, Alabama.
Cash accounts and Ledger 1884–1920. (In owner's possession.)

Clark, Edwin.
General Store papers, 1893. (Manuscript collection, Duke University.)

Coapta General Store, Coapta, Alabama.
Ledger 1923–1929. Cash Book 1888–1889. Miscellaneous papers.
Gin Book, no date.

Cohn Brothers, Lorman, Mississippi.
Ledger, Journals, Invoice Books, General Papers, 1875–1943. (In possession of Cohn Brothers.)

Coleman and Yagle, Pinckneyville, Alabama.
Ledgers 1905–1920. Daybooks 1907–1914.

Crooks, Joseph L., Pomaris, South Carolina.
General Business Papers, 1890–1930.

Doveson, D. J., Woodville, Georgia.
Ledgers 1911–1917.

Drane and Dupre, Raymond, Mississippi.
Ledgers 1866–1875. (Collection of Mississippi Department of Archives and History, Jackson, Mississippi.)

Duke, W. P.
Papers 1867–1881. (Manuscript collection, Duke University.)

Endicott, R. T., Oakland Mills, Kentucky.
Ledgers 1890–1914.

Frankenstein, F. R., Natchez, Mississippi.
Wholesale Records. Ledgers 1893–1897. (Manuscript collection, Louisiana State University, Baton Rouge, Louisiana.)

Fuller, C. C., Longmire's Store, Abbeville County, South Carolina.
Ledgers 1881–1884. Day Books 1885–1887. Cotton Books 1904–1905. Postage Records 1893–1897.
Gaskins, A. W., Nashville, Georgia.
Ledgers 1900–1920. Daybooks 1900–1920. (In possession of Gaskins estate.)
Gould, J. A. and G. W., Yokena, Mississippi.
Plantation Commissary Accounts 1866–1881.
Guidry, Odon, Carencro, Louisiana.
Ledgers 1902–1918. Daybooks 1912–1914. Invoice Books 1912–1913.
Hankinson, W. S., Yokena, Mississippi.
Ledgers 1892–1917. Journals 1893–1916. Daybooks 1898–1917. Cotton Books 1896–1898.
Hay, W. T., Pleasant Point, Tennessee.
Invoice Book 1890–1891.
Haynes, M. P., and Sons. Denson's Landing, Tennessee.
Produce Shipping Record 1909–1914.
Henderson, Brothers, Preston, Mississippi.
Ledgers 1887–1888, 1893, 1900–1911.
Henderson Brothers, Miller's Ferry, Alabama.
Ledgers 1897–1916. Daybooks 1908–1917. Cash Books 1907–1911. Invoice Books 1910–1916. Cotton Books 1897–1906.
Hunt, James A. G., Milton, North Carolina.
Account Book 1872–1891. (In possession of J. J. Lipscomb, Milton, North Carolina.)
Hyland, H. S., Yokena, Mississippi.
Ledger 1855–1860. Plantation account 1847–1877. (In author's possession.)
Jameson Company, Weir, Kentucky.
Ledgers 1902–1904, 1909–1911. Invoice Books 1914.
Jones, Ike, Blackhawk, Mississippi.
Ledgers 1879, 1883, 1891–1914.
Judice, Alice, Scott, Louisiana.
Ledgers 1878–1942. (In possession of Judice Company.)
King, Richard, Kingston, Alabama.

Ledger 1863–1876. Notes of A. McGregor. (In possession of Mrs. Atkins, Lexington, Kentucky.)

LeBlanc, Luke, Scott, Louisiana.
Ledgers 1908–1922. Journals 1906–1915. Daybooks 1912–1931. Cotton Book 1915, Inventory Books 1914–1930. Cash Books 1910–1919.

Longshores' Store, Newberry County, South Carolina.
Ledgers 1870–1890, 1904, 1905, 1911.

McElwain Store, Dunsmore, Kentucky.
Ledger 1919.

McRae, J. F., Orion, Mississippi.
Day and Journal Books 1890. (In possession of Professor E. C. Swint, Vanderbilt University.)

Marshall, C. B., Lewisburg, Kentucky.
Ledgers 1884–1885.

Martin and Johnson, Earles, Kentucky.
Ledgers 1872–1922. Journals 1904–1911. Daybooks 1903–1935. Corn Receipts 1907–1918. Tobacco Books 1889–1906. Check Books 1904–1906. General Business Papers 1869–1920.

Mayer, K. A., Lower Peach Tree, Alabama.
Ledger 1885–1892. Daybook 1881–1886. Cash Book 1889–1902. Invoice Book 1901. General Business Papers 1900–1920.

Miller, B. B., Abbeville County, South Carolina.
Miscellaneous Business Papers 1867–1890.

Moores, G. B., Waco, Kentucky.
Ledgers 1901–1930. Daybooks 1901–1930.

Morehead, J. S., Pickensville, Alabama.
Daybook 1908.

Neblett, Epes, Milton, North Carolina.
Ledgers 1888–1906. Journals 1897–1906. Tobacco Book 1889–1891. Gristmill Book 1897–1898.

Newman, W. G., and Sons, Orr, Kentucky.
Ledger 1898.

Nixon, W. D., Merrilton, Alabama.
Ledgers, Journals, and Invoice Books 1900–1912. (In pos-

session of Professor H. C. Nixon, Vanderbilt University.)

Nunn, E. F., and Company, Shuqulak, Mississippi.
Ledgers 1870–1915. (Mississippi Department of Archives and History, Jackson, Mississippi.)

Patrick, T. G., and Company, Whiteoak, South Carolina.
Ledgers 1878–1888. Cotton Books 1896–1904. General Business Papers 1878–1920.

Perry, Vestal.
General Papers 1871–1888. (Manuscript Collection, Duke University.)

Pitt, O. P., Edwards, Kentucky.
Ledgers 1904–1918.

Pitts, Harbour, Cerro Gordo, Tennessee.
Ledgers 1903–1905.

Price, R. W., and Company, Dayton, Alabama.
Invoice Book 1892–1896.

Pulliam and Connelly, Leasburg, North Carolina.
Ledgers 1869–1920. Papers 1869–1930. (Some of these papers in archives Duke University, others at store in Leasburg.)

Reed Brothers, Flat Creek, Tennessee.
Ledgers 1878–1920. Daybooks 1890–1912. Postal Records 1896. General Papers 1880–1920.

Shores and Phebus, Rives, Tennessee.
Ledgers 1904–1918. Daybooks 1904–1926. Invoice Books 1904–1931. Inventory Records 1907–1926.

Smaw, J. B., Baligee, Alabama.
Ledger 1867–1868. (Manuscript Collection, Duke University.)

Smith, William, Smithville, South Carolina.
Ledgers 1842–1845, 1868. Daybooks 1834–1846.

Snow and Demonville.
General Store Papers 1867. (Manuscript Collection in Duke University.)

Streeter, J. B., Blackhawk, Mississippi.
General Store Records, Ledgers 1866–1930. (In Possession of Streeter Family.)

Swetman, G. C., Wilbur, Kentucky.
Ledgers 1885–1912. Journal 1891–1897, 1906–1907. Daybooks 1892–1910. Postmaster's Book 1895–1908. School Trustees' Book 1888–1902. Mutual Protection Society Minutes 1888–1903.

Tolbert, John, Abbeville County, South Carolina.
Papers 1860–1910. (Author's collection.)

Tolbert, John R., Abbeville County, South Carolina.
Ledgers 1834–1837, 1870–1878, 1878–1885, 1904–1907. Papers 1860–1910. (Author's collection.)

Tygart, W. H., Nashville, Georgia.
Ledgers 1893–1915. Invoices 1900–1915. Cash Books and Daily Cost Records 1900–1915.

Vaiden General Store, Vaiden, Mississippi.
Ledger 1871.

Webb, G. M., Elberton, Georgia.
Ledger 1905–1916. Daybook 1904, 1906, 1908.

Wilkins, G. A., Gishton, Kentucky.
Ledger 1873–1875.

Williams, E. L. Chesly, Eagleville, Tennessee.
Ledgers 1871–1916. Daybooks 1874–1914. General Accounts of Estates for which Chesly Williams Was Executor 1865–1883. Eagleville and Salem Turnpiks Company, 1865–1877. School Minute and Account Books 1875–1878. Business Papers 1856–1910.

Newspapers

The Advocate. Huntsville, Alabama. 1879–1882.

Barnwell Sentinel. Barnwell, South Carolina. 1866, 1868.

The Calhoun Times. St. Mathews, South Carolina. 1930.

The Carolina Review. Lancaster, South Carolina, 1878–1879.

Carolina Watchman. Salisbury, North Carolina. 1866, 1870–1890.

The Chester Reporter. Chester, South Carolina. 1869, 1883, 1887.

The Country Merchant. New Concord, Ohio. March, 1901.
The Daily Mobile Register. Mobile, Alabama. 1887.
The Drummer. Lexington, Kentucky. September 29, 1888.
Edgeville Advertiser. Edgefield, South Carolina. 1869, 1878, 1879, 1936.
The Enterprise. Ellaville, Georgia. 1886.
The Fayetteville Eagle. North Carolina. 1868–1869, 1872, 1873.
The Federal Union. Milledgeville, Georgia. 1871.
The Gazette. Elberton, Georgia. 1866, 1878–1881.
The Green River Republican. Morgantown, Kentucky. 1888, 1891–1892, 1901–1940.
Greensboro Herald. Georgia. 1871, 1873–1877, 1880–1881, 1884–1886.
The Hamilton Visitor. Georgia. 1873–1874, 1875.
The Hillsborough Gazette. North Carolina. 1874.
The Independent. Huntsville, Alabama. 1879–1882.
Iron Age Weekly. Birmingham, Alabama. 1886.
The Memphis Commercial Appeal. Memphis, Tennessee. 1938.
The Mississippi Sun. Macon, Mississippi. 1876, 1884, 1885, 1888, 1891, 1892.
The New Orleans Picayune. New Orleans, Louisiana. 1907.
Old North State. Henderson, North Carolina. 1869, 1870.
Opelousas Clarion News (St. Landry). 1902, 1903–1909.
Republican, The Tri-weekly. Americus, Georgia. 1871.
Rural Alabamian. 2 vols. Mobile, Alabama. 1872–1873.
The Shelby Guide. Columbiana, Alabama. 1872.
New South. Elberton, Georgia. 1881–1888.
The Summit Courier. South Carolina. 1877–1878.
Times Picayune. New Orleans. 1903.
Union Times, The Weekly. South Carolina. 1886.
Union Times, The Weekly. Georgia. 1873.
The Weekly Sumter Republican. South Carolina. 1873.
The Winston County Journal. Mississippi. 1892–1930.
York Enterprise. South Carolina. 1887, 1889, 1890. 1892.

PERIODICALS

Bok, Edward. "The Patent Medicine Curse," *The Ladies' Home Journal,* 21 (May, 1904), 18.

———. "How the Private Confidences of Women are Laughed At." *The Ladies' Home Journal,* 21 (November, 1904), 18.

Browne, F. Z. "Reconstruction in Oktibbeba Company," *Publications Mississippi Historical Society* (Oxford), XIII (1913), 273–98.

Browne, William M. *The Southern Farm and Home: A Magazine of Agriculture, Manufacturers and Domestic Economy* (Memphis, Tennessee), III (1872).

Carolinian, Rural. (Charleston, South Carolina), 7 vols. (1869–1876).

Cooper, Forrest. "Reconstruction in Scott County," *Publication Mississippi Historical Society* (Oxford), XIII (1913), 99–222.

"Emigration in a New Phase," *The Merchant's Magazine and Commercial Review,* 62 (February, 1870), 115–18.

Farmer, Hallie. "The Economic Background of Southern Populism," *South Atlantic Quarterly,* XXIX (January, 1930), 77–91.

Grady, H. W. "Cotton and Its Kingdom," *Harper's Magazine,* LXIII (1881), 719–34.

Hammond, Matthew B. "The Southern Farmer and the Cotton Question," *Political Science Quarterly,* XII (September, 1897), 450–75.

Holmes, George K. "The Peons of the South," *Annals of American Academy of Political and Social Science,* IV (September, 1893), 265–74.

Hunt's Merchants Magazine. New York, 1865–1870.

Kendrick, B. B. "Agrarian Discontent in the South: 1880–1900," *Annual Report American Historical Association,* (Washington, 1920), 267–72.

Kyle, John W. "Reconstruction in Panola County," *Publication Mississippi Historical Society,* XIII (1913), 9–98.

Robison, Daniel Merritt. "Tennessee Politics and the Agrarian Revolt 1886–1896," *Mississippi Valley Historical Review,* V (June, 1918), 3–19.

Silver, James W. "C. P. James Mooney of the Memphis Commercial Appeal—Crusader for Diversification," *Agricultural History,* 17 (April 1943), 81–89.

Southern Farm and Home. Memphis, Tennessee, 1872.

White, Melvin J. "Populism in Louisiana During the Nineties," *Mississippi Valley Historical Review,* V (June, 1918).

Wilbert, Martin I. "The Purity and Strength of Household Remedies," *Public Health Reports,* 30, I (January–June, 1915), 311–317.

Government Publications

Census of United States, Eleventh, 1890.
Washington: Government Printing Office, 1891–1896. 25 vols.

Cotton Growers in the United States, Report of the Committee on Agricultural and Forestry on Condition of, the Present Prices of Cotton, and the Remedy. 53d Congress, 3d Session, *Senate Report,* 896, pt. 1.

Cotton Movements and Fluctuations. New York, 1897, 1898–1903, 1902, 1904, 1905, 1906, 1908.

Dickens, Dorothy. "A Nutrition Investigation of Negro Tenants in the Yazoo and Mississippi Delta," *Mississippi A. & M. College Bulletin,* No. 254 (August, 1928).

District of Columbia, Reports Relating to Affairs in the. 60th Congress, 2nd Session, *Document 599.* Washington, 1909.

Emergency Council, National. *Report on Economic Conditions in the South Prepared for the President.* Washington, 1938.

Kebler, Lyman F. *Adulterated Drugs and Chemicals* (Pamphlet). Washington, U.S. Department of Agricultural, Bureau of Chemistry, 1904. *Bulletin No. 80.*

Public Health Service Reprint, Purity and Strength, Household Remedies, Vol. 30, No. 5, 254–1915.

Woofter, T. J. *Landlord and Tenant on the Cotton Plantation*. Washington, 1938.

Laws and Departmental Reports

Alabama, Laws. Montgomery, 1872–1873, 1876–1877.

Mississippi, Laws of the State of. Jackson, 1876, 1866–1867.

Simpson, W. D. (governor of South Carolina). "Address to the General Assembly, November 25, 1879," *House Journal South Carolina General Assembly*. Columbia, 1879–1880.

South Carolina, Code Laws of. 2 vols., Columbia, 1902.

South Carolina, Revised Statutes of. 2 vols., Columbia, 1894.

Jones, W. N. *First Annual Report of the Bureau of Labor Statistics of the State of North Carolina*. Raleigh, 1887.

Catalogues

Ahrens and Ott Manufacturing Company. *Catalogue B,* Factory and Mill Supply. Louisville, n.d.

Baltimore Bargain House. 1899, 1900, 1912, 1914.

Birg, L. S. *Fall and Winter Clothing Catalogue,* 1899–1900.

Brief History of J. B. Coats Plant at Pawtucket, Rhode Island. Typescript, 1942.

Chamber of Commerce Publication (Official). "The International Shoe Company." St. Louis, 1937.

Garden City Watch Company, Jewelry. *14th Annual Catalogue,* 1903.

Handbill, January 7, 1876. "Fertilizer." Baltimore Manuscript Collection, Duke University.

The Implement Company Catalogue. Richmond, Virginia, 1900.

Ladies Birthday Almanac, 1900–1943. Chattanooga Medicine Company.

Louisville Fifty Years Ago, 1873–1923. Louisville, 1923.

Murray, W. H., Buggy Company. *30th Catalogue*. Cincinnati, 1915.

National Enameling and Stamping Company. *General Catalogue 17*, "Enameled Wares, Tinware, Japanned and Galvanized Wares, Etc." Milwaukee, n.d.

Progress Club, Publication of. "The 25th Anniversary, International Shoe Company." St. Louis, 1942.

Rand, Frank C. "The Modern Shoe is Solution of Problem which Bothered Man for Centuries," *Monsanto Current Events,* November, 1934. St. Louis, 1934.

Rand, Frank. "Keeping Faith." Typescript, n.d.

Richmond Cedar Works, Catalogue. Richmond, Virginia, 1895.

Robert, Johnson and Rand Catalogue, Fall and Winter, 1934 and 1935.

Rumsey, L. E., Rumsey Manufacturing Company. *Catalogue 97.* 1897.

The Silent Salesman, Hats and Caps. S. Gladstone. New York, 1899.

Tement, Stribbling Shoe Company. *57th Catalogue.* St. Louis, 1899.

Tursch and Brother. *Tinware Catalogue.* Baltimore, 1900.

Wales New Summer Catalogue, 1899. Norfork, Virginia.

Williams, Z. F. *Baltimore Merchants' and Manufacturers' Directory.* Baltimore, 1887.

Zirckel, G. A., and Company. *Catalogue.* Baltimore, 1900–1901.

Books

Adams, Samuel Hopkins. *The Great American Fraud.* New York, 1905.

Andrews, Sidney. *The South Since the War, as Shown by Fourteen Weeks of Travel and Observation in Georgia and the Carolinas.* Boston, 1876.

Arnett, Alex Mathews. *The Populist Movement in Georgia; A View of the "Agrarian Crusade" in the Light of Solid-South Politics.* New York, 1922 (Columbia University *Studies in History, Economics and Public Law,* CIV).

Arnett, Alex M., and Kendrick, Benjamin B. *The South Looks at Its Past.* Chapel Hill, 1935.

Banks, Enoch Marvin. *The Economics of Land Tenure in Georgia.* New York, 1905. (Columbia University *Studies in History, Economics and Public Law,* XXIII.)

Berney, Saffold. *Hand Book of Alabama: A Complete Index to the State, with Map.* Birmingham, 1892.

Brooks, Ropert Preston. *The Agrarian Revolution in Georgia, 1865–1912.* Madison, 1914. (*Bulletin* of the University of Wisconsin, *No. 639.* History Series.)

Brown, Harry B. *Cotton, History, Species, Varieties, Morphology, Breeding, Culture, Disease, Marketing and Use.* New York, 1938.

Bruce, Phillip A. *The Plantation Negro as a Freedman.* New York, 1889.

Buck, Solon Justus. *The Agrarian Crusade; a Chronicle of the Farmer in Politics.* New Haven, 1920.

Campbell, Sir George. *White and Black, the Outcome of a Visit to the United States.* New York, 1879.

Clark, John Bunyan. *Populism in Alabama.* Auburn, Alabama, 1927.

Clayton, W. W. *History of Davidson County, Tennessee.* Philadelphia, 1880.

Connelley, W. E., and Coulter, E. M. *History of Kentucky.* 2 vols. Chicago, 1922.

Coulter, E. M. *The Cincinnati Southern Railroad and the Struggle for Southern Commerce.* 1865–1872. Chicago, 1922.

———*The Civil War and Readjustment in Kentucky.* Chapel Hill, 1926.

Dabney, Virginius. *Liberalism in the South.* Chapel Hill, 1932.

Fay, Edwin Whitfield. *History of Education in Louisiana.* Washington, 1898.

Grady, Henry W. *The New South, with a Character Sketch by Oliver Dyer,* New York, 1890.

Hammond, M. B. *The Cotton Industry: An Essay in American Economic History*. Ithaca, 1898.

Hicks, John D. *The Populist Revolt: A History of the Farmers' Alliance and the People's Party*. Minneapolis, 1931.

Hollander, J. H. *The Cincinnati Southern Railway: A Study in Municipal Activity*. Baltimore, 1894.

Huff, James R. *Musings of an Old Sorrel Top*. Chattanooga, 1929.

Johnson, Charles S.; Embree, Edwin R.; Alexander, W. W. *The Collapse of Cotton Tenancy*. Chapel Hill, 1935.

Johnston, J. Stoddard. *Memorial History of Louisville from Its First Settlement to the Year 1896*. 2 vols., New York, 1896.

Kelsey, Carl. *The Negro Farmer*. Chicago, 1903.

Kendrick, B. B., and Arnett, Alex M. *The South Looks at Its Past*. Chapel Hill, 1935.

Mayes, Edward. *History of Education in Mississippi*. Washington, 1899.

Merriam, Lucius S. *Higher Education in Tennessee*. Washington, 1893.

Moore, Albert Burton. *History of Alabama*. University of Alabama, 1934.

Moore, James Lewis and Wingate, Thomas Herron. *Cabarus Reborn*. Kanapolis, North Carolina, 1940.

Murphy, Edgar Gardner. *Problems of the Present South*. New York, 1909.

Nichols, E. S. *Kentucky Farm Laws, with Business Forms and Business Letters*. Columbus, Ohio, 1911.

Nixon, Herman C. *Possum Trot: Rural Community South*. Norman, 1941.

Nordoff, Charles. *The Cotton States in the Spring and Summer of 1875*. New York, 1876.

Otken, Charles H. *The Ills of the South; or, Related Causes Hostile to the General Prosperity of the Southern People*. New York, 1894.

Robinson, Daniel Merrit. *Bob Taylor and the Agrarian Revolt in Tennessee*. Chapel Hill, 1935.

Sheldon, William DuBose. *Populism in the Old Dominion; Virginia Farm Politics, 1885–1900*. Princeton, 1935.

Simkins, Francis Butler. *The Tillman Movement in South Carolina*. Durham, 1926.

———and Woody, Robert H. *South Carolina During Reconstruction*. Chapel Hill, 1932.

Somers, Robert. *The Southern States Since the War, 1870–1871*. London, 1871.

The South in the Building of the Nation, "Economic History 1865–1909." Vol. VI. Richmond, 1909.

Stearns, Charles. *The Black Man of the South, and the Rebels; or the Characteristics of the Former, and the Recent Outrages of the Latter*. New York, 1872.

Tennessee, History of. Chicago, 1887.

Thompson, C. Mildred. *Reconstruction in Georgia Economical, Social, Political 1865–1872*. New York, 1915.

Thompson, Holland. "The New South, Economic and Social," *Studies in Southern History and Politics Inscribed to William Archibald Dunning*. New York, 1914.

———*The New South; A Chronicle of Social and Industrial Evolution*. New Haven, 1919.

Vail, Henry H. *A History of the McGuffey Readers*. Cleveland. 1911.

Vance, Rupert B. *Human Factors in Cotton Culture*. Chapel Hill, 1929.

———*Human Geography of the South; A Study in Regional Resources and Human Adequacy*. Chapel Hill, 1932.

Williams, Alfred B. *Hampton and His Red Shirts: South Carolina's Deliverance in 1876*. Charleston, 1935.

Woodward, Vann. *Tom Watson, Agrarian Rebel*. New York. 1938.